"Attunement is the essence of discipleship. The deeper the disciple's attunement, the more perfect an instrument he becomes for the guru's grace.
–Swami Kriyananda

Swamiji and Vijay in Hawaii 1977

The Journey of Discipleship: Learning with Swamiji

by

Lawrence Vijay Girard

Fruitgarden Publishing

"Information and Inspiration
for Living in Harmony with Life."

First Printing 2026

Centennial Celebration Edition

ISBN: 978-0-9848962-2-6

Dedication

To Swami Kriyananda

A direct disciple of Paramhansa Yogananda who has dedicated the whole of his life to the perfection of his discipleship, and in that process, brought many others to the awakening of their own discipleship.

To all who would rise to the blessing of being a true disciple.

Table of Contents

Swami Kriyananda
1977

Introduction

During seclusion in Kashmir, India, with Swami Kriyananda and Seva Wiberg, I was meditating for six to eight hours a day. We were keeping silence, only exchanging a minimum of short written notes to coordinate our needs. After my evening meditation I would sit alone at the dining table, facing an opening to the hallway while I ate some fruit.

My awareness was calm, deeply peaceful, free of restless thoughts. The food was appreciated but in no way agitating to my mind. While eating I would inwardly reach out and feel the calm of the house and its environs. Sitting in a deep soul contentment I would eventually hear the just barely audible sound of a distant door. Swamiji was coming into the house from a detached storage building that had been turned into a meditation room. His evening devotions complete he would walk down the hall so silently I couldn't hear any footsteps.

We had hung cheesecloth over the always open dining room entrance to discourage mosquitoes. The preferred technique for entering the dining room from the hallway was to part the cheesecloth with your palms touching in a kind of pronam (inward bow). As Swamiji appeared through the gauzelike material I would gaze up to see and inwardly feel Swamiji looking in to bless me goodnight.

As our eyes met I felt my heart-centered soul love commingle with him in unrestrained impersonal soul communion. For a timeless moment we rested as one in Spirit. Then with a blissful smile he would withdraw behind the cheesecloth curtain to retire for the night.

Since meeting Swamiji I had found that in his presence I was able to somehow go to him and through him to feeling Spirit on ever deeper levels. This period of seclusion, with its silence, meditation – including hours of Kriya Yoga practice – and goodnight blessings, took my spiritual life to a whole new level. It introduced me to a deep level of inner stillness which has become the bulwark upon which my relationship with Swamiji, Yogananda and God has been anchored.

The peace, calmness and inner well-being of the spiritual life has slowly but surely worked its magic on the rough edges of the personality that I have lived through in this life. I've often struggled when my personality's reactive process, over which I have had limited control, has overshadowed my soul qualities. The ability to perceive the difference between soul and ego/personality in one's self and others is a transformative tool for both self-development and service to others. The deepening of our experience of Soul/Divine consciousness and the positive expression of that consciousness through the body/personality that we currently inhabit is at the root of the spiritual life.

The Yoga teachings of India say, "When the disciple is ready, the Master will appear." So it was for me when I read *Autobiography of a Yogi* by Paramhansa Yogananda at the age of seventeen. As a new disciple I had no concept of how God through Paramhansa Yogananda would, or could, take me by the hand and heart to transform my life. Up until that time my life had been rife with inner tumult. What an incredible relief it was to discover that help was at hand. I was filled with a buoyant optimism that felt as if it would never diminish.

The joy of meeting one's Satguru (True guru – A soul who has without limit reunited with Infinite Spirit.) can sometimes delay the disciple's understanding that the spiritual life is not, and nor should it be, an easy life. Sister Gyanamata, Yogananda's foremost woman disciple, put it this way, "An easy life is not a victorious life."

Whoa! Isn't the spiritual life supposed to lead to the end of all sorrows? Well, yes...but that doesn't mean there won't be any bumps along the way or that our understanding of the value of life's challenges won't evolve beyond the usual preference that discomfort is by common definition bad.

The story is told that St. Theresa of Avila when fording a stream was unexpectedly swept into the rushing water. She disappeared for a time and her companions thought that she had drowned. When Theresa arrived cold and soaking wet on the opposite bank she suddenly beheld Jesus and asked him, "Why has this happened to me?" Jesus responded with a smile, "Don't feel bad Theresa, this is how I treat all my friends."

Entering into Jesus's playful words, Theresa responded, "Ah, no wonder you have so few!"

Theresa was practicing a precept that she shared with all her sisters: A sad nun is a bad nun! Even amidst adversity she responded with a joyful reaction. The novice in the spiritual life may not be able to maintain unshakable equanimity in the beginning, but there is an unquenchable artesian well of multifaceted well-being awaiting those who persevere on the spiritual path. So when we talk about the end of all sorrows we must look deeper than just signing on the dotted line and expecting instantaneously a complete transformation into unending bliss.

Many people equate the spiritual life with religion, certainly there have been Saints in all of the major traditions – and outside of them as well! Unfortunately there also have been many of this world's greatest tragedies associated with the misunderstanding and misuse of religious teachings. History tells us that often deep spirituality presents itself in spite of religion and not because of it. One of the reasons for this is because no matter the high ideals and good intentions of any group, people can and will make mistakes. It is the nature of our circumstances in this life for things to go what we would describe as *wrong* so that we can evolve to ever-deeper levels of that which is *right*.

Religions are often presented as a set of beliefs that you are supposed to memorize, live by and have *faith* in – meaning for most, blind belief, which means you don't find out until you die if the teachings are actually true. They also include various practices that can deepen spiritual awareness, but often this aspect of the teaching is neglected for the sake of making things easier for those who are less motivated or not adept at spiritual practice. The promotion of blind belief is one of the reasons science and religion seem incompatible to many. Often believers say "You just have to have faith," while scientists say, "Prove your hypothesis through verifiable experimentation."

When I found the yoga teachings, I discovered that they presented a bridge over the gap between science and religion by providing a methodology without a set of required beliefs. I am not referring to just the practice of Hatha Yoga (Yoga postures) but to a complete set of practices and guidelines for body, mind/emotions and spirit that lead the practitioner (Yogi) to the goal of Self-Realization.

What is Self-Realization?

One of the ways that Paramhansa Yogananda defined Self-Realization is: "Self-realization is the knowing in all parts of body, mind, and soul that you are now in possession of the kingdom of God; that you do not have to pray that it come to you; that God's omnipresence is your omnipresence; and that all you need to do is improve your knowing."

Whoa! Whoa! I have to believe in God to experience Self-realization? Are we back to blind belief?

The difficulty here is that most people define the word God in terms of what they believe, based on the story that their religion or lack of religion has told them. Each person's conglomeration of stories, opinions and limited inner experience becomes what they believe. *Belief doesn't make their distillation correct or incorrect.* Since most religions have a different story to tell and often preach that their story is the only one true story, it leads non believers to not believe and believers to just believe – thinking that believing is as much as we can do about the situation.

The Yoga Teachings don't require a person to *believe* or *not believe* in any given religion or set of beliefs, it just shifts the definition of God from being based on belief to an experienceable Universal truth. Those who teach that God is unknowable have clearly not yet had that experience. It is through direct personal communion with God that one can develop *true* faith – belief based not on opinion or hope, but on direct experience.

What is that experience?

The classical definition of God according to the Yoga Teachings is Satchidananda – Truth, Consciousness, Bliss. Paramhansa Yogananda further clarified this translation as: Ever-existing, ever-conscious, ever-new bliss. Additional descriptions of God/Spirit explain that this Eternal Infinite Consciousness has eight main attributes: Peace, Calmness, Light, Power, Sound, Wisdom, Love and Joy (Bliss/Ananda).

There is one idea that most religions will accept as a Universal truth: Love. It is further agreed that love is experienced in the heart. It would be difficult to gain a following by preaching, "I love you with all my elbow! I love you with all my foot!" It just doesn't work. Yet no cardiologist doing heart surgery has, to the best of my knowledge, ever said, "Oh, look at the love in this heart!" Perceiving love in the heart is a Universal experience that reaches beyond all races, cultures and ages in history.

Yogananda explained that the reason we experience love in the heart is that each person's soul connection to God/Universal Love, Peace, Joy is a point of intuitive perception in the heart area of the human body. Through this understanding we can come to realize that within each of us is a heart center (Anahata Chakra) which is our connecting point to all hearts...the Universal heart.

The reason that the techniques of Yoga work is that they utilize the inner mechanism of energy/consciousness flow within us. As we attune ourselves to ever-deeper levels of inner awareness we will in a very natural way experience increasing access to the eight aspects of Life/God/the Universe consciousness.

How do we know that this is true? We don't, unless we experience it for ourselves. How do we seek to experience it? We do the experiment of spiritual practice within the laboratory of our currently limited consciousness and see what happens. This is why in the Bhagavad Gita, Krishna, as an expression of the Divine, says to Arjuna who represents all disciples, "Oh Arjuna, be thou a yogi."

The Yoga tradition in ancient times was called Sanatan Dharma (Eternal expression of Truth – right action in thought and deed). Perceiving and expressing the Divine Will (Universally rooted Good/Truth) in every life experience is the essence of this path.

Why would we want to do this? Paramhansa Yogananda explained that in the most basic way, human actions can be attributed to the urge to be happy. Even the ego's instinct for self-preservation, can be seen as: I will be happier if I am alive!

People generally say, "I will be happy when I experience things that I enjoy and unhappy when I have experiences that I don't enjoy." So the most common approach to happiness is to seek more of what I like and avoid as much as possible things that I dislike. The fact that people don't enjoy or dislike the same things tells us that it isn't life's experiences themselves that determine happiness or disappointment, but our ego/ personality's reaction to life that determines how we emotionally feel.

The problem with a seek pleasure and avoid pain approach to happiness is that it simply doesn't lead to lasting happiness. No one can avoid all of the things they don't enjoy. The majority of people on planet Earth feel constantly bombarded by life experiences that lead them to negative feelings. According to their level of discontent many indulge in the use of alcohol, drugs, television and various other sense stimulants to dull/distract their discomfort.

Enjoyment through outward stimulation is by its very nature ephemeral. If we look at those who have the wherewithal to live surrounded by outward pleasures, we find that they are not generally happier. And in fact, when they discover that the experience of endless enjoyments doesn't provide the lasting happiness they expected, depression or *ennui* often ensues.

The solution to this dilemma is not a Yogic secret! It is a truth of which many people in the world today are to varying degrees aware. Just in the same way that we know that love is associated with the heart, we all know instinctively that *happiness can be found within*. Yet, how to consciously connect to inner well-being is not generally well understood. And in fact, finding lasting dynamic happiness within is seemingly out of reach for most people.

Why is this true? The essential component of life itself is eternal, never-ending, ever-new universally rooted happiness that we try to describe by using words like Peace, Love and Joy. Communion with this Cosmic Consciousness is the lasting happiness that all souls seek. This is the home that we will return to at the end of our journey through the Creation.

Yogananda described the soul as individualized Spirit. Each soul is a unique expression of Divine Consciousness. *The ego is the soul identified with the body/personality.* As human beings we are souls who have been drawn into and identified with the body/personality that we now inhabit. Most people are absolutely convinced that they are only a body/personality. Very few, even of those who sincerely believe in God, are able to access very much of their higher spiritual awareness and potential. When we are identified with our higher Self we experience our nature as a soul: Joyful Spirit with access to Universal potential. When we identify with the little self, we take on the likes and dislikes of the ego/personality and thus are subject to emotion based pleasure/pain reactions and limitations that come with life in the physical plane/material world.

Living a lifestyle that helps us to be connected to soul consciousness leads to greater awareness of inner happiness. The more we live in ego consciousness we feel disconnected from the soul's natural state of well-being. Since this is the habitual circumstance for the vast majority of planet earth's population it is considered the normal state for humanity, when in truth, it is common... not normal.

The issue at this point is not about belief. The true scientist doesn't believe or disbelieve. The scientist seeks truth and does experiments based on a hypothesis. In this case, the questions are: If the soul exists is it possible to be more aware of soul consciousness – Universal Consciousness – and will living with an increasing amount of soul awareness lead to greater lasting happiness with access to unlimited Universal potential?

The hypothesis is that the practice of a yogic lifestyle based on time-tested techniques and guidelines will provide the practitioner with ever-increasing access to Universal Truth. More specifically in this case study, the methodology will be based on the yoga teachings as they were brought to America from India in 1920 by Paramhansa Yogananda.

Paramhansa Yogananda shared the Yoga Science all across the United States from 1920 until his passing in March of 1952. Yogananda's message to the world was that each of us can experience Cosmic Consciousness directly and that the inevitable result of that communion will be the death of all sorrows in Divine Bliss. You don't have to wait until you die to find out if this is true!

When I first read the *Autobiography of a Yogi* I felt Yogananda's presence so vibrantly it was as if he was in the room with me. I kept turning back to a picture of him in the front of the book to drink in his vibrations with more focus and then push forward with reading stories and teachings that just felt like home. I had no idea that this most sacred secret to happiness was not a secret! It had been passed down in India through thousands of years from guru to disciple.

There isn't just one representative of these great truths. In each succeeding generation there have been those who have shared these sacred truths. And then once in many generations, an Avatar (Incarnation of the Divine) is born to correct directions of misunderstanding that have taken hold in mankind's consciousness and supercharge the world with powerful blessings. Paramhansa Yogananda was an avatar.

As I read Yogananda's autobiography, the sectarianism that I had associated with religion was dissipated. Here I found the antidote to modern society's endless quest to find fulfillment outside of the Self. These truths are available to all, according to each person's level of interest. Through these great ambassador's of Truth who have experienced what they are sharing, millions of lives have been and will be uplifted.

In 1949 Paramhansa Yogananda gave a speech at a garden party in Beverly Hills, California. James Donald Walters, later to become known as Swami Kriyananda, was present at that moment of spiritual history. Of Yogananda's words that day Swami Kriyananda wrote in his own autobiography *The New Path*:

> I remember especially how stirred I was by a talk he gave at a garden party in Beverly Hills on July 31, 1949. Never had I imagined that the power of human speech could be so great; it was the most stirring lecture I have ever heard.
>
> "This day," he thundered, punctuating every word, "marks the birth of a new era. My

> spoken words are registered in the ether, in the Spirit of God, and they shall move the West.... Self-Realization has come to unite all religions.... We must go on – not only those who are here, but thousands of youths must go North, South, East and West to cover the earth with little colonies, demonstrating that simplicity of living plus high thinking lead to the greatest happiness!" I was moved to my core. It would not have surprised me had the heavens opened up and a host of angels come streaming out, eyes ablaze, to do his bidding. Deeply I vowed that day to do my utmost to make his words a reality.
>
> Often during the years I was with Master he exhorted his audiences on the subject of this cherished dream of his: "world-brotherhood colonies," or spiritual cooperative communities – not monasteries, merely, but places where people in every stage of life could devote themselves to living the divine life.

There were 800 people at that garden party, but only one person in that group made the inner commitment to help those words to become a reality: Swami Kriyananda.

In 1967 Swami Kriyananda purchased the property that became the Ananda Meditation Retreat and in 1969 started the first Ananda World-Brotherhood Colony, which has since been called for simplicity's sake, Ananda Village. Located on approximately 1,000 acres in the foothills of the Sierra Nevada

Mountains near Nevada City, California, Ananda Village is the international headquarters of what has become a worldwide group of disciples who are dedicated to living and sharing the ideals of "plain living and high thinking" that Yogananda taught. Along with emphasizing the need for the personal experience of God's presence in meditation, Yogananda also spoke of the practical value of using spiritual principles to achieve success in every life endeavor.

There are, as of this writing, Ananda Communities in America, Italy and India, totaling about 1,000 resident members. Ananda Sangha (Ananda – Divine bliss or joy and Sangha - fellowship) is the name of this truly international group of people from all walks of life who have discovered the joy of living spiritual instead of material values. There are also many thousands, possibly millions, of people who connect to the teachings of Paramhansa Yogananda through the Ananda Temples, Meditation Centers and Meditation Groups around the world, as well as, Swami Kriyananda's many books, audio recordings and video programs.

Ananda's online presence is a gift to mankind, serving devotees worldwide. Ananda.org is a portal which provides free access to an incredible resource of inspiration and spiritual education, including online courses, free online books, articles, blogs, videos and much more.

Swami Kriyananda's journey from birth to American parents who were at that time living in Romania to the doorstep of his Guru's ashram in 1948 at Mt. Washington in Los Angeles, California, and then going on to represent the teachings of Yogananda around the world, is chronicled in his deeply inspiring autobiography *The New Path,* and in *A Place Called Ananda.* So I needn't fill you in on the details covered in those works.

My own reading of Yogananda's *Autobiography of a Yogi* in 1969 and subsequent arrival at Ananda Village in June of 1972 I have shared in book one of T*he Journey of Discipleship* Series, titled *Traveling with Swamiji.* In that volume I described how I arrived at Ananda and my experiences with Swami Kriyananda and life at Ananda Village up to the fall of 1977. The narrative in this volume starts where the previous volume leaves off. I had recently returned from an epic seven and a half month trip around the world with Swami Kriyananda.

My purpose here is to share with you a practical view of the spiritual life as I have lived and understood it under discipleship to Paramhansa Yogananda and the guidance – and friendship – of his direct disciple Swami Kriyananda. It isn't that I am personally of much interest. It is the subject of discipleship and the very real challenges that present themselves along each soul's journey, bathed in the light of Swami Kriyananda's example and the teachings of Paramhansa Yogananda that gives value to this tale.

Swami Kriyananda didn't come into this world alone. He drew to himself a family of spiritual seekers who have followed loyally and joyfully in his footsteps. I am blessed and humbled to be included in this august group. This family isn't so much a fellowship of followers, but of leaders who have learned through his example how to follow in the highest way. This spiritual family is now a dynamic power that is living and sharing the ancient tradition of Sanatan Dharma worldwide through the Path of Self-Realization.

I remember hearing a Chinese proverb: May you live in interesting times! As a young man I would have taken this as a thought of blessing, for I was intensely interested in all that this world has to offer. But now I realize the wisdom of the curse that this proverb is meant to be. This world is designed in such a way as to draw us into its web of outward involvements so that we don’t take the time to develop our ability to see the truth of life underneath the surface of the Lila (Divine Play). We are compelled by forces that we can't perceive to seek happiness outside of ourselves.

Paramhansa Yogananda and Swami Kriyananda have written extensively on the details about how the Creation was made and how it works. I won't be attempting to duplicate what has already been so beautifully and powerfully expressed in words wiser and more poetic than I can offer. At the same time, I will need to explain at times the *what’s* and *why’s* that are guiding the issues being discussed. It should be understood that further study of those subjects would be of great benefit to those who have not yet been exposed to them.

It has been my observation over the years that many people have a very unrealistic view of what the spiritual life should look and feel like on a day to day basis. I was certainly one of these people even after many years on the path. The distance between our aspirations of oneness with God and the day to day ups and downs that we experience leaves us without a clear sense of where things stand. How am I doing? Am I headed in the right direction? How long is this going to take?

Why haven't I experienced Samadhi (Conscious oneness with God) yet? What am I doing wrong? What can I do to improve my life? What should a life of discipleship look like? Do I need the help of others on the path? The questions are endless.

We all have preconceptions and expectations that float on the waters of our optimism – and sometimes desperation, yet those very thoughts are colored by the limitations from which we are seeking to free ourselves. One of the great values of spending time with other spiritual seekers is that they can help us to develop a comfortably realistic perspective while we traverse the terrain of our lives. We can learn from the way others have faced their challenges and we can offer support or be supported by others as the needs of the moment present themselves.

Through close observation of Swami Kriyananda I have discovered in him and the way that he approaches life, many opportunities to understand and improve myself. As a result of these observations I have come to realize that it isn't only Kriyananda's prodigious talents and innate spirituality that are of benefit to us who aspire for self-improvement, but also through the way that he has faced his own life challenges. In his courage, compassion, humility, kindness, tenacity and loving dedication to right action, we can find ideas and inspiration for improving our own lives.

If Swami Kriyananda were born perfect, well that would be beautiful, but he has never claimed perfection, omniscience or even any kind of greatness. One of the things that I admire most about him is that as long as I have known him he has simply been himself. He has adhered to his best understanding of what is right in his life no matter how challenging that path may be.

As I describe some of my observations about Swami Kriyananda please don't think that I am being critical of him. It is true that I haven't agreed with every choice that he has made, but then his choices were not mine to make, they were his. I know for a fact that he hasn't agreed with every choice that I have made, but he has never loved me less or pulled away from me because of that.

It became clear to me one day that if I wanted others to accept and love me just the way that I am, I need to offer the same towards them. As Jesus taught: *Do unto others as you would have them do unto you*; one of the great, most basic, teachings.

Since the day of Yogananda's prediction that the idea of spiritual communities would "spread like wildfire" much has happened in the world. In the 1960's and 1970's there was a cultural and spiritual revolution in America that gradually made its way around the world. In the 1980's and 1990's the fall of communism and the rise of the internet – bringing truly global communications – has given access of information and misinformation to all nations.

We now live in the 21st century, our world is truly a planetary community which is tied together not only economically, but by the realization that each of us has a part to play in the future of mankind. But, like many families, when you get too many relatives in a limited space life can and often does erupt into pandemonium!

The Path of Self-Realization is both the truth that all of life is at its core a spiritual experience as well as a body of specific practices that are applied creatively according to the individual needs and abilities of each person. No matter what techniques a yogi practices, there are specific attributes of experience and expression that will naturally occur as the soul reaches towards spiritual freedom.

Patanjali, known as the father of the modern yoga – since he lived only a little more than 2,500 years ago! – is the exponent of Ashtanga Yoga or the Eight-fold (or eight-limbed) path of Patanjali. He described eight stages of spiritual evolution: Yama (non-violence, non-lying, non-stealing, non-sensuality, non-covetousness), Niyama (cleanliness, content-ment, self-control, self-study, devotion to God), Asana (posture – the ability to sit still in meditation), Pranayama (the ability to access and control one's inner prana – lifeforce/energy), Pratyahara (the ability to interiorize one's awareness), Dharana (the ability to be inwardly absorbed), Dhyana (meditation – single pointed concentration on an aspect of Spirit or a specific technique) and Samadhi (Conscious oneness with Universal Consciousness – God). These natural stages of soul identification are both goals and guidelines for the spiritual aspirant.

These teachings are a part of what is called Raja Yoga, the Yoga of Kings. The king of a nation must take into account the unique needs of all its citizens. Thus it is that Raja Yoga recognizes that each soul is a unique expression of Spirit. We are each manifesting our own blend of intellect, heart and actions. So Raja yoga includes Gyana yoga (Discrimination that leads to wisdom), Bhakti yoga (devotion that leads to Prem - Divine Love) and Karma yoga (Actions that lead to soul freedom instead of ego bondage). Added to these three kinds of yoga are the techniques of meditation that accelerate the aspirant's potential for deep magnetic inner communion with Spirit.

Along with the timeless precepts of the yoga teachings, Paramhansa Yogananda taught a specific meditation technique – Kriya Yoga – for greatly speeding up the process of spiritual evolution. This technique is so effective that when practiced properly, along with a lifestyle that supports the goals of Kriya Yoga, a practitioner actually has a chance of achieving Self-Realization in this lifetime.

In order to absorb more fully what spiritual freedom in this lifetime means, imagine a very long journey. How long would that journey be? Would it be a year? Ten years? Fifty years? A lifetime? One thousand lifetimes? A million lifetimes? It says in the ancient scriptures of India that once the soul becomes identified with the limitations of the Creation it takes 100's of millions and possibly billions of years to once again become fully identified with infinite Spirit. While this teaching can be quite sobering, Yogananda said that once the soul fully realizes that communion with God is the pathway to ending this long journey, the soul is almost home. A technique like Kriya Yoga and the Path of Self-Realization are incredible keys to the completion of each soul's epic adventure.

In my wildest imagination I couldn't have scripted the twists and turns that have presented themselves in this life. It is only because I have been blessed by the guidance and support of Swami Kriyananda and Paramhansa Yogananda that I am able even to comment on these subjects in what hopefully will be a useful way. For myself, I have never known a person in this incarnation that I have loved or respected more than Swami Kriyananda. It is that simple for me. The Ananda Spiritual Family is my spiritual family. We might wrestle occasionally as siblings are wont to do, and on occasion get a psychological bruise or two, but the unity in mind and heart that we have shared through our discipleship is for me sacred ground. From this basis, I will be presenting the most true to Truth version of my story that I am capable of expressing. It is not an account where life never gets messy, but an expression that will, with love, respect and my most sincere prayer, be helpful to those of you who journey with me. May you find greater insights into your own discipleship and tools to face the challenges in your lives with greater understanding, hope, dignity and ananda (Divine joy/bliss).

Let us now, consciously, open our hearts and for a time walk side by side in divine friendship: if we do so, the path of self-realization will be much more fun!

Namaste – Spirit in me bows to Spirit in you.

Lawrence Vijay Girard
2005

Chapter 1

Seeking Truth

**"And ye shall know the Truth,
and the Truth shall make you free." —John 8:32**

The first time I met Swami Kriyananda he was speaking to a group of about fifty souls in the temple at the original Ananda Meditation Retreat in the foothills of the Sierra Nevada Mountains, near Nevada City, California. A number of times during his talk he prefaced statements by saying, "The Truth is...", followed by a universal principle connected to the subject at hand. Over time I learned that the precepts he shared were based on teachings that he had received at the feet of his guru Paramhansa Yogananda.

Paramhansa Yogananda defined Truth as: *That which corresponds exactly with reality.* It is important to understand that reality is not reliant on our opinion: It *is* what it *is*. Reality is not a stone, but a flowing river, simultaneously eternally the same yet ever-new. Yogananda also taught that Truth is *center everywhere, circumference nowhere;* so to know Truth we must connect to that Universal center.

This brings up a natural question: Where did Yogananda learn what he shared with the world? Initially he learned it from his guru. Where did his guru learn it from? From his guru. And so this has been the yoga tradition handed down from guru to disciple for thousands of years.

According to the educational doctrines that prevailed when I was growing up, learning is the process of memorizing information provided by others, thus a good education would be dependent on reliable content and a good memory. The body of knowledge that I was offered in school was almost always presented as fact and not opinion.

Over time I began to realize that the "truths" I was being served in the public classroom were at best only occasionally factual, such as in math, spelling or dates in some of history, more commonly the scholastic fare was partially factual and mostly conclusions based on opinions – which were often later found to be incorrect in a range from slight distortions and misunderstandings to intentional gaps and outright lies. Had my teachers made the simple statement, "Here is our current understanding of this subject." Or, "Some people say/think this and others say/think that." It would have provided a more beneficial learning environment. Students could have begun at an earlier stage to learn and practice the value of coming to their own conclusions through a dedication to seeking and speaking truth.

The teachings of yoga were not passed down through the generations simply as intellectual information. Universal Truth must be approached not only by the brain, but connected to directly from within, as Yogananda taught, through the soul's power of knowing: intuition. Here are some thoughts on the subject from the original *Autobiography of a Yogi* in which Swami Sri Yukteswar, Yogananda's guru – who he called Master, is referring to this subject:

> Sri Yukteswar related one of his own experiences in scriptural edification. The scene was a forest hermitage in eastern Bengal, where he observed the procedure of a renowned teacher, Dabru Ballav. His method, at once simple and difficult, was common in ancient India.
>
> Dabru Ballav had gathered his disciples around him in the sylvan solitude. The holy *Bhagavad Gita* was open before them. Steadfastly they looked at one passage for half an hour, then closed their eyes. Another half hour slipped away. The master gave a brief comment. Motionless, they meditated again for an hour. Finally the guru spoke. "Have you understood?"
>
> "Yes, sir." One in the group ventured this assertion.
>
> "No; not fully. Seek the spiritual vitality that has given these words the power to rejuvenate India century after century." Another hour disappeared in silence. The master dismissed the students, and turned to Sri Yukteswar.

> "Do you know the *Bhagavad Gita*?"
>
> "No, sir, not really; though my eyes and mind have run through its pages many times."
>
> "Thousands have replied to me differently!" The great sage smiled at Master in blessing. "If one busies himself with an outer display of scriptural wealth, what time is left for silent inward diving after the priceless pearls?"
>
> Sri Yukteswar directed the study of his own disciples by the same intensive method of one-pointedness. "Wisdom is not assimilated with the eyes, but with the atoms," he said. "When your conviction of a truth is not merely in your brain but in your being, you may diffidently vouch for its meaning." He discouraged any tendency a student might have to construe book-knowledge as a necessary step to spiritual realization.

During Yogananda's years of training in Sri Yukteswar's ashram they studied the Yoga Sutras of Patanjali. They progressed so slowly to new lines under Sri Yukteswar's guidance that Yogananda occasionally expressed moments of impatience. This went on for some time until one day Sri Yukteswar said that the lessons were finished. Yogananda was very surprised and protested that they had not covered all of the sutras (Threads of thought).

Sri Yukteswar then explained that more important than learning the meaning of each individual teaching is the ability to connect to Truth directly. Through direct intuitive perception the yogi can connect to the central Truth of any idea or circumstance. This deeper approach to accessing Universal understanding and potential allows us to not only absorb the teachings, but to perceive how to apply them in any given situation. This is the difference between information/knowledge and wisdom.

Since all disciples are not equal in their absorption of the inner and outer teachings, we should realize that not all teachers are able to express Truth equally. This doesn't mean we should judge others, but we do want to learn to discriminate, so that we don't just believe everyone who speaks on any given topic. Gradually, as we grow spiritually a feeling of Truth will resonate within. This is where the saying, *It has the ring of truth,* comes from. At the same time, we shouldn't assume that a positive feeling makes our opinions true – through observation of our inner perceptions over time we will see when they are correct and when we were mistaken This inner education will eventually lead to being able to trust our intuition.

What makes the teachings of Paramhansa Yogananda reliable? Firstly, the way he lived and manifested what he taught. He didn't just *"Talk the talk"*, he *"Walked the walk"*. The example of how he lived and the qualities of blessing that flowed through his life are still expanding in this world today. Secondly, Yogananda accessed Truth directly, when he wanted to understand the essence of anything in life, he didn't go to the local library and read a book or search the internet (Which of course didn't exist during his lifetime!), he dived deep in meditation and communed with the Universal storehouse of knowledge and wisdom. And finally, should we just take his word for it? No, we should verify the Truth of what he taught by practicing it ourselves and experiencing the result in our own lives.

Something that I noticed about Swami Kriyananda was that he was very careful to differentiate between statements that he had heard Yogananda say or that Yogananda had written, and extrapolations or opinions that were the result of his own distillation of the subject. In both cases he commonly tried to include what the traditional yoga teachings said about the subject and the line of reasoning that he or Yogananda had followed in coming to the given conclusion. At no point did he ever say that we had to believe or agree with what he presented. We were always on our own to decide what to do with the ideas that he shared.

In Western style education we are told that there is only one right and true answer to any question. In India Truth is like a diamond; one Truth with many facets. Again, the key in the yogic view is to go to the center of any issue and consult inwardly with Universal potential. From that inner communication, many different possibilities may present themselves.

One day I was standing in front of the reception center at Ananda Village with Swamiji (Kriyananda) and a small group of friends. I don't recall the general subject that we were talking about but I remember that at one point in the conversation Swamiji looked at one of the women in the group and said, "One day you are going to make my songs famous." The woman was certainly the best singer in our group at the time, we all believed that what Swamiji said would come to pass, but it never did. So was Swamiji speaking untruth?

This question came up in my mind many times over the years because Swamiji would often predict how many people would come to a program or how many books would be sold. His predictions were almost always higher than the actual results. Swamiji's explanation for this was that he was putting out an energy flow, an affirmation, that could help his words to manifest. And that if he didn't do this even fewer people would come and fewer books would be shared. In the case of the singer, Swamiji was affirming a potential, not guaranteeing an outcome.

Yogananda explained in his book *Scientific Healing Affirmations* that we should affirm things that are not yet manifest in our lives so that they can become true through the inner power of affirmation. When we broadcast vocally, first loudly and then more silently with intense inwardly concentrated energy flow we can tap into Universal consciousness/energy flow, thus helping to bring a potential truth into a manifested truth.

In Patanjali's Yoga Sutras he explains that when the yogi has perfected the stage of *Non-Lying*, whatever the yogi says will become Truth, the Universe will respond accordingly. This is one of the reasons why Masters don't easily give their word. Their word once given, must come true. This natural power of the soul is not accessible at the beginning of our journey through the Creation and must be reawakened through the practice of always expressing the highest Truths of which we are currently capable.

Truth starts with the outward facts, but then dives deeply into the central reality of what is taking place from both inward and outward perspectives. It also takes into account the karmic energy flows of the totality of the circumstances – of which few are fully aware. The greater our inner attunement to Universal Truth, the more often we will be able to perceive and express Universal Will or God's Will – the highest good of the moment.

A further aspect of this subject is that Truth is directional. Swamiji sometimes used this example to help us understand the subject (I am paraphrasing.):

If Mahatma Gandhi came to you one day and said, "I think I will stop serving my country selflessly and go out, find a job, make a lot of money, build a big house and put my feet up to enjoy the rest of life." You would respond by thinking, "That is too bad."

On the other hand, if a bum off the street said the same thing, "I have decided to stop being a bum, I am going to go out, find a job, make a lot of money, build a big house and put my feet up to enjoy the rest of life." You would pat that person on the back and encourage them with a smile. The same life choice would be a positive direction for one and a negative direction for the other.

Truth doesn't require us to do things that we aren't yet capable of doing. At the same time Truth is challenging us to do things that we haven't yet accomplished. It is said that God will never give us a test that we can not handle; though at the time we may think that the situation is beyond our ability to cope. The space between can and can't is caught up in the intricacies of karmic flow and is unique to each circumstance.

There are also things in life that just simply aren't ours to do. The teachings say it is better to fail attempting to follow one's own dharma (right action) than to succeed in following the dharma of another. "One incurs no sin in trying to fulfill his own duty –Bhagavad Gita 18:47." All children aren't expected to accomplish the same thing in the same way at the same time. So it is with discipleship. Everyone is at their own level, moving at their own pace, traveling their own unique path.

At Ananda there could sometimes be a reversal of perspective. The people who were busy taking the teachings out to the pubic would sometimes feel that they were doing so because they weren't advanced enough to stay at home and meditate. At the same time, some of the people that stayed at home felt that they weren't advanced enough to go out and share. Gradually we learned not to compare in that way. Over the years we noticed that people would eventually find the ways that were best for them to serve. And no matter what that service looked like on the outside, if they were doing it with the right attitude on the inside it would lead to seasons in their lives that were more outward or more inward, and that this was the natural ebb and flow of life.

Spiritual growth is connected to expansion and contraction of consciousness. If we are moving in a positive, self-expanding, greater soul perception direction, all is well, and the details of what that looks like on the outside are secondary. If we are moving in a negative, self-contracting, ego identification increasing direction, it won't be beneficial. It will lead to a disconnection from inner well-being and a shrinking of soul perception.

Truth is a higher level of factuality. Truth is beneficial. Sometimes Truth is easy. Sometimes Truth is very difficult. Swamiji often used the example of visiting a patient in the hospital. When you see them it might be factual to say that they look really bad, but in most cases it wouldn't be helpful to say so. It would be more Truthful to offer something that represented a positive direction, like: You are looking better today! Or, I am so glad you are going to be okay! The creative application of good manners is a part of expressing Truth in life. Thus the ancient general guideline: If you can't say something nice, don't say anything at all.

It is a common practice in modern society to use "white lies." These are falsehoods that are tossed out sometimes for well meaning reasons and at other times for selfish manipulation. These are not positive affirmations, but negative bursts that destroy our ability to access our highest soul potential.

Sometimes unpleasant things must be said in life and it would be an untruth not to say them. Yogananda's guru Sri Yukteswar was known to be a strict disciplinarian, he didn't baby his disciples with kid gloves, he gave it to them straight and if they couldn't handle it, they were free to leave...Ouch! Yogananda was known to give a good dressing down to disciples that had requested him to do so when necessary. But keep in mind, a Master has no personal motive or ego irritated reaction to a disciple's mistake. He doesn't want to take vengeance for the inconvenience of a situation. The guru, like a surgeon, sometimes needs to use a knife which may cause temporary discomfort, but never to injure, only to heal.

How does the guru know when to discipline and when to console? How do we know what to do in any given situation in life? Most people live according to the personal preferences of their ego. They have created habit patterns over many lifetimes which are reinforced by their reaction to experiences in this life. So they don't consider so much as react to life. The devotee is taught to inwardly stand back from our personal preferences and the ego's knee jerk reaction, and to inwardly attune to the "Truth" of the moment. We ask inwardly, "What would be most beneficial in this moment? What is the Truth/Divine view of this situation? What is God's will? At Ananda we often ask, "What is trying to happen?"

The impression that this process might give some people is that all spiritually advanced people would come to the same Truth in the same situation. This would be incorrect. There is such a thing as simultaneous Truth. A collection of diamonds may look to the untrained viewer to be all the same, but to the experienced gemologist they are all unique. Every person, place and situation in life reflects the ever-new nature of the Creation. If we look at life through the perspective of each person we will see something different. If we look at the inner center of anything we will find God's view, which takes into account every variable of all the components involved. This Universal view may offer one solution or many different solutions, each of which can be consistent with Truth. It is even possible that what we might perceive as our own wrong action can end up being an action that needs to happen for the sake of a larger Truth that we can't currently see. There isn't just one way to do good in life.

In my early years on the path I was at a loss much of the time as to how I should proceed. This is why the yoga guidelines are so essential for newcomers. They give us a practical framework in which to make our best guess until deeper understandings present themselves. Once I met Swamiji I was very eager to get his guidance on any and every aspect of my life, and I told him so. His reaction was to rarely give me any specific advise. Swamiji wanted us to connect *within* to God and Yogananda's guidance directly and not to rely only on him. He considered our relationship with God/Guru to be holy ground on which he tread lightly.

When asked, "What is the best yoga posture?" Swamiji replied, "Standing firmly on your own two feet!"

This is the goal of all spiritual practice, to live inwardly connected to the Divine and outwardly manifesting the Divine Will for your life. God wants to keep the Creation going, so souls are welcome to wander around as long as they desire. At some point along the way the soul gets tired of the endless ups and downs of the material plane, like riding a roller coaster too many times, the soul begins to gag on the endless repetitions and disappointments. At that point, when the soul call becomes sufficiently powerful, the guru appears and the endgame of our journey through the Creation begins.

Of course, just like in chess, it takes more than one playing to determine a grand champion. As disciples we will have to begin living in such a way as to expand our awareness of soul perception and avoid getting drawn into actions that lead to binding us in ego/personality consciousness. We come into each new incarnation with tendencies from our past lives that are integrated with the DNA of a fresh body. If we carry strong spiritual karma (Seed tendencies from past lives.) we will be given opportunities to continue in that direction. If we have previously bonded with a satguru – True Guru – we will be guided consciously by that Divine expression.

A new incarnation has advantages and disadvantages. Most commonly people forget their previous incarnations, which means they won't be overwhelmed by their past shortcomings – a plus – but it also means they might have forgotten their spiritual quest – a minus. The reawakening of interest in the spiritual life is of uncertain timing. This is one of the reasons yogis want to accomplish as much as possible once they do come onto the spiritual path.

Another challenge is figuring out what is going on in life. What is life's purpose? How do I fit into that purpose? Not many people figure that out on their own. In this regard Swami Kriyananda was quite unusual, he actually thought it through and figured it out. He wrote in *The New Path*:

> I found myself concluding, for reasons both objective and subjective, and for the sake of mankind generally as well as for my own sake, that what I wanted, what all mankind really needs, is God.
>
> The question returned to me with increasing urgency: *What **IS** God?*
>
> One evening, taking a long walk into the gathering night, I deeply pondered this question. I dismissed as absurd, to start with, the popular

notion of a venerable figure with flowing white beard, piercing eyes, and a terrible brow striking fear into all those who disobey Him. Science has shown us an expansive vastness comprising countless galaxies, each one blazing with innumerable stars. How could any anthropomorphic figure have been responsible for creating all that?

What, then, about fuzzy alternatives that had been proposed to suit the abstract tastes of intellectuals? A "Cosmic Ground of Being," for example: What a sterile evasion — what a non-concept! Such formulas I considered a "cop-out," for they gave one nothing to work with.

No, I thought, God has to be, if nothing else, a *conscious Being*. I had read alternate claims that He is a *dynamic force*. Well, He had to be that, too, of course. But could it be a *blind* force, like electricity? If so, whence came human intelligence? Materialists claim that man's consciousness is produced by "a movement of energy through a pattern of nerve circuits." Well! But intelligence, I realized, is not central to the issue anyway. Intelligence implies reasoning, and reasoning is only one aspect of consciousness; it might almost be called a mechanical aspect, inasmuch as it is conceivable for something electronic to be devised that will do much of his reasoning for him.

René Descartes' famous formula: "I think, therefore I am," is superficial, and false. One can be fully conscious without thinking at all. Consciousness obviously exists apart from ratiocination, and is a precondition for any kind of *thoughtful* awareness.

What about our sense of I-ness: our egos? We don't have to ponder the question objectively. We simply *know* that *we* exist. This knowledge, I have come to understand, is intuitive. Even a newborn baby making its first cry doesn't become self-aware *because of* that cry. It requires self-awareness for it to suffer! Even a worm demonstrates self-awareness: prick it with a pin, and it will try to wriggle away.

Obviously, then, consciousness is at least *latent* everywhere, and in everything. God Himself *must* be conscious, and, having created everything, must also have produced it out of consciousness: not out of *His* consciousness, for consciousness cannot be something He possesses: He *is* consciousness: Essential Consciousness.

What about self-awareness? This, too, must be inherent not only in all life, but in everything. We are not merely His creations: We *manifest* Him! We exist, because He exists.

To "cut to the chase": all of us, as His manifestations, have the capacity to manifest Him more or less perfectly. Surely, then, what we need is to deepen our awareness of Him at the center of our being.

What a staggering concept!

I recalled the days I had spent watching the ocean surf break into long, restless fingers among the rocks and pebbles on the shore. The width of each opening, I reflected, determined the size of the flow. Similarly, if our deepest reality is God, might it not be possible for us to chip away at our granite resistance to Him, and thereby *widen* our channels of receptivity? And would not every aspect of His infinite consciousness flow into us, then, like the ocean, abundantly?

If this was true, then obviously our highest duty is to seek attunement with Him. And the way to do so is to develop that aspect of our nature which we can open to Him. The way to do that, obviously, is to lift our hearts up to Him, and to seek His guidance in every thought and deed. In so doing He *must* – since we are a part of His consciousness – assist us in our efforts to broaden our mental channels.

I realized, now, that true religion is no mere system of beliefs, and is a great deal more than any formalized attempt to wheedle a little pity out of the Lord by offering up pleading, propitiatory rites and prayers. If our link with Him consists in the fact that we are already a part of Him, *then it is up to us to receive Him more completely, and express*

Him more fully. This, then, is what true religion is all about!

What I had seen thus far of religious practices, and eschewed in disappointment, was not *true* religion, but the merest first, toddling steps up a stairway to infinity! One might, I reflected, devote his entire life to this true religion, and never stagnate. What a thrilling prospect!

This, then, would be my calling in life: I would seek God!

Once the soul remembers that seeking and communing with God is Life's purpose, figuring out how to do that comes next. In this case, for Swamiji and many others in the Ananda Spiritual Family, reading *Autobiography of a Yogi* has been a common turning point. There are some exceptions, but the overwhelming reaction to that book by most members is *Wow! That man knows God!* Followed by, *I am going to do what he says because I want to know God!*

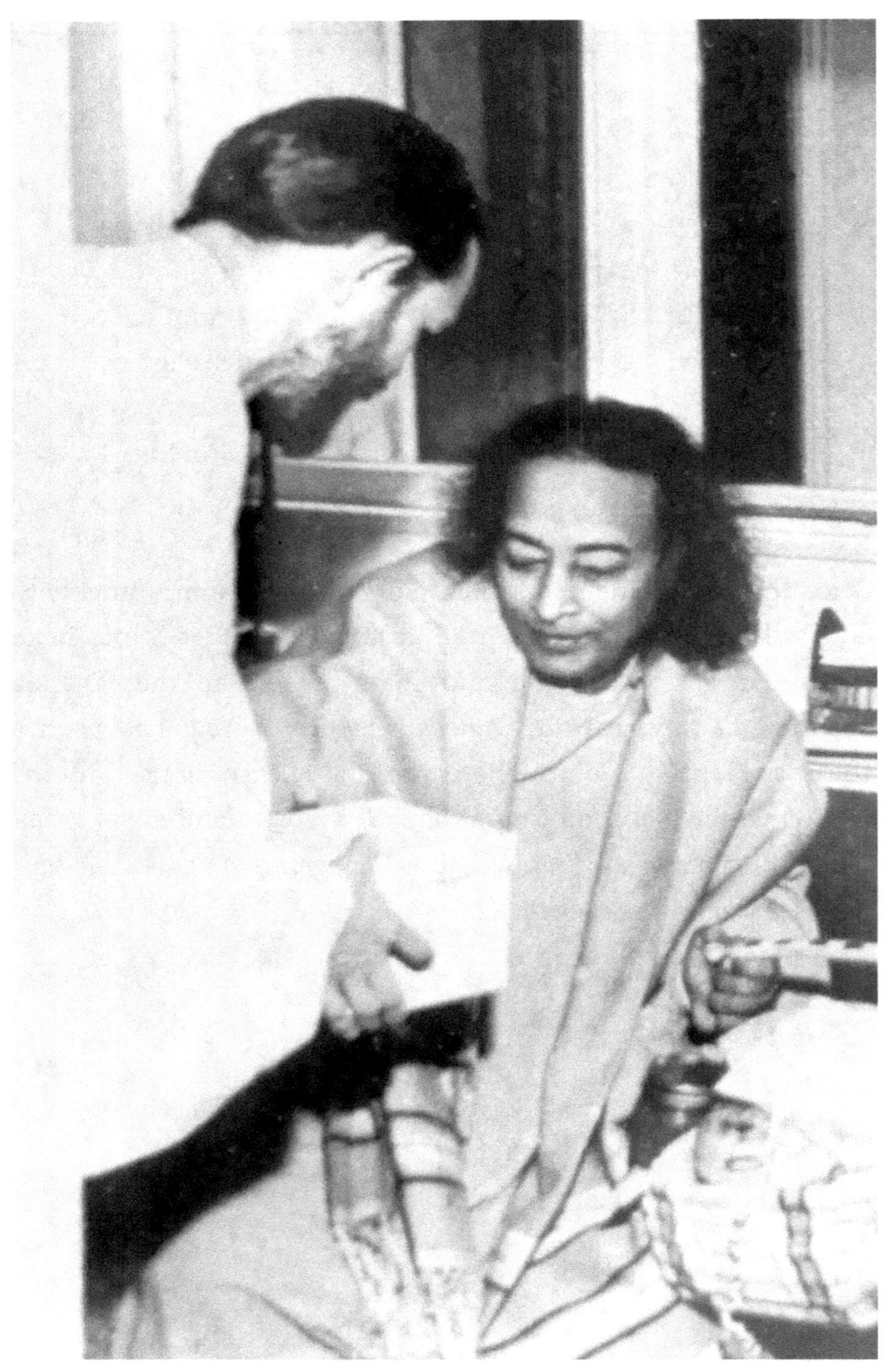

Chapter 2

Ananda Spiritual Family

"All time is wasted that is not spent in seeking God."
—Lahiri Mahasaya

One day Swami Kriyananda told a group of us the following story:

> There was a man in India who came home to find his wife in a state of distress. When he asked her what had upset her she explained, "My good friend's husband is threatening to take the vow of sannyas (renunciation) and leave the family to fend for itself!"
>
> The husband then replied nonchalantly to her statement by saying, "Don't worry, he won't do it."

> This seemingly flippant response left the man's wife wondering if her husband knew more about the situation than she did, so she asked, "Why do you say that?"
>
> "Because that isn't the way a person who is serious about renunciation acts," he replied.
>
> "Well, how does a person serious about renunciation act?" the wife then asked.
>
> "Like this!" the husband responded.
>
> Then before the wife's astonished eyes, her husband stripped down to his loin cloth, circled her three times, and walked out the door never to be seen again.

If we assume that the new renunciate didn't know ahead of time that the subject of renunciation would present itself that day, it would appear that he didn't do any conscious planning for his response. He simply spontaneously reacted to the moment as he saw it and made a choice.

One of the ways that life can be described is as a seemingly endless series of choices. In the spiritual life we want to become more consciously aware of the choices that we make. We want to understand the potential ramifications of our choices and then make conscious decisions based on how they will affect our expansion towards spiritual freedom versus our contraction into material world bondage.

The value system of materialism is based on likes and dislikes which are ruled by the ego's mantra, "What's in it for me!" This represents a contracting or limiting consciousness.

For these choices we use words like: self-indulgent, selfish and ego driven. Because of the dual pleasure/pain nature of life, even if a choice results in short term pleasure the Universe will always balance it with an equal and opposite displeasure (pain). Even more injurious to achieving our goal of lasting happiness is that constant immersion in life through the senses, it distracts us from accessing our potential for infinite non-fluctuating yet ever-new soul bliss. The value system in the spiritual life is based on trying to expand our consciousness beyond sense consciousness so that we can once again be fully identified with the inwardly accessible Universal well-being of Spirit.

Like most people, as a boy I made decisions based on what I desired. I sought pleasure and excitement under the general heading of what was fun from my point of view. I did my best to stay away from things that I didn't like. And since it is virtually impossible to completely avoid things we would rather not do, life for me was an endless series of ups and downs. I wasn't passive as I grew up, so I began to vigorously seek the things I liked. The only problem was that no matter how much fun I had, it always had an end. When it ended I would gradually feel let down. Then I would once again seek a new way to feel up again.

This endless series of ups and downs began to frustrate me. I was tired of it all. I wanted to find some point of rest, a place of peace. I sought to love and be loved. I wrestled with the question of life's purpose. I began to yearn for a resolution to my angst. Little did I know that this yearning would activate a universal response to the needs of my soul.

Sometimes in a person's life there comes a turning point, a time of choice when the life consequences of a chosen path are substantially larger than our common every day – What shall I eat for dinner? – choices. Just like the man who renounced his family in the story that Swami Kriyananda related, we may be faced with a truly life defining choice.

One day I found Yogananda's autobiography sitting on the dining table of a home in which I was a guest. As soon as I saw Yogananda's picture on the front of the book I felt a chord of connection chiming in my heart. Reading that book was for me a truly life defining experience. Yogananda's description of the way life is made and how the whole Creation works just made so much sense to me. As I read his revelations about the Universe my inner knowing kept saying: Yes, it must be this way! When I turned again and again to his picture, looking into his eyes, I could feel his Spirit with me and I knew that it was the presence of Truth.

Along with many delightful and amazing stories, Yogananda revealed the nature and purpose of life. He spoke of the power of maya (delusion), which is the Universal force that tries to keep our consciousness bound to the limitations of this world. He told the tale of the soul's journey through the Creation by explaining the process of reincarnation. He described the ancient tradition of yoga and presented the soul liberating technique of Kriya Yoga. Most importantly, he spoke of the guru/disciple relationship, its purpose and essential place in the process of Self-realization. I hadn't even read the whole book when my soul inwardly resonated with a sacred recognition: Paramhansa Yogananda, you are my guru, I am your disciple.

Swami Kriyananda's response to reading *Autobiography of a Yogi* in 1948 was to catch a bus and travel straight from New York City to California. On the day of his arrival, when he found himself in the presence of Paramhansa Yogananda, his first words were, "I want to be your disciple."

That evening James Donald Walters was taken to live at Mt. Washington in Los Angeles, California (The headquarters of Self-Realization Fellowship – which is the organization that Yogananda started in 1925). There he began his spiritual training under the direct tutelage of Paramhansa Yogananda. During the last three and a half years of the revered Master's life he was transformed from a neophyte to being ordained as a minister, sharing the teachings at Sunday Service and authorized to initiate new disciples into the sacred technique of Kriya Yoga.

After Yogananda's passing in 1952 Kriyananda continued to rise in the organization. He was put in charge of all SRF (Self-Realization Fellowship) meditation groups around the world. He traveled internationally, becoming SRF's best known speaker, was given the position of vice president and placed as the only man on the SRF board of directors.

In 1958 Swami Kriyananda was sent to India to help revitalize YSS (Yogoda Satsanga Society) the Indian arm of SRF. He spent four years in India and spoke to thousands as a representative of his guru. And then in 1962, because of what in retrospect can only be called God's Will – which unfortunately manifested as the kind of political infighting that you wouldn't expect, but all too often find even in spiritual organizations – Swami Kriyananda was unceremoniously kicked out of the organization that his guru had started.

Once again I remind you that the spiritual life is not for the faint of heart. The release of the soul from the grip of the delusion that we are an ego/personality and not an unlimited expression of infinite Spirit is a powerful struggle. Until a person is completely free from the power of this world, we are at risk for suffering the ups and downs, twists and turns, that are the building blocks of life in the physical world. Even the great Avatars (Fully liberated beings that come back to this world with a Divine mission.) like Krishna, Buddha, Jesus and Yogananda, all accept and experience the outward challenges of this world when they are here. The only difference between them and us is that they are fully identified with their universal reality and are able to live inwardly untouched by the outward polarities of life in a physical body, while our awareness is tied to our life through the limitations of the senses and personality. So while our fairy tale view of the spiritual life might be something like floating in the clouds while listening to heavenly music as the hustle bustle of this world flows harmlessly around us, the fact is that while our inner joy grows, we will also experience growing pains.

All of these years later, with his almost endless list of accomplishments to prove his worth, it is easy to see why Swami Kriyananda needed to be outside of the SRF organization. Kriyananda's boundless energy and creativity simply didn't fit in the confines of SRF's institutional approach. But at the time of his separation from SRF, Swami Kriyananda couldn't see the blessing this change would become, he could only feel the pain. He had spent 14 years serving in SRF. His whole life was dedicated to serving his guru and he couldn't even imagine life without that service. Yet even more challenging was the act of betrayal that his spiritual family had enacted upon him. His brothers and sisters in God, who he loved and was loved by, had somehow turned against him and cast him out.

One of the strange truths of life is that often things that we call "good" can't happen unless something that we would describe as "bad" happens first. This is part of the Universal balancing act that I mentioned earlier. It is one of the great lessons of life that is learned when we not only understand intellectually, but embrace wholeheartedly the truth that, as Yogananda said, "All life circumstances are neutral." It is how we respond to our life experiences that determines their positive or negative value and not the details of the experience itself.

Another disadvantage of the limited awareness in which we commonly live is that we can't see the bigger picture. We aren't aware of the incredible way in which life is integrated. The need for one person's karma to be fulfilled is matched with another person's or situation's magnetic resonance. Interactions on both microscopic and macroscopic levels are always in harmony with a Universal justice that our limited perceptions simply can't grasp.

I bring this subject up because the separation of Swami Kriyananda from SRF has dramatically affected the lives of all connected with Ananda Sangha and SRF – though the majority of SRF members are probably unaware of this fact.

When I arrived at Ananda in 1972 it was a requirement of Ananda membership that you had to also be a member of SRF. The love and respect that the devotees at Ananda expressed for everyone in SRF was very deep and sincere. Swami Kriyananda often spoke of his days at Mt. Washington with affection, inspiration and without recrimination. In the early years of Ananda there appeared to be a "live and let live" policy from SRF in regards to Ananda and Swami Kriyananda.

I myself became a member of SRF shortly after reading the *Autobiography of a Yogi* and received their full course of lessons by mail. I received Kriya Yoga Initiation in June of 1971 at the SRF convocation which was at that time held at the Biltmore Hotel in downtown Los Angeles, where Paramhansa Yogananda had experienced his Mahasamadhi. (A yogi's final conscious exit from the body.) The Kriya initiation ceremony was led by Brother Mokshananda (bliss through liberation) and along with about 300 other souls I felt blessed and deeply thankful for the opportunity to advance my spiritual practices.

I arrived at the Ananda Meditation Retreat in June of 1972 and received Kriya Initiation from Swami Kriyananda that summer, at the end of Ananda's traditional Spiritual Renewal Week. I found the Kriya ceremony to be powerful like the initiation with SRF, but it was also less formal and much more personal, like with a close family. At Ananda I found that my inner life began to push forward in earnest. I had spent years wanting to meditate, reading about meditation, thinking about meditation, and talking about meditation, but had spent relatively little time actually meditating. When I arrived at Ananda I found a group of people who didn't just talk about it, they did it. The influence of the groups meditative enthusiasm infected me to the point that I actually meditated as well.

People who don't meditate simply can't imagine the short and long term benefits of the practice. And in most cases, meditators that don't meditate with others on some kind of regular basis aren't maximizing their efforts. It wasn't until I was embraced by Ananda's magnetic aura that I found the support I needed to get myself inwardly on track. Daily meditations that sometimes included yoga postures and almost always included devotional chanting were the staple of the way we lived. I found that I was gradually able to penetrate beneath the restlessness of my mind and experience an inner up-welling of peace and well-being that, as I mentioned, I had only talked, read about, and occasionally touched.

I am not saying that it was easy. Even with the group support I struggled with mental restlessness. But when it was good…oh, was it good! The thing about experiencing the joy of Spirit within ourselves is that it quenches the soul's thirst for peace and bliss without having the bitter aftertaste of let down that comes with outward excitements. Instead of sparking a fire of outward desires spiritual upliftment warmed my heart in an embrace that even though it receded in intensity, I never felt abandoned, just thankful.

While the foundation of life at Ananda is the regular practice of meditation, when I arrived at Ananda I found a group of about 90 people who were living a very active lifestyle. Along with supporting the spiritual aspirations of each individual, the community also included a variety of businesses that were necessary to support the group's financial needs.

There was never any attempt to force people into a preconceived mold. Each person was responsible for expressing their lives in ways that met both their own personal needs and the needs of the group. So instead of the misconception that some people had of Ananda as a commune where everyone walked side by side hugging all of the time, I found a diverse group of rugged individualists who had been drawn together by the incredible power of Yogananda's presence and Kriyananda's absorption in and dynamic expression of that presence.

Having passed through the 1960's as a teenager, I had explored all that those heady years had to offer. Certainly I had met many good people before I arrived at Ananda, but none of them had what I needed to nurture and guide the needs of my soul. When I met Swami Kriyananda, I knew that I was in the presence of a man who expressed the substance and value of Yogananda's teachings. As I opened my heart to what God had to share with me through him, I found that not only did he feed my intellectual need to understand the spiritual life, but even more importantly, I found that simply by being in his physical presence I was, well, at peace…I was happy.

Once I had met Swami Kriyananda I began a practice that I learned by observing the others who spent time with him. When I was near him I would inwardly open myself up in attunement to God through him. I would mentally reach out with mind and heart to "feel" Spirit in and through Kriyananda. This inner process of attunement is an essential component in the spiritual life. Through this inner link I very quickly passed thru the "getting to know you" evaluation stage of a relationship and found myself fully immersed in the realization that this was and would be the most dear person in my life. There were many layers of meaning in this observation. In Kriyananda I found a father, mother, brother, friend, elder disciple, teacher, guide, example and transforming presence.

As I spent more time around Kriyananda I began another practice that I had observed others doing. There were two ways of addressing Swami Kriyananda that were used by those close to him. The first way was: Sir. It represents the esteem in which he is held, but also the truth that the highest relationships are rooted in impersonal Spirit. I don't mean impersonal and unloving, I mean unlimited loving because it is based in omnipresent Spirit and not simply human affection – which as we can clearly see in this world, is subject to change.

The second way of addressing Kriyananda is Swami or Swamiji. At the time of his formal vow of renunciation James Donald Walters chose the name Swami Kriyananda which means divine bliss through the practice of Kriya Yoga, or alternately divine bliss in all actions. A swami renounces the little self of personality to embrace the Universal Self of omnipresent Spirit, thus becoming the master of his ego identified little self in communion with his Universal Divine Self. When addressing a Swami without using his full name it is the custom (though not mandatory) to add the suffix of ji (sounds like gee). Thus Swami becomes Swamiji. Although ji is an expression of respect, it can also be an expression of endearment. So those who feel so inclined address Kriyananda with the title and endearment of Swamiji.

From Ananda's inception there began to grow around Swamiji what can only be described as a spiritual family. When a person arrived at Ananda you didn't know if they were there for a day, a year or a lifetime. Most often, they didn't know either. So it was interesting to watch how people reacted to the intensity of Ananda's spiritual environment. Initially most people began to relax and experience levels of peace that they had not previously known. But after varying lengths of time you could see their past involvement with the world trying to say, "Okay, enough of this peace and joy! Let's get back to the real action!" Then an internal struggle would ensue and the outcome was all too often that the person would leave.

The attracting power of the world and the outward flowing momentum of our past is a formidable force. Those at Ananda who fully embraced the protective power of the group's spiritual practices through active participation were able to fend off many potentially distracting attacks of worldly desires. Year after year it was seen that when a person began to withdraw from their active involvement in the group energy they would gradually and sometimes dramatically spin away from Ananda's center.

When members moved away from Ananda they sometimes expressed negative energy towards Ananda and Swamiji, but no negative judgment was sent towards the person leaving. Swamiji's attitude of divine friendship towards all demanded that his heart reach out with love and compassion. This wasn't an act that Swamiji put on, but a natural expression of his soul nature. Most importantly he respected each person's need to choose their own life.

In a long running race each stage has its own risks. You can fall when leaving the starting blocks. You can twist an ankle by not paying attention to the path. You can wander out of your lane by loosing focus. You can push yourself too hard in the beginning and fail to have the staying power to finish. You can fail to do the work that is necessary for success. You can doubt yourself and your training, thus sapping your determination. And when the end comes near and your reserves are spent, you may lose faith and then who can say what will happen? The good news is that every soul will eventually finish the race of their passage through the canvas of God's Creation. But it is only those who are spiritual champions that will finish in this lifetime.

The tools and training techniques of the Path of Self-Realization have proven over the millennium to work. Each of us can choose to make this our final lifetime if we make the right spiritual effort. Yogananda used to say, "You have to live anyway. Why not live in the right way?" And Yogananda's guru, Sri Yukeswar said, "Everything in the future will improve if you make the right spiritual effort now."

One of the things that I didn't fully grasp when I started consciously on the spiritual path, was that I would never be alone. Every religious encounter that I had growing up held God at a distance. As far as I could tell, the religions of the world taught that God was unknowable and occasionally performed miracles in this world to remind us that He was up there, somewhere, lurking around, so we had better be careful about how we act! When I discovered the ancient tradition that

Paramhansa Yogananda represented I found that this "God at a distance" approach was not the tradition of Yogis.

Interestingly, the teachings of yoga – which are a direct path to knowing God – do not require a belief in God. This is because yoga is a science. It only requires that we take the time to investigate in the laboratory of our own consciousness the hypothesis that something that we haven't yet fully understood might be going on in there. Once we begin to practice meditation we will start to see life with an inner sensitivity that had been previously inaccessible because of mental restlessness. In the calmness that comes from deep meditation we will begin to experience for ourselves the truth of God's joyful and loving presence.

God is by definition omnipresent, so if God exists, God must always be present; it is only our spiritual blindness that keeps us from seeing God everywhere. It was Swamiji's example that gave me a greater understanding about how to step forward and work with God as not just a presence, but as a participant in my life. Most of the spiritual leaders I met came across as "know it all's." They didn't in most cases actually say they knew it all, they just acted as if you should get that they did. Swamiji simply wasn't like that. He never claimed that he knew it all, and when speaking he would sometimes actually say, "I don't know for sure, but I think," or "In my opinion" such and such is true. As I have said, he was very careful to separate the teachings as he had heard them from Yogananda, from his personal extrapolations.

Swamiji's expression of honesty and humility without considering that others might think less of him for not knowing something was in itself a mark of his greatness and an important lesson for us. Honesty is the bedrock of the spiritual path, without self-honesty our construct of self will eventually come crashing down like a house of cards. Humility is not a weakness but a strength, and is an essential ingredient for those who want to achieve spiritual freedom. Taken to its state of perfection we can hope that we will experience what Yogananda said once when praised for his humility, "How can there be humility when there is no consciousness of self?" Yogananda had fully transcended the little self even though he kept it going. He was fully identified with the Infinite Self. In infinite consciousness even positive qualities are limiting. So the satguru is described as *triguna rahitam,* beyond the three qualities that make the Creation: Tamas (downward pulling/contracting), Rajas (activating – in either contracting or expanding direction) and Sattwa (elevating, expanding).

The practical truth is that while we as devotees want to live always aware of the Divine Presence, most of us aren't yet able to do so. So the key is to work with our current level of perception in the best possible way while we strive to improve our intuitive connection to Spirit. Spending time with other devotees and especially advanced disciples is extremely beneficial for this purpose.

The ability to see more of God's hand underneath the surface of our lives is one of the first things that I noticed about life around Swamiji. There was an air of spiritual anticipation constantly present no matter what we were doing. It was this twenty-four hours a day, seven days a week, every moment of every day and year approach to living not only for God, but with God, that completely transformed and supported my own efforts to do the same.

As a part of Swamiji's process to live in harmony with God's view of his life, you could see him occasionally stop during a conversation and focus more fully his attention on the spiritual eye (An energy center at the point between the eyebrows.) You could tell that he was inwardly consulting his intuitive connection to Spirit on a deeper level. The development of this inner connection is key to accessing our Spirit guided creative potential. Simultaneously it is also true that when a devotee harmonizes their life with Spirit, they will often automatically act in beneficial ways without conscious volition. So in a sense we are working our situation from both directions. We consciously seek to be aware of making the best choices in life while we also develop the ability to do so without consciously thinking about it.

Many people think that the key to achieving all of our goals in life, no matter if they are material or spiritual must be complex, but it is actually quite simple. When I discovered and became a part of the Ananda spiritual family I joyously entered into the group practice that solves all life challenges. As Jesus Christ said, "Seek ye first the kingdom of God and His righteousness, and all these things shall be added unto you."

Chapter 3

Young Monks

God alone! —Sister Gynamata

During the formative years of Ananda there was a spiritual intensity that was inspired by Swami Kriyananda's dedication to living for God alone. In many ways the group was like a person who had withdrawn from society and was living in seclusion. Members lived in cabins, tepees and trailers that ranged from simple to very primitive. We lived very close to nature in those days. Most people lived without running water or indoor plumbing, electricity and telephones. Wood was the most common form of heating and kerosene lamps or candles lit the night. Many did not own cars.

Although each of Ananda's members has their own version of "*How I arrived at Ananda*" the most common thread is that they had reached the point in their lives where they wanted to dedicate themselves to knowing, loving and serving God. They also recognized that they needed a supportive environment and spiritual guidance in order to do so most effectively. When I arrived at Ananda I discovered that the bedrock of Ananda's group culture was the spirit of inner renunciation. All of Ananda life revolved around three basic components: service, meditation and satsang (Fellowship with Truth).

Like a gaggle of chicks around the mother hen, our lives swirled around Swamiji who pushed steadily forward in his determination to serve his guru. Swamiji led a class on Saturdays and services on Sunday at the Meditation Retreat. During the week he often held a spontaneous satsang with spiritual discussion, chanting and meditation at his dome-shaped home at the community monastery named Ayodhya (The capital city of King Rama during India's golden age).

Whenever we met with Swamiji we were all intensely focused inwardly. True listening is not just a mental process, but an opening of the heart, a form of intuitive embrace. In order to listen fully one must release thoughts of other activities or one's personal opinion on the subject, and simply receive both the information and vibration of what is being shared. When Swamiji would speak of God and Guru it was like listening to heavenly music that poured over our souls and released us for a time from the strings that kept us tied to this earthly world.

The pleasure that we had in spending time with Swamiji wasn't the same as when "hanging out" with a friend. Even though we thoroughly enjoyed being with him and could laugh until tears were streaming down our cheeks, we were always in school. In every moment and experience we found fresh opportunities to understand how we could improve ourselves and our understanding of the teachings. We had before us a living example of discipleship and we sought to learn as much as we could from him.

Through my experiences in school I was used to teachers: Instructing. They would in essence tell you what to think and test to see if you had memorized their words. As I mentioned, Swamiji didn't so much teach us as inform and inspire us. He never required that we agree with anything he said. He simply shared with us his understanding of the teachings and left us to come to our own conclusions. His style of communication helped us to begin the process of developing within ourselves a direct inner connection to Truth rather than just parroting his words. So while he did educate us in the teachings, he more importantly, taught and encouraged us to access Truth directly.

When you combine our group's general withdrawal from the hubbub of society, our immersion in a life of service, the time that we spent in meditation and the practice of Kriya Yoga, and the influence of Swamiji's presence and guidance, you come up with a recipe for cooking devotees. Occasionally people would find the environment too spiritually hot and take a vacation to let off steam. Usually, they came back from those trips, but sometimes they didn't. It was a reality check for everyone when someone that we felt a deep bond with left the family. We realized that we wanted to push ourselves spiritually, but not so hard that we couldn't maintain the long view. Swamiji often guided us to give our best efforts, but that we should also use our common sense.

Each of us at different times explored the benefits of fasting, keeping silence and periods of seclusion. We discovered that like the yoga postures, stretching to the point just past comfort was beneficial. We also learned that if you stretch too far and injure yourself it can slow you down rather than speed you up.

Ananda Village is just that, a joyful village, where people strive to live in harmony with each other and all of life. In the village there are businesses, schools, shops, homes, temples and places for recreation. During those early years, even though the community was designed to include householders (couples and families) along with monks and nuns, in the 1970's there was an undercurrent that official monastic renunciation was the quickest path to knowing God. Another way to say it is typically American, "Go big or go home!"

This emphasis on individual monasticism occurred in spite of the teaching in the Bhagavad Gita where Krishna explains to Arjuna that the path of the householder is actually the higher path, because the devote who is successful in that path is able to keep their inner spiritual awareness without succumbing to the restlessness that usually attends involvement in the world. Of course it is also a more difficult path because of those outward involvements.

The fact that Yogananda and Kriyananda were swamis (monks) certainly was a strong influence, in spite of the fact that Lahiri Mahasaya (The father of Kriya Yoga in the modern era.) was married – as was Swami Sri Yukteshwar (Yogananda's guru) before taking monastic vows. There was also the factor of youthful exuberance that did not take into full account the totality of one's karmic circumstances and wanted to go all the way to God as quickly as possible.

I had been married and divorced since my arrival at Ananda in 1972 (A story which I tell in book one, *Traveling with Swamiji.*) My good fortune had taken me around the world with Swamiji to England, Ireland, Scotland, France, Switzerland, Italy, India, Thailand, Bali, Australia, Fiji and Hawaii. In the fall of 1977, having recently returned from our world tour, I had moved a small trailer to the monastery and set myself up in order to embrace the next step in my life. I didn't have any specific prospects at the time. I was floating on the blessings of my time spent in deep seclusion in India with Swamiji, while trying to figure out what to do next in terms of service and supporting myself financially.

Swamiji had a global vision for Ananda's future. He had said a number of times in recent months that it was time for Ananda to expand its horizons. The next logical step was to reach out across America. Swamiji began to arrange a cross country tour for the rapidly approaching New Year, in which he would put on lectures and promote his recently published autobiography *The Path* (The current updated version is called *The New Path.*) Little did I know that Swamiji had other plans as well.

I wrote in Chapter 29 of *The Journey of Discipleship: Traveling with Swamiji*:

> It was in November that the monks held a dinner in honor of Swamiji. There was a

performance of Handel's Messiah taking place in Nevada City at the same place where we had the big fundraising concert after the fire. It was arranged to have a dinner in their dining hall with Swamiji before the performance. As we all sat at a long table Swamiji spoke with enthusiasm about touring across America in the spring, just as he had envisioned when we were in India. He was on fire for bringing Master to the world.

Toward the end of the dinner Swamiji began to speak of starting Ananda's first outreach center. He thought that Sacramento would be a good place to start. Then he wondered aloud, "Who should we send?"

I don't know if everyone at the table looked down at their plate when Swamiji spoke of sending someone to Sacramento, I was too busy looking at my own plate to see what the others were doing. It is common knowledge that eye contact is an offer of interest. I wasn't about to volunteer and I didn't think anyone else was either. Then I heard Swamiji suggest out loud, "Maybe we should send Haridas and Vijay!"

Upon hearing my name I had to look up. I found Swamiji looking at me with one of those "I think you should do this!" looks and a big smile.

Of course I was honored to be asked to help start the first center outside of Ananda Village. I should have been thrilled, but I found it was a poignant moment because on one hand Swamiji was giving me the nod of approval that I had been seeking from him, while on the other hand that approval would guarantee I wouldn't see him as often. Even though I knew that he was in my heart, I couldn't help wanting to be in his physical presence.

Even so, Swamiji's words rang with the tone of truth. I smiled back and nodded a wholehearted, yes. As I thought about it I realized that the times I had been happiest – other than being with Swamiji and/or in seclusion – were the times when I suspended my personal desires about life and lived fully to serve Master (Paramhansa Yogananda). This was the example that Master and Swamiji held up to us and I knew from experience that it worked.

Haridas (Servant of God) had arrived at Ananda in 1969 and was about one year older than me. He had grown up in Manhattan Beach in Southern California, just a stone's throw from Malibu, where I had lived for many of my teen years. We hadn't spent a lot of time together, but we were fellow monks, lovers of God and we had plenty of energy and enthusiasm: What else did we need?

Well, we needed money! Of which we had very little. Somehow we scraped together enough money to rent a house on Boone Lane in a southeastern section of Sacramento. We particularly liked the street name because one of Swamiji's fellow disciples at Mt. Washington had the name Daniel Boone (Yes, this is true!) Once we had rented the house we arranged for an inaugural program at the Sacramento YWCA with Swamiji. On December 9, 1977 we held the first official program of Ananda Sacramento.

In preparation for moving to Sacramento I had spoken to Santosh (contentment), a fellow monk who had been teaching Raja Yoga classes in Sacramento during the previous year. I asked him if he had any students who might like to participate in the new center. He gave me a list of possibilities and then pointed to one name in particular, Toni Gloria Liebermann. He said, "Call her first, she is family."

My first official duty as co-leader of the Ananda Sacramento Center was to have dinner with the Liebermann family. Little did I know what would be behind the door of this Sacramento beginning, only years later would I be able to look back and marvel at the way life had unfolded before me with the shadow of God's hand by my side.

The Liebermann family lived in a barn shaped house that Toni's husband, Richard, had built in the city of Roseville, about 15 miles northeast of Sacramento. The home was cozy with the warmth of Toni's Italian heritage. As soon as I met Toni I knew Santosh was right, she was family. Over the years at Ananda, we had begun to recognize in the faces and hearts of people that we met, a radiance of harmony and commonality that felt like family. It was like meeting an old friend that you just hadn't seen in a while. It didn't always mean that they were followers of our particular spiritual path, though often it did, but it always meant that they were devotees in the family of souls that transcends the particulars of outward style and resonates with the Universal oneness in which we all live.

Toni and Richard had two well behaved young children, Daniel (9) and Cristi (7). During dinner I spoke of our plans for the Ananda Center in Sacramento. Toni expressed much enthusiasm. I left their table that night full of great food and thankful that we already had at least one strong local supporter for the center.

Not long after our arrival in Sacramento we decided to transform the garage into a temple. I had seen this done at the home of Satya's (Truth) son's house in Reno, Nevada. They had turned their garage into an SRF meditation chapel. So we created double walls and insulated them well. When complete the room was very quiet: protecting us from both the noises of the neighborhood and from drawing too much attention to our group chanting. We installed carpeting on the floor and the pictures of the Self-Realization line of gurus, Babaji, Krishna, Jesus Christ, Lahiri Mahasaya, Swami Sri Yukteswar and Paramhansa Yogananda on the altar. We couldn't figure out what to do with the washer and dryer since the hookups were there in what had previously been the back of the garage, so we just threw a large blanket over them when they weren't being used. Several of the ladies at Ananda teased us for years about this.

When we inaugurated the new chapel, about forty people both new members and some supporters from Ananda Village, came to bless our humble beginnings. Over the next few years that chapel became a powerful place of sadhana (spiritual practice.) Eventually it became teasingly and lovingly known as "the Garage of the Eternal Religion". And thus began an incredible series of experiences that enriched our lives, nurtured our souls and made us ever more aware of God's active presence in our lives.

Haridas and I established a very clear chain of command when we started the center. God and Guru were in charge, all we had to do was figure out what they wanted us to do! We were committed to doing God's Will, but as Haridas said years later, "When I lived in Sacramento with Vijay I was amazed to find out that God had two wills! The one He told Vijay and the one He told me!"

Our basic modus operandi when dealing with issues large or small was to seek inner guidance about how to proceed. If we didn't have a clear feeling about what to do we used our intelligence and common sense in the best combination that we could, while constantly checking our inner connection to Spirit for a feeling of rightness. Since we realized that neither of us was likely to know clearly what to do all of the time we agreed that we would avoid trying to impose our own view on the other. As an example: We agreed that it was a good thing to meditate together at 6 am every weekday, but we also agreed that if you didn't show up that was okay too. Ananda has never been a place for too many rules. As Yogananda said, "Too many rules kill the spirit!"

Shortly after our arrival in Sacramento Haridas and I discussed how we would support the center financially. We realized that it wouldn't be easy to bring in enough income through classes and Sunday Service donations, but we both felt strongly that for a period of time we should try. So we didn't go out and get jobs right away. We applied ourselves to setting up as many classes as we could, as quickly as possible and hoped for the best.

With Toni Lieberman's help we set up a public lecture at the Roseville Parks and Recreation District. It would be Haridas' first public lecture. As I remember it there were about 25 or 30 people in the audience. Boy did he sweat! Poor Haridas was wound up like a top ready to spin. But once he started speaking, his good-hearted nature and natural humility endeared himself to the audience. By the end of the evening we had enough new students to start a series of classes.

We lived in day to day wonderment as somehow we had just enough money to eke by during the first few months. At this time we consciously practiced a basic principle of prosperity. If you want money to flow through your life you can't be afraid to spend it (Not irresponsibly, but for a worthy purpose!) even when you don't know where the next dollar will come from.

On Sundays we would have an offering during the service and the five to twelve attendees would donate small amounts. One Sunday the donation represented the only money that we had. We decided that the best thing we could do was spend it in order to prime the pump for more money to flow our way. So we bought some food for the refrigerator and went to the movies! We didn't always do this when money was short, each time held its own truth, so we sought at those times to feel inwardly what we should do. All I can say is that every time we did it, somehow over the next few days, money that we didn't expect would arrive. Not a lot! But just enough.

Once it was the end of the month and we didn't have the rent money. The rent was due no later than the 5th of the following month or we would have to pay a $20 late fee. We didn't want to pay the penalty but we didn't have enough money. We sent as much money as we could with a note explaining that we would send the rest as soon as possible. The 5th was a Sunday and so theoretically we could bring the money to the landlord on Monday and it would still be okay.

Haridas and I discussed the situation. We decided that we had done as much as we could, though we continued to listen inwardly for any new ideas that might present themselves. Well, on Sunday after everyone had left I went to count the collection. We had been getting between $5 and $25 each week. As you might guess, I got quite a surprise. There was a check for $200! With a nonchalant smile I told Haridas to look in the basket. As soon as he saw it we both started to laugh. It was a good play! We had also needed money to put out a promotional mailing and the check covered that and the balance of the rent with seven dollars to spare.

Another time we found ourselves in the same *no rent money* situation and we were fairly convinced we wouldn't have the money on time, so Haridas decided to call the landlord and explain the situation to her. After saying that we didn't have the rent money he quickly added, "But we are praying for it!"

The landlord's sweet response was, "Well, I will pray too!"

That Sunday after service we quickly realized that there would be no large donation to save the day.

In 1976 I had taken a course in piano tuning and repair. So one of the ways I could bring income into the center and still have a flexible enough schedule for teaching classes was by purchasing an old piano, fixing it up and selling it for a profit. We created a little workshop out behind the house and while Haridas refinished the cabinet I worked on the piano's mechanical parts. Once we had finished fixing it up we moved it into the temple and made an instrumental recording of Yogananda's chants while Haridas beautifully played his own arrangements. That recording was enjoyed for many years by devotees until it was eventually updated.

I should digress for a moment and mention that the tape recorder that we used for that recording also came to us through Divine intercession. We desperately needed a tape recorder to listen to a sample of a radio program that Swamiji had created. After giving the situation some thought there didn't seem like there was anything we could do except pray – not having the time or funds to drive to Ananda just to listen to the half hour tape.

One evening shortly thereafter a fellow in Haridas' evening class at the center started talking to me. Out of the blue he said, "Oh, by the way, I have a reel to reel tape recorder that you would be welcome to use whenever you need it." So not only did we listen to the tape of Swamiji, but we used the recorder to record Master's chants, which we probably wouldn't have thought to do if we hadn't had that tape recorder to use.

So that day when we once again needed the rent so badly I decided that the piano was our piggy bank and this was the day to cash it in. Haridas helped me put the piano in a covered trailer that I had bought for moving pianos. I then announced, "I won't be home until it is sold!"

I drove to a not too distant corner on which I knew there was a gas station that was closed Sundays and pulled out a poster sized sign: Piano for Sale. It took about two hours. The first person to stop bought it! I made the arrangements and drove home to get Haridas to help me deliver it. Soon we were at a friendly woman's house, squeezing the piano through a narrow passageway. It was because of a number of these precarious piano deliveries over the years that Haridas began a tradition of teasing me about working with pianos, he said, "Why don't you do violins? They are a lot easier to carry!

With the piano in its chosen spot at its new home we received the money and made pleasant conversation. Somehow the subject of Ananda came up and the woman surprised us by saying, "I've been there!" We couldn't help smiling on the way home. God had once again come through for us. We had exactly the amount that was needed for the rent!

Haridas and I both had old clunker cars. We eventually decided that it was time to upgrade our transportation. So as usual…we prayed. Within two weeks one of our center members, Dave Howe, donated a car. We couldn't help laughing and thinking that Divine Mother (God is both Heavenly Father and Divine Mother. Paramhansa Yogananda often prayed to God as mother.) was a jokester because the car was a little red MG sports car! Not exactly what you would expect a monk to drive around town! Nevertheless, our prayer had been answered! When we did finally upgrade the cars, we added to our prayers the thought that sports cars probably weren't what we needed!

Life at the Sacramento center wasn't always fun and games. Occasionally people would arrive with serious life challenges and we were expected to help them. At one point a couple came several times to meet Haridas for marriage counseling. While we did take their situation seriously, we couldn't help laughing at the idea that a young monk would be giving marriage counseling to a middle aged couple. At the same time, I wasn't surprised that Haridas did help them. The teachings of yoga are so central to the way that life is made, that no matter what aspect of life you consider, the principles of yoga still apply and can provide very practical solutions.

One day while purchasing gas at the corner station we learned that there had been a shooting nearby. The attendant asked, "What do you think about that shooting? Well, the truth was that we had no thoughts, because we didn't know it had happened! We didn't watch television or listen to the radio. Even though we lived in a large city we were very isolated from the mainstream of society. So after that we started getting the newspaper delivered so we would know at least a little about what was going on in the world.

We often had visits from Ananda members who were traveling to or through Sacramento. Once, Asha (Hope) and Lakshmi (Goddess of prosperity.) came to visit. Haridas and I lived by the basic philosophy that we should try to feed anyone who came to visit. So when the ladies called to say they were dropping by I began to think about what we might offer. Soon mischievous ideas were hatching in my mind.

I pulled a package of store bought oatmeal cookies out of the cupboard and put them on a cookie sheet. Then I put the sheet in the oven to warm them. When Asha and Lakshmi arrived they were greeted at the door by the aroma of baking cookies. I informed them that their timing was perfect as we were just taking a fresh batch out of the oven.

The ladies were quite impressed when we brought out the cookies. They looked at the perfect warm brown roundness that was exuding a pleasant aroma and their eyes became wide with wonder. They couldn't believe that we had made these cookies. Then when they tasted them and found a very pleasant flavor and texture they began to compliment us on our fine baking, which was high praise since both were quite accomplished in the kitchen.

We had great difficulty holding in our mirth. No sooner had they finished applauding our prowess in the kitchen then we broke into uncontrollable laughter. When we were eventually able to stop laughing long enough to tell them what we had done, they also laughed for a long time.

During the year of 1978 we made steady progress in growing the center. Our numbers weren't large, twelve to twenty people at Sunday services and more when we had special events. Eventually we had enough cars parked on the street that one of the neighbors complained and started spreading rumors that we were a *cult*. It was then that we learned an important lesson about living in the suburbs: People consider the car spaces in front of their homes to be a part of their private space. If you invade that space too often they will rebel.

So right away we had our members and visitors park down the street and around the corner, when they came for classes and services. One day I came to the door of the house and there were a lot of shoes on the porch, no sign of cars on the street and only the slightest hint of sounds coming from inside the house. Certainly no one could complain about that!

But the neighborhood had become unsettled because one particular household was stirring things up. Haridas decided to face things head on and go visit the couple. The husband of the house was a businessman and the wife a psychologist. As soon as Haridas arrived the woman began to grill him about what we were doing. He calmly explained our purpose. When he mentioned that we taught classes and occasionally counseled people she felt that as a trained psychologist she was on solid ground and demanded to know, "What is your training? What makes you qualified to do these things?"

Haridas answered simply, "We are not qualified. Only a true spiritual Master is qualified, but we do our best." His honest and unassuming answer instantly took all of the air out of the woman's sail. By the time Haridas left she had wished us well in our efforts.

It is true that we hadn't attended a university for training as ministers. And we had not been officially ordained as ministers at that time; Jyotish (Inner light) Novak, the director of Ananda under Swamiji was the only legal minister besides Swamiji. But it would not be true that we had received no training. We had both spent years at Ananda, which was a far more practical and intense spiritual training ground than any university of which I have ever heard. And while the specifics of ministerial protocol were never officially discussed, the ability to flexibly express positive caring thoughts from a yogi's point of view was a basic component of the Ananda way of life.

When it was decided that we would come to Sacramento I had initially expected, and then hoped, that Swamiji would sit us down one day and give us some advice on how to proceed, but he never did. His way was to let us learn by doing. I believe that he knew we would ask if we had any serious needs. Except, one day a couple of months after we started the center, during a spontaneous visit he was looking around the place and just before leaving, he turned back to us and said, "If I may, I would like to give you boys some advice."

I thought, okay, here they come, words of wisdom to be etched into the mind. I wished I had a tape recorder rolling. Oh, well. We responded eagerly with, "Yes, please tell us what you think." Then Swamiji smiled with a twinkle in his eyes and said, "Boys, keep the place clean!"

Chapter 4

Sacramento Adventures

In God We Trust
— Official motto of the United States of America

The first year of the Sacramento center was filled with a joyful intensity. We felt like young soldiers on the front lines of a war between the forces of dark restlessness and the light of calm inner peace. The daily battle of keeping one's personal equilibrium while working hard to get people into our yoga classes, and then teach the classes as well, was challenging. Haridas and I had our own ways of keeping personal balance.

Our most common way to recharge when we felt the need was to go back up to Ananda Village for a few days. It was about a 90 minute drive to the Village – which in itself was pleasant, because it quickly passed from urban sprawl to open countryside. We usually took turns so that there was always someone at the center to take care of things. But during that first month our local group was so small that we went up to the Ananda Meditation Retreat for the traditional all day (8 hours) Christmas meditation on December 23rd and then stayed for the Christmas festivities.

Christmas at Ananda is a beautiful balance of inward absorption at the all day meditation, followed the next day by a party with Christmas caroling on Christmas Eve. And then the sweet Spirit permeated fellowship on Christmas day during the service in the Meditation Retreat Temple, gift exchange and banquet in the next door Common Dome. The day ending with an open house at Swamiji's dome at Ayodhya. I found that the high vibrational charging during this time could boost my inner weather for months. It was the perfect counterbalance to the busy lives we were experiencing in Sacramento.

Not long after I arrived at Ananda I envisioned being able to share the yoga teachings with others. I thought that giving classes would be the ultimate job; spiritually uplifting and serviceful. I had not given thought to the other parts of teaching, like getting students into the classes and then being properly prepared in body, mind and spirit to present the teachings in the best possible way. I also hadn't thought about the need to support the students between classes. Our arrival in Sacramento gave us an opportunity to experience firsthand the diverse challenges that are part of being a minister.

In the beginning Haridas and I would share the loftiest view of the spiritual life that we could access. Gradually we realized that we were giving the students more than they were ready to hear. So we toned down our presentations under the general philosophy of "Less is more." This seemed to be a good thing, but when Swamiji came to Sacramento to give a public lecture it got us into a bit of trouble.

Since this new discovery that *less is more* was so fresh in our minds, we decided that it would be good to share our insight with Swamiji just before he gave his talk at a local church. At the time I didn't think much about it, we were just trying to be helpful. As we explained that we thought he should shorten his presentation, Swamiji just nodded while listening. He then went on to give his talk for the regular length of time, which as usual, was deeply inspiring and no one wanted it to end.

Swamiji never said a word about our presumption in offering guidance on public speaking. Most people would have put us in our place; after all, we were two young novices with pitifully little experience. Yet it was so like Swamiji not to be in any way negatively reactive to others. He always stood centered in himself and never seemed to feel the need to be defensive or superior towards others no matter what they said or did.

I remember a time in Vancouver, BC, when we participated in a large spiritual symposium. Swamiji entered the large hall while another speaker was leading the group in song. There was only standing room available in the large hall so Swamiji stood close to another man.

Suddenly the man next to Swamiji asked him accusingly, "Why aren't you singing?"

Swamiji answered, "I don't feel like it and I don't want to do it insincerely."

The fellow then asked, "Why are you being so defensive?"

Swamiji then answered patiently, "I was just answering the question you asked."

"Well, it sounds to me like you are being defensive!" the man retorted.

"Well then, the defense rests!" Swamiji returned with a smile.

Swamiji simply couldn't be baited into an argument, because he never took the comments of others to his ego. He always weighed the words of others on the scale of Truth. And then responded according to the positive expression of Spirit to which he had dedicated his life.

Swamiji probably would have never said a word about our suggestion that he shorten his presentation, but years later I asked Swamiji what he thought of our advice. In response, he looked at me with a smile of somewhat nostalgic humor and said, "I thought you guys were pretty cheeky!"

Our classes included the instruction of a series of exercises that Yogananda developed called Energization Exercises. These exercises increase one's ability to access and direct inner life force through the focusing of the will. When doing the exercises the muscles are tensed and relaxed as the practitioner turns on and off the energy flow with concentration and will power. Along with the benefits of greater energy and less tension in the body and mind, the skills learned in the exercises lead to improved abilities to both meditate and deal with daily life.

One day I was scheduled to be on an interview television program with Swamiji. The taping was scheduled at a time just after the ending of a yoga class that I was teaching at American River College. I knew that the timing was going to be very tight so at the end of class I left as quickly as I could. I then proceeded to change from my yoga postures clothes into something more appropriate for television as I drove with excessive speed down the freeway.

The television station was in the downtown area of Sacramento and I wasn't exactly sure how to get there in the quickest way – this was way before cell phones and map apps! Fortunately the traffic was not heavy, because at one point I began to pass the correct off ramp and in a panic hit the brakes and actually backed up on the freeway – something that I had never done and have never done since!

By the time that I reached the front of the station building the peace of yoga practice had been left behind somewhere on the freeway; my mind was a whirlwind. I knew that I was late and Swamiji would be put in an awkward position. As I came bursting into the reception area of the station a person behind the desk instantly knew who I was and just pointed me in the right direction while I ran down the hall buttoning my shirt.

Just before I reached the door to the studio I realized that I needed to put myself in the right frame of mind or there wouldn't be any purpose to my being there. So I did something that I had learned from Swamiji and the energization exercises. I stopped right before the door, stood absolutely still, put my mind at the point between the eyebrows and took what we call a double breath (short and long inhalation through the nose, followed by a short and long exhalation through the mouth). As I did this I willed my body, mind and spirit to enter a state of calm inner connection. I then took hold of the doorknob and walked into the studio as if this was just another easygoing day. I smiled as I greeted Swamiji and the host, sat down where they were already sitting on the set and we immediately started recording the program.

As usual, Swamiji answered the host's questions in a way that communicated beautifully the vibration and value of the yoga teachings. At one point the host asked me how I ended up being a follower of these teachings. In my mind I shouted, "How do you expect me to answer a question like that in two or three sentences?" But out of my mouth came a relatively short stream of words that were apparently acceptable because no one called out, "Cut!"

Afterwards everyone was smiles and handshakes. I had never before experienced such a dramatic instant switch of conscious. My mind hadn't just slowed down, but my whole being had been flooded with peace. It was not only a great experience, but a valuable lesson.

In the spring of 1978 Haridas and I reassessed our decision not to get outside jobs and decided that it was time for a change. Our financial situation was such a struggle that it was beginning to drain our energy rather than providing more energy to grow the center. We didn't expect that God was going to just drop a whole pile of money on us as a donation so we got practical and found gainful employment. Haridas found a job at a local non-profit group that had an auditorium that they rented out. He became the maintenance *Jack of all trades*. Based on my piano tuning background, I searched in the phone book for musical instrument stores. The first one that I called "just happened" to be looking for a piano salesman.

I couldn't help laughing at the turn of events. I was still teaching yoga classes and leading Sunday services, but I was also driving downtown each day with the rank and file of Sacramento in a suit and tie to sell pianos at Cochran's Pianos and Organs. Of course I had sales in my blood. My father was a salesman and so was his father. And sharing the teachings of yoga was sales in a way. We sold a way of life that leads to happiness and freedom in Infinite Spirit. Unfortunately people were more likely to let loose of their hard earned cash for a piano rather than eternal freedom in God.

One of the great things about life is that you never know what is going to happen next. At Ananda I had learned to look for God's hand underneath all life experiences. I was soon to find that God had His hand in with piano sales as well.

It wasn't very long after arriving at Cochran's that I struck up a conversation with the single parent of a young girl who attended piano lessons at the store. The girl's mother attracted special attention because she had come into the store with a beautiful sandy colored dog. I soon learned that the dog's name was Fibber and his steward was Carmen. I explained to Carmen that I was a new salesman. She asked me how I enjoyed working for the store and one thing led to another. The next thing I knew I was showing her a piano. She then became not only my first customer in the store, but also a friend.

It wasn't long before Carmen had heard about Ananda from me. One day she came to the center and then just kept coming. Fibber came to the center as well because he was Carmen's constant companion: Fibber was a guide dog. Along with Carmen, Fibber sat quietly during meditation with everyone else.

I had never spent any time with a blind person before I met Carmen. We had a number of frank talks about what her life was like. I was inspired by her resolve to embrace life instead of retreating. Once Carmen asked me an unexpected question, "Vijay, would you take me to the movies?"

It had never occurred to me that a blind person would want to go to the movies. Apparently it hadn't occurred to the ticket person at the theater either. She looked at us like we were nuts, but sold us tickets. I don't remember what movie we saw. It was a matinee with few other patrons in the theater. We sat in the very back and while Carmen listened to the soundtrack I gave her a running dialogue of what I could see on the screen. I felt like a radio announcer at a sporting event, trying to paint a picture of the action with words. It was actually a lot of fun.

Carmen became a disciple of Paramhansa Yogananda and received Kriya Yoga initiation. Eventually she moved to Ananda Village and lived there for a number of years. I can't help wondering how Carmen would have found her way to Ananda if I hadn't taken that job. Certainly God could have worked it out, but I was thankful to be a small instrument in that process. After all, that was why we had come to Sacramento in the first place.

Working at Cochran's provided a number of other experiences of interest as well. One evening that summer I was working the afternoon/evening shift that kept me in the store until nine pm. Just before closing time a very large man came into the store. I was alone and felt a slight tingling of discomfort, but there wasn't anything to do but greet him with a smile. He soon introduced himself as the store's piano tuner. I instantly relaxed and wondered why I had felt trepidation. The next thing I knew he was showing me his gun that he kept in a shoulder holster under his coat. That widened my eyes a bit! I only saw him a few times after that. A few weeks later, on the fourth of July, he committed suicide by shooting himself.

The man's suicide made me wonder if I should have been able to tell how troubled he was. Could I have helped him in some way? I found it humbling and it reminded me that I had much to learn about life.

After working for some months I was transferred to Cochran's second store which was conveniently closer to home. One afternoon while I was working in the store with a senior salesman a man entered holding a baseball bat. The visitor then addressed the senior salesman with accusations of sleeping with his girlfriend. As the clearly angry man started working his way through the pianos and organs on the sales floor, the salesman began to back away saying, "She isn't with you anymore!"

Dealing with an assailant holding a baseball bat was not in the training that I received upon arrival at the store. I was dumbstruck as to how I might help as the salesman headed out the back door followed by the assailant. Once they were past me

I called 911 and then went out the back of the store to see what was happening.

When I arrived behind the store the two were yelling at each other and the salesman was on the ground receiving a number of kicks, not fighting back. I took a few steps towards the situation but was unsure about what to do. When the assailant saw me he raised the bat and said, "You want some of this?"

Well I didn't want any of his bat, but I didn't see how I could stand there and do nothing. I shouted out that I had called the police and that it might be time for him to leave. I wasn't worried about the police finding him since the salesman knew exactly who he was. Apparently my mention of the police helped because after a couple more kicks he and his bat got into a car and drove away.

Afterwards the salesman begged me not to tell Mr. Cochran about what had happened. He was afraid he would lose his job. So I didn't say anything. The salesman said he was just glad that the guy hadn't used the bat on any of the pianos!

That experience reminded me that life on planet earth is fraught with unexpected dangers. It bothered me that I felt so helpless to offer assistance. I certainly had no desire, nor the skills, to fight the man. I also didn't feel able to diffuse the situation with spiritual energy alone. It made me think, without coming to a clear conclusion at the time, about what, besides chanting AUM (A mantra that represents the cosmic sound of the Creation.) out loud and bringing peace to the situation. I wish I had been able to do more.

Swamiji once told us a story about the time when he was still in SRF and a man with a knife had threatened to stab one of the monks. He said that he had jumped in front of the other monks and told the man strongly, "You will have to get through me to do it!"Apparently those words of strength were enough to diffuse the situation. I always wondered what Swamiji would have done if the man had pushed forward.

The scriptures say that it is right to fight for a dharmic (righteous) cause. The scriptures also teach Ahimsa – non-violence, turning the other cheek and loving thy enemy. Modern military leaders say a strong military is the best deterrent. Certainly I believed that spiritual strength is the best defense for all life challenges, but that doesn't mean that physical strength is never appropriate. As you will see later in my tale, this is an area that my life has led me to explore in more depth.

One day I decided I needed more exercise and gave some consideration as to what I might do. This turn of thoughts led me to investigating local sports facilities. That in turn led me to a club that had racquetball courts. Soon I was running around the court like a gladiator, swinging my racket and gleefully bashing into walls.

I had played some tennis in my teens, but found that I had difficulty following the ball with my less than perfect vision. With racquetball I discovered that the shorter racket and the blue ball with white walls were a comfortable match. Along with the strenuous exercise I enjoyed learning to predict where the ball would end up based on the trajectory and speed with which my opponent had hit the ball.

As my ability to play racquetball improved over the months I ran into an unexpected dilemma. The guys who play racquetball at the sports club are generally quite committed to winning. When they lose they can become quite upset. As a devotee I was happy to let them win, but I couldn't improve my game by losing all of the time.

At Ananda when we played sports we played as hard as we could, but we never got angry or felt bad if someone else won. In fact we were happy for them when they played well! Often Anandites will applaud the efforts of their opponents as much as their own. When I was with guys in the city I had to deal with their swearing and complaining when the game didn't go their way. Eventually I began to think of them as little children who couldn't help themselves: that helped.

I played racquetball for a number of years and became a better than average player. I would often play on what is called the challenge court. This is where you sign up as a challenger and play the winner of the previous match. If you lose you can sign up again and wait your turn. As long as you keep winning, you get to keep playing.

Some of the players were so good that they would keep winning until they were tired and then voluntarily leave. Others never won and spent much more time waiting to play than playing. Over time I worked my way up the ladder of racquetball success. While my general level of play rose, occasionally I would have days of brilliance and also days when I looked like had only just taken up the sport.

Most of the time I didn't care about what others thought of my play, I was just out to have fun and get exercise. But occasionally some of the regulars would get on my nerves. One day I was having an off day and the player that I was challenging began to deride my play to my face. He acted as if I was wasting his time. He had worked his way up onto a high perch of superiority when the Universe decided to intercede.

My opponent had been hitting serves that were very difficult to return. I had missed a number in a row and he was almost laughing at me outright while he looked at me with disdain. I wasn't upset, just determined to do my best in spite of his negative attitude.

The next serve was my opponent's fastest serve of the night. And to my horror it came in a blur right between my legs. I never had a chance to think, my body just reacted. The next thing I knew my racket was behind me and hitting the ball back between my legs towards the front wall. It was a completely reflexive action. My return landed on the front wall in a perfect kill shot (A shot that it is impossible to return.) I was stunned. The audience behind the glass wall was stunned. My opponent was stunned.

I didn't win that game, but that opponent never made fun of me again.

The zenith of my racquetball career came some years later when I was once again on the challenge court. Over time I worked my way up so that I could actually play with the man who was acknowledged by all as the best player in the club. He was the undisputed king of the challenge court. I had played him a number of times previously and been beaten soundly each time. I didn't mind him winning. I enjoyed the challenge of improving my game.

One day I entered the court and experienced what some sportsman call "the zone." This is when you can do no wrong. It was like my body and mind effortlessly knew what to do and each time I hit the ball it did exactly what I intended. At first the king didn't know anything different was happening. I had pulled ahead of him several times in the past, but every time he really applied himself he overwhelmed me.

When we started our match the king was quite relaxed with confidence. I quickly pulled out to a 7 to 2 lead in the 15 point game, he acted unconcerned. When my lead became 10 to 3 his attention began to focus and he started to put on the heat. By the time the score was 12 to 5 he was sweating profusely and beginning to grumble. We began to have ferocious rallies and took turns serving a number of times with no points scored – since you have to win your serve to score.

The players observing the match began to realize that it was taking the king of the court longer than normal to beat me. When the score became 13 to 7 in my favor the king's grumbling turned to cussing. At 14 to 9 he made a supreme effort and pulled himself up to 11. And then the game was over, I had won.

The fallen king shook his head in disbelief as he walked away. His friends were confused when I didn't leave the court. It took some time for it to sink in to the king's courtiers that I, lowly player that I was, unworthy of their respect, had accomplished what most of them had never done, I had defeated the king.

In many ways that feeling of being *in the zone* is the way devotees feel when they are in tune with the positive flow of their own lives. In the beginning I thought that it would be necessary to intellectually know the right thing to do all of the time. But as Swamiji has said to me more than once over the years, "I don't always know the *why*, but I have learned to trust the inward guidance that I feel." Living in the conscious unbroken flow of that inner connection is a major goal for the yogi.

In the end, the most valuable thing that I got from playing racquetball was literally the actual lengthening of my physical life. One day after showering I was approached by a man at the racquetball club. We had the following conversation:

"Excuse me," the man said somewhat uneasily.

"Yes?" I responded.

"This is a bit awkward," he said slowly, as if considering exactly how to communicate what he wanted to say, "My name is Dr. Goetz and I am a dermatologist. I am not in the habit of checking guys out in the shower, but I couldn't help noticing that you have a good sized black spot on your back. Are you aware of it?"

This certainly was an unexpected topic of conversation. I had noticed a spot on my back, but it was not in a place where I could easily see it, and in any case I didn't really care about it. I answered, "What about it?"

"Well, it may be nothing, but I would encourage you to have it looked at," Dr. Goetz then said.

"Okay, may I come to see you?" I asked.

Dr. Goetz shuffled a little and said, "I am not trying to solicit your business. I just felt I should say something. It may be nothing, but then it might be something."

I could tell that he spoke sincerely. I told him, "Look, I really appreciate what you are saying. I don't have anyone that I have seen before. So it really doesn't matter who I see, I may as well see you."

Dr. Goetz gave me his business card and I made an appointment to see him the next week. Soon I was on the examination table face down and he was cutting a dark spot the size of a quarter out of my back. He felt that it should be sent in for a biopsy. When I went to pay I was totally surprised to be informed that there was no charge! Talk about Divine intersession! I was amazed. I spent some time trying to convince Dr. Goetz to accept payment, but he steadfastly refused. He wouldn't even let me pay the lab fees for the test on the specimen.

A few days later I was back in his office and he sat me down to give me the results of the biopsy. Everyone knows that when a doctor sits you down to talk the news probably won't be good, so I sat down with some concern.

The bad news was that the specimen had been found to be malignant. The good news was that he was pretty sure the cancer had not spread. He described it as a stage one malignant melanoma. As a prime body type for skin cancer – red hair and light freckled skin – who had spent many years in the sun while surfing, it wasn't too surprising.

Dr. Goetz then went on to say that in order to be sure, I should have a surgeon do what basically amounted to an exploration of the area to make sure there weren't any stray cancer cells. So I made the arrangements and one morning

Haridas dropped me off at the hospital and that afternoon Toni Liebermann picked me up and drove me back to the center.

They used a general anesthetic for the operation. I had never experienced that before. They wanted to give me a tranquilizer before hand, but I told them it wasn't necessary. When the anesthesiologist came in and found me calmly lying on the operating room table he asked, "Do you meditate?" I answered, "Yes. Why do you ask?" He replied, "It would explain why you are so calm."

I was then told to count backwards starting from ten. I thought it would be interesting to try and resist the anesthesia, but my effort was a complete failure, the next thing I knew I was fighting my way out of a mental fog while lying on a bed in the recovery room. I was groggy for a few minutes, but then my head cleared and I was fine. A few days later I was given the good news that no additional cancer was found. The bad news was that along with a sizable scar on my back, the surgeon and the hospital did charge me: plenty!

I have no doubt that this episode was Divinely directed. The odds of a doctor approaching to help me in this way and then refusing compensation are just too remote to chalk it up to chance. And given that I could not easily see the offending spot, it is probable that it would have continued to grow until doing who knows what damage. I do believe that Dr. Goetz at minimum extended my life, and possibly saved it. And thus, racquetball was truly a lifesaver.

THE BOYS PRAYED —
SACRAMENTO RESTS SECURE…
WITH THE ANANDA YOGI BOYS.

Chapter 5

More Sacramento Adventures

"From joy I came, for joy I live, in sacred joy I melt again."
—Paramhansa Yogananda

It was just a few days after the operation on my back that I had the opportunity to travel to southern California with Swamiji and a small group of Ananda members. Swamiji was scheduled to give several lectures. It was during his appearance in the ashram (A place for practicing the spiritual life.) of a man who had lived at Ananda Village for a short time that the absolutely funniest thing that I have ever seen connected to Swamiji happened.

After our group arrived at a relatively small two story shopping center we were led upstairs to a large room in which about 150 people were sitting on the floor facing the altar. The men were on one side and the women on the other side – this is a common practice in India. While Swamiji met privately with our host for about twenty minutes, the rest of our group sat down and enjoyed the in progress kirtan (Group chanting).

Many of the devotees were wearing Indian clothes and there was an atmosphere of joyful anticipation as everyone waited to meet Swamiji and hear him speak. The group vibration was very sincere and we felt right at home. I observed that there were two large padded chairs on the sides of the altar – presumably one for our host and one for Swamiji.

I should mention that Swamiji was not a man of ostentation. He never put on a special face when he was in public. He was always simply himself: calm, centered and eager to help others when the opportunity arose. How he was treated by others – whether praised, blamed or ignored (which didn't happen often) – had no visible effect on him. If praised, he recognized that God was the doer, so all praise should go to God, and if blamed for some wrong, he would humbly consider if it were true, in the hopes that he might improve himself if he had made an error. If ignored, he was happy to keep his own company. No matter how people treated Swamiji he was always gracious. He would never respond in a way that put others down, even if they – in the opinion of lesser souls – darn well deserved it!

At Ananda I found a group of people who were intensely aware that the Universe was consciously responding to the needs of every moment. No matter what was happening we observed that circumstances were somehow led by unseen forces to resolve themselves in the best, and sometimes most humorous, way.

When the host and Swamiji entered the room the group rose out of respect. As I looked into our host's face I saw an American man in his mid to late thirties, dark hair, dressed in white Indian attire, and carrying himself with an air of self importance. His personality was so on the surface of the situation that it stood in dramatic contrast to Swamiji's calm and inwardly connected demeanor.

After directing Swamiji to one of the large chairs in the front our host moved to the other chair and sat down comfortably. He then began the program by speaking in such a way as to aggrandize himself as he praised Swamiji. I looked over to see how Swamiji was receiving this oration of praise and I noticed that Swamiji seemed much more concerned with trying to find a comfortable way to sit in his chair than what our host was saying.

Yogis prefer to sit with a straight spine away from the back of the chair so that the energy in the spine can flow freely. But between the depth of the seat and the curve of the back, Swamiji seemed unsure about how to use the chair most beneficially. Adding to his challenge was the fact that the chair was capable of rocking back and forth.

Just as our host was achieving a crescendo of fervor I saw that Swamiji had come up with a solution. He placed his hands on the arms of the chair, lifted his body up like a gymnast, crossed his legs Indian style and then lowered himself down. Swamiji seemed quite pleased that he had come up with a good solution. And for a moment he sat facing forward perfectly still with a wide smile. What added to the humor of what happened next is that Swamiji's face never changed or even twitched from that smile of calm contentment.

There was a pause of rest after Swamiji's seat adjustment and all seemed balanced in equilibrium. Our host kept right on pontificating without any knowledge that something else was about to take place. As I watched Swamiji I observed that the chair began to very slowly tip backwards. It became clear that Swamiji's center of gravity was placed just behind the balance point for the chair. This motion was so gradual that it took Swamiji a moment to realize what was happening. Like a slow motion movie the chair began to tip further and further back.

As the angle of the chair moved I saw Swamiji place his hands on top of the arms to grip them, but he made no attempt to escape the inevitable. He just sat there like a smiling sphinx as the chair tipped backward until it fell to the floor with a padded thud. Even after the chair landed Swamiji didn't move, he just smiled up at the ceiling as if nothing at all had taken place.

When our host looked over to see what had interrupted his soliloquy he was absolutely mortified. He jumped up out of his chair with admirable speed and height. He then raced over to make sure Swamiji wasn't injured and helped him get up. The pain of genuine horror that I saw on our host's face gave me good reason to have compassion for him. But I was too busy trying to stifle the mirth that was intensely in need of escaping my mouth. My only regret is that in the name of good manners I couldn't take full advantage of the moment and roll over laughing. It was just so funny!

Please understand that I mean no disrespect to our host, in general I think he was doing good work there. After this incident Swamiji gave a very inspiring talk and then answered a number of questions from the audience. The group was extremely open to Swamiji's words and vibration – which says a lot about the totality of what they were receiving in their ashram. It was just our host's tendency towards self-importance that drew a particularly humorous response from the Universe. The next day we had lunch with him at a restaurant by the beach. He was buoyant with the blessings of Swamiji's presence and we were happy to see that all was well.

Sharing spiritual teachings with humble confidence is truly an art. Not every great soul has the ability or the responsibility to share the teachings intellectually. It is also true that intellectual sharing isn't the only or even the most important way to share. It is through the transformation of one's own consciousness first, that will then lead a devotee to share in the way that is right for their own life and the souls they serve.

In Sacramento we tried to offer a variety of ways that people could participate. Along with Sunday services and regular hatha and raja yoga classes, we did a variety of other activities. We had picnics at a local park, we took river rafting trips, and we had potluck lunches after Sunday service. There were special occasions as well. We had Thanksgiving dinner together and once we celebrated the Jewish Passover. At Christmas time we had a tree trimming party and sang carols. The thing that made all of these activities special is that they always carried an undercurrent of connection to God. The

Ananda way of life doesn't require outward excitement for the experience of joy. In fact, we are taught to practice the truth that joy is within us and that we should share that joy by bringing it out into the world.

Along with our spiritualized social activities we took to heart Yogananda's statement: Seclusion is the price of greatness. Spending time away from a busy life to focus completely on God without distraction is an essential part of deepening spiritual development. Once we had a strong core group we offered our first day long silent retreat.

We all know that much can be accomplished in a short time when we give our complete attention to a project. Cleaning up the garage or even painting a house can be done quickly if approached with energy and concentration. A day of spiritual seclusion can accomplish much in just the same way. Consciously keeping silence, chanting and meditating, listening to a spiritual discourse, reading spiritual words of wisdom, these are all things that take on deeper value when dedicating a whole day or more to intense immersion in inward connection to Spirit.

Our first retreat had seven attendees. Along with our spiritual practices, in the afternoon we planted some tomatoes in remembrance of Yogananda's early years at Mt. Washington, when finances were so tight that at one point they planted tomatoes and had to eat tomato soup, tomato sandwiches, tomato salad and any other way of serving tomatoes that they could come up with.

There gradually developed a small group of ladies who would come for 2 hour advanced hatha yoga sessions. We would practice one of the basic Ananda Yoga routines that usually took about forty-five minutes to complete. Instead of adding more poses to fill in the additional time we would extend our holding of each pose. So each pose became a time of meditation rather than just stretching. Once we had adjusted to this extended rhythm we began to go deeper into the poses than ever before.

At the end of each session we would lay in Savasana (The corpse pose – laying on your back, palms upward, with arms to the sides.) and go into deep relaxation by consciously switching off the energy that animates the body. Instead of going into subconscious sleep our awareness would then expand out in a dynamic state of freedom from the body. I would sometimes completely lose track of time and wonder how long I had been floating away on waves of peace. Then we would finish the sessions by sitting up and meditating.

We also instituted a weekly three-hour meditation. It was beautiful to see people who had not long ago approached a thirty minute meditation with trepidation, arrive eager to dive deep in Spirit, and be reluctant to leave at the end. The key to meditation is sitting absolutely still and learning to focus completely on one of the techniques. Once you learn to focus completely for five minutes, five hours is within your grasp.

When the end of August arrived I made my way back up to Ananda for Spiritual Renewal Week. This was a full week dedicated to sadhana, meditation, and daily classes on the yoga teachings with Swamiji. On one evening Swamiji would pull out his guitar and sing some of the songs that he had composed. His voice and the melodies of his songs would touch our hearts and we would inwardly soar on the wings of his inspiration. There were cute little children's songs like *Little Cathy* and soul stirring songs like *What is Love?* and *Through Many Lives*. Swamiji's music was like none that I had heard before. He was somehow able to capture the perfect balance of meaningfulness without being preachy, spacey, quotey or smarmy like much of modern "spiritual" music I had heard around that time.

Haridas and I had been taken to a concert where they essentially played bible quote inspired Rock n' Roll. It was just gaining popularity at the time. What those musicians didn't know, that Swamiji was teaching us, is that music is an expression of the consciousness of composer and performer. Music that is born of emotion and restlessness, even with well meaning words, will not lead to upliftment, but at best to emotional catharsis. Truly uplifting music should lead to inner silence and not outward emotionalism. It isn't enough just to quote scriptures, but we should connect to Spirit directly and express that relationship in ever-new ways as inspired by that inner connection. The very nature of the way electric guitars and drums are used in most popular music, creates a restless agitation of the mind that makes deep inner perception more difficult.

Kriyananda was also able to convey upliftment without the spacey feel that was prevalent in new age music at the time. Even Swamiji's most active songs took us in some subtle way to a point of stillness in our hearts. This inner connection to Spirit through music was his purpose and in that he was a true maestro as he conducted our spirits up into the realms of inner joy and love.

On Friday we held an Indian Banquet which was a tradition that Master started at Mt. Washington. When the glorious food had been eaten with inwardly connected moderate overindulgence, Swamiji would share stories of banquets with Master and we would be inwardly swept up into the Yogananda/Kriyananda oneness with God vibration that was at the root of Swamiji's life's gift to the world. In these moments our sense of time and space were suspended, we were inwardly transported into Master's living presence and we felt as if we were in the room with him. It thrilled our souls and our hearts overflowed with God love.

On Saturday of Spiritual Renewal Week we held a Kriya Yoga Initiation. Newcomers and the previously initiated would arrive at the temple dressed in white, keeping silence and calmly ready to receive the blessings of that sacred ceremony. This was the spiritual highlight of the week and it never failed to powerfully inspire us toward greater effort in our meditations and thankfulness in our hearts for the blessing of finding our guru and spiritual path.

I wrote a letter to Swamiji just before returning to Sacramento:

> Dear Swamiji,
>
> Such a joy this week has been. Just what the Divine Doctor ordered!
>
> Since I won't be here on Sunday (We have Sunday Service in Sacramento), I feel inwardly renewed, outwardly refreshed and mentally ready to continue the battle joyously.
>
> Truly a wonderful Spiritual Renewal Week!

May God ever increase the blessings that flow to you and through you.

With much love,

In Master, Vijay

When December arrived that year I was fortunate enough to spend about two weeks in seclusion at Santosh's cabin at Ayodyha. It was my first real seclusion since being in India with Swamiji the previous year. The quiet of the forest was soothing to my soul and with Swamiji in his dome just up the hill I felt at peace. I wrote a song with the following words that expresses my experience during seclusion.

Listen, Watch and Hope by Vijay Girard

Listen, to the silent voice, it speaks.
Listen, to your throbbing heart it leaps.
It tells of joy that we know must be true
And guides our lives to the things that we must do.

Watchful, for the things we need to know.
Watchful, for the seeds we need to sow.
To plant within the soil of our hearts,
A tree of living kindness which to everyone imparts.

Hopeful, as the early morning sun.
Hopeful, in the knowledge of best been done.
We know that He who stands above
Can see that He is the one we truly love.

The Christmas season in 1978 found us shuttling back and forth from Sacramento to Ananda for as many of the activities as we could. Our group was still too small for a dynamic all day meditation, so we again attended the eight hour meditation at the meditation retreat. On Christmas day we bathed again in Swamiji's words of wisdom. After the traditional Indian food banquet we melted into bliss as Swamiji spoke of Master and Christmas at Mt. Washington.

It always amazed me to see how Swamiji could just spontaneously express truth in fresh ways. Even though I have heard him speak on any given subject a number of times, he never says something the same way twice. While his stories enchanted us, he wove us in his web of love for God and our hearts soared on wings of oneness in the bliss of Spirit.

I received a very touching note from Swamiji dated Christmas 1978. He wrote:

> Dear Vijay,
> Thank you for your friendship and support, and for the wonderful spirit you have shown. May you be increasingly filled through the New Year, and forever, with Master's love and bliss.
>
> In his love,
>
> S. Kriyananda

In the afternoon on Christmas day Swamiji invited the whole community to his home. We gathered in his dome, mingling, laughing and generally enjoying each other's company the way families do. I don't really know if Swamiji had planned it previously in his mind, but at one point Swamiji gathered a few people together and said that we needed to have a meeting. We went downstairs to his small apartment below the main floor of the dome.

Once we had settled with ears eager to hear why we had been gathered, Swamiji announced with a smile, "We need to appoint some new ministers!"

Up to that point, as I mentioned, Jyotish was the only legally ordained minister beside Swamiji. We were all taken completely by surprise.

Swamiji then asked, "Who shall we choose?"

Again we were shocked into silence. What did we know about who should or shouldn't be a minister? As we attempted to recover our wits Swamiji continued without us.

"How about Jaya?" Swamiji said. We all nodded in silent agreement.

"How about Binay?" Swamiji added. We all nodded again.

Finally our brains got into gear and a few additional names were discussed.

Then Swamiji looked at me with a smile and said, "How about Vijay?" When everyone started laughing I assumed it was a good thing, so I laughed as well. After all, I wasn't about to say, "No, thank you Swamiji. I will pass on that."

While a few more names were discussed I realized that Haridas, who was not present, had not yet been mentioned. So I spoke up.

"Of course, Haridas as well!" Swamiji reacted with another smile.

Soon there was a new batch of ministers. I couldn't help wondering at the perfection of Swamiji's timing. It was a Christmas blessing that I never could have anticipated. It didn't really change anything about the way we lived, to me it was a sign of Swamiji's belief that we would represent Master and Ananda in a beneficial way, and for that expression of support I was deeply touched.

I also could never have guessed what the circumstances would be in which Haridas and I could first use our minister's cards as a way to help a situation. I would have thought that it would be for a marriage or maybe a christening. Even a funeral would have been my thought before what actually happened.

One day we received a call from a young man who needed our help. He had come to the center regularly so we weren't surprised to hear from him. What we didn't expect was when he asked if we could come down and bail him and is buddy out of jail! So there we were on our first official task as ministers, down at the jail house. The boys had been arrested for a fairly minor infraction, so it wasn't like we were saving career criminals from Folsom Prison. We felt a bit like the parents of a child that has had a bout of youthful bad judgment. We picked them up and put them in the car. After shaking our heads in appropriate dismay for as long as we could stand it, we then burst into laughter!

Along with Toni Liebermann we had an enthusiastic group, including Steve Phelps, Dave Howe, Dan Houser, Carmen Quintana, Erwin Rupert, Mark Monson, Tom Sheehy,

John Dyer, Laura Adee, Theresa Meredith, Carol Bies, Susan Fiddyment, Julie Baker, Marilyn and Marilee Beckwith, and Sanaka (who had lived at the village for some time).

It was Marilee's mother, Marilyn, that gave Haridas and I our most challenging ministerial opportunity. Marilyn, like Carmen, was visually impaired. Some months after her first visit to the center we were happy to hear that she had found a life partner: Fred Grimes. The new couple asked Haridas to be their minister at the wedding and he agreed.

The wedding was a joyous occasion and everyone wished them a happy life together. So when Haridas received a phone call from Marilyn just two days after the wedding he was surprised to find her extremely upset. Soon it came out that while on the honeymoon, Fred, had a heart attack and was now in the intensive care unit of a Sacramento hospital.

It would be terrible for this to happen to anyone, anytime, but on your honeymoon? It was truly mind-bending. Haridas jumped right in with supporting Marylyn and family at the hospital. They spent hours in the hospital chapel praying and they kept someone at the hospital twenty-four hours a day. After four days everyone was exhausted. Fred appeared to have stabilized somewhat and they decided to take a day off from their vigil to get some much needed rest.

In an effort to recharge himself Haridas went up to Ananda Village for the day. I was working at Cochran's downtown store when I received a call with the news that Fred had died. Haridas couldn't be located immediately. Marilyn was at the hospital and she wanted me to come right away. I left work with a hurried explanation and drove to the hospital. I was so focused on getting there as quickly as possible that it wasn't until I approached the hospital parking lot that it finally occurred to me that I had no idea what to do. How do you console a bride that has lost her husband after a week of marriage?

I didn't fail to think at some point that we might have anticipated this. It was most likely the fervent prayers for Fred had been keeping him in the body. As soon as they had relaxed their efforts, nature – guided by the karmic elements of the situation – had taken its course.

While a part of my mind wished that Swamiji had given us some specific instructions for just such a situation, I knew he had taught us to work positively with whatever presents itself in life, so I pushed forward with calm concern.

When I arrived on the proper floor I was ushered into the hospital chapel where the staff Chaplain was consoling Marilyn. Part of my mind was thinking, "Let this trained Chaplain handle this, I will just stand around in the background!" It wasn't that I didn't want to help, I just had no clear idea about how to help in the best possible way. And I wasn't encouraged when after asking Marilyn how she was doing, she wrapped her arms around me and broke out into a convulsion of sobbing.

I don't suppose there was anything I could have said that would have brought about a different result, but I couldn't help mentally kicking myself for messing things up right away as I hugged her.

When Marilyn calmed down I discovered that she had not yet gone in to view the body; she had been waiting for me to come with her. I can say that I didn't hesitate, but inwardly I was praying that I wouldn't fail in my duties. I had never seen a recently deceased body before. I had once seen a cadaver during an eighth grade field trip and another time I saw a dead man lying on the street as the car I was in drove by an accident. But those aren't the same as being right up close and personal to the dead body of someone that you have known personally.

We entered the room where Fred had been prepared for our visit and I led Marilyn right up to the bedside. She reached out and began to caress Fred's face as tears flowed freely down her cheeks. Marilee (Marilyn's adult daughter), the Chaplain and I stood back and let Marilyn have this moment in as private a way as possible. As I watched the poignant scene I looked at Fred and was surprised, although I don't know why, to see that he had a beatific smile on his face. He almost didn't look dead, he looked like he might be sleeping.

I reached out with my inner awareness and tried to touch the Truth of the moment. As I looked inwardly into Fred's face I began to feel flooded with happiness and freedom. I was instantly convinced that Fred was experiencing this same joy now that he was free from this physical world. The juxtaposition of this inner joy with Marilyn's grief was quite dramatic.

I wanted to tell Marilyn that while I understood her reason for being sad, she should realize that Fred was now experiencing joy and she should be happy for him. But I couldn't make myself say it. I didn't think she could handle it. I wasn't willing to take a chance.

After a few minutes Marilyn asked me to do a ceremony. I had known that things might come to this, but I didn't at the time know exactly what to do, so I made it up as I went along. First the four of us held hands over the body. Then we prayed and I recited the Gayatri Mantra. I figured you can't go wrong with a Sanskrit mantra for the liberation of the soul.

I then decided to read Yogananda's astral ascension ceremony. The hospital Chaplain held the book open for me so I could still hold hands with the others. I began to read Yogananda's words and everything was going fine until I found myself reading words like dust, bones and ashes. It started to get too graphic for standing right over the body, after all the body was still warm and Marilyn had been touching him. My mind began to race with trying to figure out what to do. I then took a leap of faith and began to extemporize words that I thought would be appropriate for the situation.

As part of my mind sought words of solace to share with Marilyn, in another part of my mind I could see that the Chaplain had been following along as I read and must be wondering what I was doing, since I was no longer reading from the book. The Chaplain never said anything and in the end I feel that Marilyn felt supported in that moment of trial. I have no doubt that Fred was supported because I felt what I believe was his bliss during the whole experience.

The next day Haridas was back from the village and he guided the grieving family every step of the way through all of the funeral arrangements, including officiating at the funeral and graveside services. I can't imagine anyone doing a better job. It was a dramatic reminder of the impermanence of physical life.

I later learned from Swamiji that the Gayatri Mantra is the correct mantra to use for those who are passing from this world. When possible it and/or the chanting of Aum – sounds like Om – should be done in the right ear of the deceased.

Passing into and out of this physical realm of the Creation is not generally well understood. In western society we have done our best to separate ourselves from all that we don't understand and/or define as unpleasant, of which death is the ultimate expression. It is helpful for loved ones to realize that the journey of the soul from this material world to the astral world (Heavenly for souls of higher vibration and hellish for souls of lower vibration.) can be confusing for the one in transition. While it is appropriate to express the grief of parting, it is important that we don't hold our loved ones back once it is their time to go. It is most productive to pray that God's Will be done, and act as a conscious channel for blessings of love and joy to flow to any soul that has departed from the physical body.

Chapter 6

Even More Sacramento Adventures

"Learn to laugh at yourself". –Swami Kriyananda

"You have come to earth to entertain and to be entertained." –Paramhansa Yogananda

We always enjoyed it when our friends from Ananda Village would come and visit us in Sacramento. Vidura (Wise: a trusted minister of the Pandavas in the Mahabharata.) was very enthusiastic about running and staying healthy. So when he came to visit we would sometimes go jogging with him. One time he convinced us to go on a juice fast, so we drank only juices for three days. His next recommendation was that we go for a colonic treatment in order to cleanse the colon.

Anandites were always trying various unconventional ways to stay healthy or heal a physical challenge. Swamiji was often trying unconventional healing techniques so there was a general openness for such things. Nothing was too bizarre. I personally had never been particularly interested in doing many of the things that I heard others were trying, but somehow Vidura convinced Haridas and I to give it a try. Vidura found a place that wasn't too far away and so we were soon seated in a small reception area waiting for our turn.

I had never experienced a colonic so I wasn't sure exactly what to expect. I had been given an enema once when ill in Hawaii and I figured it would be similar to that. Well, I won't go into all the details, but let me just say that it was nothing like the little enema that I had been given in the past. It included the inserting of a metal tube that was in my opinion way too large. I mean, way, too large!

Even though I had never had a colonic I could tell that this office was not a top of the line operation. As the first victim, I lay on the table during the procedure mostly wondering what I might do in a playful way to pay Vidura back for this indignity. I briefly considered cutting my session short, but then decided that I would endure it and let the others do so as well.

When I came out I didn't say a word I just smiled like all was well with the world. I sat and read a magazine while Haridas took his turn. When Vidura asked me how it was I just shrugged my shoulders like it was no big deal and said, "Okay."

When Haridas came out I could see the shock on his face. He didn't say a word as Vidura went in for his turn. Once Vidura had disappeared into the office Haridas and I looked at each other, having difficulty in controlling the laughter that wanted to burst forth but needed to be held back in the name of good manners.

When Vidura reappeared we could see his eyes were also open a little wider than normal. We all kept up a proper decorum while we paid for the treatment, but no sooner had we left the building then we all broke out into laughter. Haridas and I teased Vidura about colonics for many years after that day.

Anyone who has participated in the role of teacher, no matter in what field, knows that not every student is interested and/or capable of absorbing all that the teacher has to offer. Most of the time Haridas and I practiced our "less is more" philosophy when teaching. I should clarify that for us, less-is-more didn't mean watered down teachings, it meant emphasizing inner stillness, devotion and attunement rather than an overly intellectual approach to the teachings. When it came time to offer our first Yoga Teacher training program I experienced the difference between quantity and quality of students. Well, I should say, student! You see, there was only one student in the course: Toni Liebermann.

Toni had grown up in an Italian family in Brooklyn, New York. It must be difficult to get more Catholic than that! After graduating from art school she married and went with her husband to a military base in Amarillo, Texas. There she began to explore a larger view of life – since we all know that everything in Texas is bigger! – and discovered not only an expanded view of Christianity through a local bible study group, but also came into contact with the teachings of yoga.

I asked Toni how she found Ananda and the teachings of Paramhansa Yogananda one day and here is what she said:

I attended my first Hatha Yoga class in 1971 in Amarillo, Texas. I was taking exercise classes at the local YWCA and signed up for a class at the suggestion of a friend. She told me that she was enjoying the class and she thought that I would as well. At the time, I had no idea what Hatha Yoga was so I had absolutely no preconceived ideas of what to expect. I came out of my first class with the distinct impression that I had worked with my body in the most satisfactory way; in that every body part seemed to have gotten the attention it needed. I continued with these classes until our family moved to California in 1974.

Once we were settled in Roseville, I began looking for a yoga class to take locally, but I couldn't find one. I called the Roseville Parks and Recreation Department and spoke to the Director. I asked him if they had any yoga classes scheduled. He replied that he did not know what yoga was. When I explained that it was a type of exercise, he told me that he was looking for an instructor to teach a regular exercise class and would I be willing to do it? Well, I said yes, since I was desperate to find some way to get into a class.

My first classes were one hour long consisting of 30 minutes of jumping jacks, etc. and then 30 minutes of "stretching". It did not take long for my students to mention that they enjoyed my classes, especially the "stretching" part. The practice of yoga was not well known then, so I told them that what they were doing was called Hatha Yoga. They immediately asked me if I offer a full yoga class. When I suggested this to my Director, he was very open to it. He said that if there were enough students who would sign up for such a class then he would be willing to put it into the schedule. So began my career as a yoga instructor.

The teaching went well. I learned a lot, not only about how to share my subject, but I became increasingly aware of the more subtle changes that were taking place in my consciousness. I knew that this practice was based on the teachings of India. I did not know what those teachings were, but my desire to explore them continued to grow. Also, I realized that if I wanted to continue to evolve as a teacher, I needed to get some formal training. In preparation for this, I committed myself to some serious Bible Study because I wanted to have a good grasp of the tradition I had practiced from childhood, so that I could compare what I would learn of yoga with a teaching I already trusted.

I began to look for a class to take that would advance my knowledge of yoga. I eventually learned that there was a Raja Yoga class scheduled at the YWCA in Sacramento. I was told that this class included some philosophy as well as instruction in the postures. I signed up right away. When the day came to attend the class, I arrived early. I found a young man very busy putting up a table and placing many items on it which were for sale. The items included books, records, audio tapes, and incense. He was very friendly and started talking to me. He asked me why I had decided to take this class. I related my story to him and then asked, "Have I come to the right place?" He smiled at me and said, "Yes, you have come to the right place."

I had assumed that this man was the instructor, but he explained to me that he had come along to help the teacher, but the teacher himself was meditating before class started and would be out shortly. I immediately liked what I heard. He told me that his name was Keshava (Another name for Krishna.) and the teacher's name was Santosh (Contentment).

Santosh had scheduled a series of four week sessions and I attended all of them. I so resonated with what he was saying that I digested the information more deeply every time I heard it. More importantly, I saw a light in Santosh's eyes that told me I had found that which I had always longed for without knowing its name. I still could not really articulate this impression very clearly, but I knew that I was going to pursue these teachings with fervor. At the end of the third class

Santosh motioned me to the side of the group for a private word. He simply said, "I would like to recommend a book to you, I think there is something in it for you." He said nothing else, so I had no preconceived ideas of the book's contents or about the author, but I set out to find a copy.

On a day shortly after this, I entered a local bookstore looking for a book entitled *Autobiography of a Yogi* by Paramhansa Yogananda. What I found that day was a featured display of the book on a table that held hundreds of copies, all face up, staring at me. I stepped back, and somehow knew that my life would be different once I had read it. But, if you can believe it, I did not buy the book that day.

My husband (at the time) had been eyeing my new found interest in yoga warily. He was feeling increasingly threatened by my interest in something he did not understand and could not share. I instinctively knew that going further in my studies was going to present further problems in this area. I went home without the book but I could not put it out of my mind. I woke up the next morning knowing to my core that I had to push forward, so I took a deep breath, resigning myself to an uncertain future, went back to the store and bought the book.

Once I had the book in my hands I literally could not put it down. I remember having the book tucked under my arm as I vacuumed the carpet! It took me four days to complete my first reading. The book was like nothing I had ever read before; it felt so alive. I remember thinking, "This man knows God. He is not talking about dry facts; he has actually experienced what he is talking about." I knew then that what I had always wanted was to know God as this man knew God. I also realized that he could show me the way to reach that goal. This was in 1976 and I believe I became a disciple that day, although I did not realize it at the time.

After completing those classes with Santosh, I invited him to come to Roseville to give a Raja Yoga class to my students. He did come, bringing Nitai, Prahlad, and Danny with him at different times. This was how I first met so many of the Ananda monks. I enjoyed meeting all of them because I deeply respected the spiritual commitment that they each had made. I wanted to make that commitment, also. Peggy Morgan was one of the students who took Santosh's class in Roseville. This was the beginning of our long association with Ananda.

It was a little later that year that Santosh suggested that it was time for me to come up and visit the Community. I took along a group of my students for this big adventure – this was a radical thing for suburban housewives to be doing!

Santosh gave us a tour of the village and then he took us up to the Seclusion Retreat where Prahlad was waiting for us in the temple.

Prahlad led us in yoga postures and a short meditation. We then went into the dining room where a delicious meal had been prepared for us. The day was wonderful! I felt very joyful.

At about 3 p.m. the students began to feel that it was time to leave in order to be home by 5 p.m. for their families. I myself was having difficulty thinking about leaving. My feet felt glued to the ground and I could not move. I had to be practically dragged to the parking lot for our departure.

Peggy and I signed up for Swami Kriyananda's lessons by mail after those Roseville Raja Yoga classes. In 1978, we took Kriya Initiation together. By the time we took this step, my resonance with Master's teachings had already grown very deep. Yet, on the night of initiation, it went still deeper. By the end of the ceremony I found that a subtle change had come over me. It was as though Master had overshadowed my very being with His presence; he was in me and around me. That sense of His presence within me has never left.

As I began to discuss the teachings of Raja Yoga with Toni I found that she was not only intelligently receptive, but inwardly open. As I have mentioned, the study of Yoga cannot be successfully accomplished with only the intellect. It isn't enough to learn the facts and figures of the tradition. It is essentially an experience that at its root is a process of attunement, absorption and vibrational transformation.

It is the act of conscious inner connection to universal Truth itself that is the key to real understanding in life. In the West we are taught that the memorization of information is an education. In Yoga it is the process of learning how to access our highest potential inwardly that we seek to perfect. Once we have learned to inwardly connect to life itself, we will be following a path that leads past knowledge to the direct perception of intuitive wisdom.

A number of Ananda members, including myself, had been raised in Jewish families and were unfamiliar with the perspectives of other traditions. Here is what Toni had to say when years later I asked about her Catholic background and "Bible Belt" experience:

> When one is raised in a particular tradition, all that one learns is colored by the characteristics of that style. For this reason, the move to Texas was extremely important for me in that it showed me a larger world. At the invitation of my next door neighbor, I attended a Women's Bible Study group at the local Baptist Church in Amarillo.
>
> The group consisted of women of varied Christian denominations. I was the only Roman Catholic. As we got to know one another, we

discovered that we were all women of deep faith. We all loved God and desired to live holy lives. That was why we were there studying the Bible.

We sought instruction and inspiration in order to know what God wanted of us. We also realized that we had each been told at one time or another that our denomination was the only true teaching. A look around the room showed us that there was something wrong with that idea. We acknowledged each other's paths and, over time, grew to respect each other. There were a few, however, who still weren't too sure about the Catholic in the group. They related having been told that all Catholics were Communists!

This experience was eye-opening for me. I began to see myself as a Christian instead of a Catholic Christian. However, to the alarm of many in the group, I began suggesting that we were Jewish Christians. I could not separate the two in my mind because it seemed that one must accept the God of the Jews for the Christian teachings to be considered valid. I pondered this idea for years, expanding it later, after studying the teachings of yoga. At one point I decided that I was a Jewish Christian Hindu Buddhist Yogi. That was the day that I left all labels behind forever.

I also asked Toni many years later about her experience of our teacher training course and she said:

First of all, I was so grateful to you for taking this project on. I was not free to go to Ananda to attend the program there due to family obligations. You offered to give me the training I desired in a way that would work for me. That told me a lot about how Ananda did things.

All of my early experiences with Ananda showed me that people were there to help me and would work with my circumstances. Prakash (Inner light) was the overall coordinator of the Ananda Yoga Teacher Training Programs at the time and he was amenable to the arrangement, so all together we made it work. That is why, till today, I am especially sensitive to the time and cost of classes for my low income students.

I was still new to the teachings and had not yet had time to digest the information in the lessons and assimilate it into a cohesive whole. I had not yet had the benefit of attending Swami's classes which always help to solidify understanding. But you accepted me where I was at the time and did not make me feel like a fool when it was clear that I was not fully following what you were saying. Your patience made a big difference because I developed a trust in you that gave me the time and inclination to persevere with our classes. I really did want to learn what you had to share. So, of course, I ended up getting a very great opportunity which none of the other

> YTTC students at the Community were receiving; one on one discussions.
>
> I know now that those classes were good for you, too. You were able to teach in a style that suits you, that is, to dialogue instead of to lecture. It sure worked for me, because I could easily stop you and ask you to clarify or expand on the topic as needed. My studies with you allowed me to get my Certification in good time. More importantly, my studies with you gave me further insight into the "way of the devotee".

Toni might be the only one in Ananda's history to have received a private Yoga Teacher Training Course. But that is what we did. She would study the materials from Swamiji's course on Raja Yoga (At that time it was called 14 Steps to Perfect Joy.) and then we would discuss what she had read. Simultaneously she was a regular participant of hatha yoga classes, Sunday services and other center activities. And she was already a hatha yoga instructor, so she knew how put classes together and communicate successfully with her students.

From my point of view it was a pleasure to share with someone who could handle so much of what I had to share. There was an openness in Toni's mind that had no barriers. I never sensed a "Prove it to me!" attitude in her, but only a "Why is it so?" interest when she didn't understand something. After several months of weekly meetings Toni received the first Ananda teachers training certificate which was given to someone who hadn't lived at Ananda Village, dated July 30, 1979 and signed by Swami Kriyananda.

Along with sharing the teachings with others, Haridas and I were still in school as well: I literally, and both of us figuratively. When I was in India with Swamiji during spring and summer of 1977 he had read the long letters I was sending back to the Ananda Community. One day he commented to me that the letters were pleasant to read but that the spelling and grammar needed a lot of work. He suggested that I take an English writing course when we returned to America. So once we had the center going I enrolled in a class – which I passed!

Haridas and I were complete novices at running a center so we were always trying to be open to fresh ideas about how we could do a better job. One day Haridas came across the acronym SPIDOG – solving problems in the directions of goals. Since one of our main goals at the time was to support the center financially, this new inspiration turned into the SPIDOG Cleaning Service. The idea was to do clean-up for new construction sites. Our first job was to clean the windows of a new custom home. Haridas had negotiated a flat rate for the whole job. So we arrived ready to buff those windows to a shine as quickly as possible. We had extended handle squeegees, buckets, soap, rags and a ladder.

I think we might have started in by counting our chickens before the eggs were hatched. Our first look at the windows gave us the impression that Haridas had negotiated a fantastic rate. We were all smiles as we went to work. Unfortunately we hadn't taken into account the practical reality that the windows weren't just dirty, they had been splattered with some sort of greasy product that was really difficult to get off the windows. Our soapy water wasn't even beginning to cut through the stuff!

Soon Haridas and I were deep into a discussion about how to apply SPIDOG to this unexpected situation. We needed help and we needed it soon. I guess Divine Mother wanted to take the dollar signs out of our eyes, because the clock was ticking and were weren't cleaning. It didn't help our speed that we couldn't stop laughing at this unexpected state of affairs. Here we were, two perfectly capable young men and we couldn't get some windows clean. At the time, it seemed pretty funny.

We eventually decided that Haridas needed to go off and find the right cleaning equipment. I kept on washing while Haridas was gone but didn't make much progress. About an hour later Haridas returned with unexpected supplies. He had a big stack of used newspapers and a can of kerosene.

At the hardware store Haridas had explained our dilemma to the man behind the counter. The man smiled with a knowing nod of the head and then proceeded to give Haridas a lesson in window cleaning; which included the esoteric teaching that newspaper was the tool of choice for window cleaners in the know and kerosene was the proper solvent to take care of the gooey spots on the glass.

Even with these high teachings and techniques of window cleaning it took us most of the day to get the job done. It was definitely not easy money! But it was incredibly funny! We had a lot of fun that day and we have enjoyed remembering the story many times through the years, so I think in the end we did get paid pretty well. Though now that I think about it, it must have been somewhat traumatic, because it was the one and only job we ever did as SPIDOG Cleaning Service!

I thoroughly enjoyed living with Haridas. His joyful creativity always brought a smile to my face. He often approached challenges from unanticipated directions. In an effort to find new members Haridas started calling people at random from the phone book. He started with the Z's instead of the A's. The next thing we knew there was a man named Jeff Zender coming to the center. Jeff became a disciple, took Kriya Yoga initiation and was a strong supporter of the center.

One day Haridas and I were brainstorming about how to get more students into our classes. According to our creative calculations it would be less expensive to pay them to come than it is to advertise. But you would have to advertise in order to let them know you are willing to pay them…so that knowledge wasn't as helpful as we would have hoped.

Each of the people that came to the center was very special to us. We were deeply aware of the divine play that was going on underneath the surface of our interactions with people. Finding the spiritual path and then turning it into the way that you live your life is the most important kind of healing that can take place in life; not the healing of the body, but the healing of the soul. That we could in some small way help others along their quest for inner freedom was our sacred task.

In spite of all the good that was taking place in my life at Ananda Sacramento, during the fall of 1979 I found that an interior unrest began to develop within me. A disciple's inner weather will naturally fluctuate at times so at first I assumed it was a temporary feeling, but after a few months I realized that change was percolating. I wasn't sure what that change might be, so I began to open myself up to whatever might be next for my life.

Christmas that year was once again a season of deep inspiration. Along with the blessings of the all day meditation there was also much fun. For a number of years the monks had made a practice of being Santa's helpers to hand out Christmas presents. They were also in the habit of putting on a skit that was filled with "insider" Ananda humor.

Anyone who has put on seasonal programs knows that it is difficult to make each year better than the previous year. That year the monks were feeling their oats and came prepared to accomplish new heights in Ananda entertainment. Little restraint was used during these presentations; any subject was fair game for finding a humorous perspective.

During the past two years Swamiji had spent many months touring across America to bring Paramhansa Yogananda and the Ananda way of life to the attention of as many people as possible. During one tour Prahlad and Santosh would travel ahead of the group, getting Swamiji's books into local stores and making various arrangements for Swamiji and the group that traveled with him. In some cities the presentations were very well attended, but in others there might be only a few people present.

No matter how many people came Swamiji always made his presentation. His only purpose was to serve his guru and help anyone who was interested in growing their spirit. He had no attachments about what that service should look like. As long as everyone did their best, with the balance of right attitude and attention to practical details, Swamiji felt that he had done his part. It was up to God to determine how many people came and what they did with his humble offerings.

Well, to get back to the skit, for some reason the monks thought it was funny that Swamiji would come to a town and only a few people would show up, so that was included in the Monks thespian expression. In all fairness, it does seem a little funny that God would send one of His best representatives and then not provide an audience. At the same time, anything that would disrespect Swamiji's efforts was seen, unfortunately in retrospect, to be inappropriate. So it was that that year, was the last year, of the monks Christmas skits.

It should be mentioned that to the best of my knowledge the end of the skits didn't come from Swamiji. As far as I know he wasn't even remotely bothered by the reference. Swamiji almost never responded to other people's mistakes unless he felt that he could help them in some way. How others treated him was observed, but rarely reacted to. Needless to say, this was a moment of poor judgment on the part of the monks, possibly due to a mild case of over familiarity.

I got confirmation from Swamiji that there were no hard feelings in a very unexpected way at a Kriya Yoga initiation ceremony. During my early years at Ananda I had occasionally overheard Swamiji whispering words of encouragement to a few of the initiates after blessing them during the ceremony. These were sharings that I probably shouldn't have been poking my ears into. He said things like: Master is pleased with you. And, God is pleased with your devotion. Of course, I hoped that in the future I might get similar feedback during the Kriya Ceremony.

I remember that one day for no particular reason I was thinking about ham. Being a vegetarian, that wasn't a common thought in my mind. I didn't think anything of it at the time, it was just a passing thought out of seemingly nowhere. A few days later there was a Kriya Ceremony. Having taken Kriya from Swamiji numerous times since coming to Ananda I felt comfortable with making the offerings of fruit, flower and donation, followed by stepping forward for the blessing at the spiritual eye. After the blessing we open our hands to receive blessed rose pedals from Swamiji. Normally Swamiji didn't engage in eye contact when giving the rose pedals. He was acting as a channel for Master and wanted to maintain inwardness.

On this occasion, as I prepared to receive the rose pedals I opened my eyes to make sure my hands were positioned properly to receive the pedals. As I did so I saw a soft smile come to Swamiji's face and then he leaned forward and whispered in my ear, "God loves hams just as much as He loves other people."

I had to put my reaction on hold while I walked back to my seat. And of course once I got there I couldn't make any noise because it might disturb others. I was very calm as a result of being at the ceremony, but I really wanted to laugh out loud! God had set me up with the thought about ham as a food earlier in the week and then got me again through Swamiji about being a theatrical ham. Once I had chewed on the whole thing for a few minutes I realized that *God loves hams* and *I am a ham*...God loves me...Sweet!

The yogi doesn't seek acknowledgment for any success in life, but when it arrives unexpectedly it is greatly appreciated. Years later I was told by someone traveling by car with Swamiji from San Francisco to Ananda, Swamiji said, "Let's stop in Sacramento to give encouragement to Vijay." And as a part of that conversation he also commented: "Vijay's devotion is pure."

"IN MEMORY
OF MASTER'S EARLY DAYS
WE CHEERFULLY PLANT TOMATOES."

Chapter 7

Sacramento Center Adieu

Your spirituality must be tested in the harsh cold light of day.
–Sister Gyanamata

When I first moved to Ananda I thought that I had spiritually *arrived.* I would now live a happy life in the forest while I merged with utmost speed into the infinite joy of Spirit! Such is the naivety of the young devotee. When we think of Paramhansa Yogananda's life we think of bliss in God, we conveniently forget how hard he had to toil while bringing these teachings to America and that finances were a major challenge for many years. In the early years of Ananda, a local lumber company tried to steal Ananda by foreclosing on a debt that was not even late and Swamiji had to figure out in a hurry how to come up with the money.

In my early years at Ananda, like others before me, I experienced what old timers at Ananda, with a nostalgic smile, call the "honeymoon" period. The struggle that comes from knowing that you don't fit into the meaningless treadmill that so many people call life is dissolved by the joy of finding a spiritual family of like–minded lovers of God. The months and sometimes years of deep inspirations and soaring joy seem like they will never end. The spiritual life, for a time, may give the impression that suffering and challenge only exist in the past.

Discomfort in life can take many forms. It isn't always an illness, accident, financial loss or an unpleasant relationship. Sometimes it is a feeling of restlessness or a cloud of confusion that keeps inner peace from filling one's heart. At other times it is finding a fork in the road of life and not knowing which way to go.

Many times over the years I have seen that the day I think "Things are going well!" is often followed quickly by an unexpected challenge. While at the same time, when life looks dark and I wonder if I can possibly take another step forward, there will unexpectedly appear a light in my life that I could not have anticipated.

The yogi isn't instantly freed from the pleasant and unpleasant karmic winds of their past, but they are gradually freed from being affected in the same way as in the past. I had grown up in a society that supported living in my emotional response to life, to smile with my likes and frown with my dislikes. As a yogi I was learning to live underneath the surface of my emotions, in a calm centered place of peace in my heart. So if I didn't feel that inner calmness, I asked myself, "Why?"

Life is in many ways like rafting down a river that you have never been on before – or at least you don't remember having been there before. Sometimes the waters of our lives are calm. At other times we are caught in rapids with large boulders in the stream and crashing waves. And we never know what is around the next bend.

Toward the end of summer in 1979, having just completed my tenth year as a disciple of Paramhansa Yogananda and in my seventh year at Ananda, I began to experience an inner restlessness. It was a natural time for me to take stock of how my life was going. The Sacramento Center was now established and while there was still much to be done, I began to feel hemmed in; I began to long for new horizons. It wasn't that I had anything specific in mind, I just knew that I felt a need that wasn't being fulfilled.

It was also around this time that Toni began to share with me some of the challenges that she was facing in her home life. Her spiritual life had blossomed since finding Ananda and the practice of Kriya Yoga had deepened her ability to feel God's presence. Her two children, Dan and Cristi, had come many times to the center but her husband came only once. It was clear that he began to feel threatened by Toni's growing involvement with Ananda. Eventually he turned actively against her participation and she felt inwardly forced to make a choice.

I was very careful when I spoke to Toni about her marriage. I felt strongly that it was important I didn't sway any decision that she might make. Even though I felt that her discipleship would not be deterred by her husband's negative feelings, I knew very clearly that she had to make this decision on her own.

My role as a minister was to help her find her own truth and not to tell her what that truth might be. This is something that I had observed about Swamiji. Even though there were many people who came to him for advice he very rarely told them what he thought they should do. If he did say something specific, they were under no obligation to follow his advice.

Once a woman asked Swamiji for a spiritual name and after some time Swamiji gave her the name Kripa, which means Divine Grace. But the young woman didn't like the name because it sounded like the word creep – as in an unpleasant person. So Swamiji happily accepted her feelings and came up with a new name, which she did accept.

There is another lesson to be considered from this new name story: attunement to the spiritual flow of energy into one's life. When we don't accept that which God gives us, we may become disconnected from that which is most beneficial to us. It is interesting to note that the woman who couldn't receive the blessing of the first name that Swamiji gave her didn't stay at Ananda all that long after receiving her new name.

There was another factor that made life in Sacramento challenging for Haridas and myself. We were young men who had in our spiritual enthusiasm attempted to leave our sexuality and any desire that we might feel for female companionship behind us. We had both, along with eight or ten others, taken vows of brahmacharya – a conditional vow of renunciation. In my own mind, this vow of renunciation didn't so much represent what I should give up in life, but represented my desire to be as dedicated as I could to living for, serving and knowing God. When I took the vow I didn't really think about whether I could actually handle life as a brahmachari (Someone who has taken a conditional vow of renunciation – which usually includes celibacy.) or even if I in the ultimate sense should. I believed it was a good thing to do at the time so I just did it.

Our lives in Sacramento brought us into contact with the mainstream of society. Haridas and I both had jobs in which we used our western names and the people we worked with knew very little or nothing about our affiliation with Ananda. While it was a great opportunity for us to spiritually challenge ourselves it was also impossible to not be aware of the many ways that we could become distracted from our spiritual purpose.

In January of 1980 I approached Swamiji with the news that I wanted to move back to Ananda Village. I didn't have a clear sense of what I should do next, but I knew that once I started moving forward with my life opportunities would begin to present themselves.

I was deeply touched by the wonderful satsang and going away gathering that took place at the Sacramento Center after the announcement that I was moving back up to the Village. The group had really bonded during the first two years. When Steve Phelps gave a goodbye speech with tears in his eyes I had one of those special moments when I was reminded of all the good that God was doing through Ananda. I didn't feel he was crying because of me, but that we were all so appreciative of the blessings that had come into our lives through Yogananda's and Kriyananda's efforts.

I received this letter from Jeff Zender a couple of months later:

3-15-80

Dear Vijay,
Greetings! I hope this letter finds you deeply centered in the Spirit. Enclosed are pictures from the Maha-good bye party. Please accept them as a small token of appreciation from me for the tremendous amount of inspiration that I have drawn from you. In you I have seen what it means to truley have the compass of the minds always pointing toward God. But more than that, God has blessed me through you — through association with your concioueness, and for that I am deeply grateful to the infinite Lord. May God bless you with His eternal rapture and joy.

In Divine Friendship I Remain

Jeff

I did feel a bit guilty abandoning Haridas, but not so much as to not move forward! I was confident that he could handle the job, so knowing that our growing Sacramento family was well cared for I made preparations to move back up to the monastery at Ananda Village.

The men's monastery was a hodgepodge of dwellings on a forested slope just west and below Swamiji's dome. I had previously taken seclusion at various times in Prahlad's trailer, Haridas's tepee and in Santosh's wood, tar paper and plastic "cabin." So I knew the layout well. What I didn't know is where I would live.

Housing at Ayodhya was very limited. The whole community was under strict control by the county as to what building we could or couldn't do. I decided that I wanted to build a small cabin at the monastery but needed permission to proceed. And the cabin I wanted to build would be bigger and nicer than anything that existed at the time. Knowing this was a very controversial issue I wrote the following letter to the village council and all of the monks:

> Dear Friends,
>
> I am hesitant to write this letter. I hope that it may clarify any questions about my situation. As you all know I have recently moved back to the village. It's hard to believe that it is almost three years since I've actually lived on the land for any length of time.
>
> A brief history will describe my previous living situation. Having lived at the meditation retreat since my arrival in 1972, I moved into a small trailer at the village in the spring of 1976. After the fire that summer I moved into an 8 x 12 foot screened off (with clear plastic) portion of my piano repair shop in the barn. Where I lived until my departure in April of 1977 for (sigh!) a most pleasant trip around the world with Swamiji (and other fine traveling companions!). Upon our return in October I was given a brief month's respite and then jettisoned off to Sacramento for the next two years.
>
> Anyway, as you can expect, I'm beginning to feel like a reincarnated YoYo!

It has very often during the last two years been the case that upon arrival at the village for whatever brief period of time, I have been unable to find suitable accommodations and either sped back to civilization, I mean Sacramento, or spent the night on a rather dirty floor somewhere.

What all this is blowing up to, is that I feel a great need for a place to call Vijay's space at Ananda.

So, what to do?

It is my hope to live at Ayodhya. I have discussed with Nitai the various possibilities as related to my peculiarities as a person. And the up and up is that there seem to be two choices. One is that I build a cabin and the other is to bring in a trailer (while taking out an existing one).

I understand that the situation with the county is an unpleasant one. And out of kindness to you all I would just as soon get a trailer, but to be honest, the idea of living in a trailer is most unpleasant for me: almost to the point of unable.

That may seem strange, but as I have lived in several trailers for varying lengths of time it has been my observation, for myself at least, that they are something to be avoided: sort of the way a big dog reacts to living in a one room apartment – confining to say the least.

What I propose is a 16 by 20 foot cabin, built to code: simple, but nice.

As I am sure that this will cause considerable heated discussion I can only say that I am sorry to be the cause of it.

Your consideration of this matter is much appreciated and regardless of your decision I would like to thank you for your serviceful attention to myself and the community.

In Divine Friendship, Vijay

My intent was to build my cabin on the site of a very primitive hut that Ramdas (The servant of Lord Rama.) had built. Prakash had also lived there for some time, so I needed to be sure they were done with the place. My idea was to use some of the foundations, which included a stone wall and a meditation cave. Other than those parts I would build a new structure.

Having sent my letter off to the village council, I went into seclusion in order to prepare myself for the next step. I soon received the following letter from Nitai:

Vijay,

At the meeting we worked out an understanding where you could "upgrade" an existing structure at Ayodhya. Remember the word upgrade. The more you stick to this term in describing your plans, the easier things will be.

The next step is getting Prakash to agree, and Ramdas. It will be your responsibility to contact them.

The final step is getting your plans approved by me. As we work towards an agreement you should know that 16 by 20 seems immense to me. The closer you can come to the existing square footage the easier it will be for me to agree. You might think about sleeping lofts and other space saving ideas.

Enjoy your seclusion. May Master bless all your efforts – spiritual and material.

Joy, Nitai

I didn't envy Nitai in his position as head of the monks. At the time the group was young with supercharged enthusiasm and a limited sense of the best way to use all that energy. Trying to keep us all headed in the same basic direction was no easy task. He didn't ask for the position. In fact the story about how he ended up becoming the head monk is a classic in the way that Swamiji often worked with us.

I believe it was in 1971 or 1972 and there were a handful of monks living at Ayodyha. They would meditate each morning together in a tepee located below Swamiji's Dome. At the time there was no one in charge so people would just come and go as they pleased. One day Swamiji arrived unexpectedly at the morning meditation. He sat down in the back and meditated with the small group. Normally people would just get up and leave when they wanted to, but with Swamiji sitting in the back Nitai realized that no one really knew what to do. So eventually after some time of internal struggle Nitai decided to speak up and end the meditation. It was soon after that meditation that Swamiji put Nitai in charge of the monks.

Once I got my foot in the door concerning the cabin, I just kept wiggling it until I got what I felt was reasonable. It wasn't that I intended to build a palace, but compared to the shacks, trailers and tepees that were currently in vogue, it isn't surprising that some people thought I did. I was actually on a very tight budget, so I did everything I could to save on materials.

I found out about a lumber mill where you could buy 2x6 studs at a very cheap price because they were only six feet long. So I made the walls, floor joists and roof beams with those six foot boards in various combinations. I did buy longer 2x8's for the roof joists. I used plywood on the floor, siding on the exterior walls and sheet rock inside. The walls were well insulated and I built a counter for cooking and eating in the small kitchen area. By the time I was done I had a basement bedroom with meditation cave and upstairs living room with wood burning stove and kitchen area. Soon I had electricity and one day that spring I sat down and looked out my picture window at the wide Yuba river valley below and thought, "Wow, Nitai was right. I did build a palace!"

I thoroughly enjoyed my new home for about two or three months and then life swooped me up and dropped me off at Ananda's attempt to create a community called Oceansong near Occidental in Mendocino County, California. Peter and Maria Meyers had a large property on rolling hills that overlook the Pacific Ocean. They invited Ananda to help start a community there and so a handful of intrepid Anandites moved from the village, set up canvas yurts and started again at square one.

Vidura, Durga and others spearheaded the project. I was sent down that summer to help in the organic garden which produced fresh food and some income for the endeavor. When I arrived at Oceansong I found Santosh wandering among rows of lettuce under the guidance of our head gardener, Dave Warner (later named Devarshi). Soon I was wandering in the rows of veggies playing farmer for the summer.

It was a big day when Dave said we could drive the tractor. There was some loading to be done with the bucket that went up and down on the front of the tractor. What guy doesn't like to move dirt with a big motor driven bucket? Little did we know what Dave was up to!

It was a long drive to the loading area, one guy on the tractor and two in the truck. We arrived at a place that sounded like a convention of turkeys, only to learn that that is exactly what it was, it was a turkey farm. There was a roof with open air sides that covered what looked like a square city block of turkey pens. Next to this turkey housing was the biggest pile of turkey droppings you could ever imagine. Dave informed us that these droppings were just what the garden needed.

So it was our job to scoop up the turkey poop and drop it in the back of the truck. Dave failed to mention that the driver of the tractor would be the recipient of an almost endless shower of turkey dropping dust as the motion of the bucket and the pleasant breeze of the day created a whirlwind of windblown particulate that found every opening in face and clothing that wasn't zipped shut. In other words, we ate turkey poop! The stuff was really smelly too! Of course we couldn't stop laughing and that made things worse because it is hard to keep your mouth closed while you laugh!

And wouldn't you know it, since I didn't want to live in a trailer at Ayodhya, I found that my accommodation at Oceansong was a very small trailer in a very big barn!

There was a strong sense of family at Oceansong and I found the earthy work in the garden soothing to my mind, though I still felt like I was in some sort of transition. Building my cabin and working in the garden had kept me physically busy, but I didn't feel settled in my mind.

Living at Oceansong was a little like being at summer camp. Along with my duties in the garden; I went to the beach that could be seen in the distance on a clear day and even did a little surfing. I rode on horseback through the tall brown grass and along the fences some evenings. We ate lots of fresh vegetables from our gardens and homemade farmer's cheese. We occasionally drove to town for dinner and a movie. We had Sunday services and group meditations. It was beautiful, but it didn't feel like home to me, so at the end of the summer I moved back to Ayodhya.

My experiences there inspired me to write a song about life at Oceansong.

Oceansong by Vijay Girard

The early morning mist rises upon the golden land.
The rolling hills embrace with tender loving hands.
The ocean sings, you can hear the mighty roar.
The oceansong wings, into the sky it soars.

Silent, whispered wisdom, sunlight through the dew.
Capturing moments, a sense of loving you.
The day begins with a lovingly offered prayer.
We live our lives in service and in that thought we share.
The ocean sings, you can hear the mighty roar.
The oceansong wings, into the sky it soars.

Recently planted flowers growing towards the light.
A garden of human forms, mystical in flight.
The world will change, but loving remains the same.
In living close to Mother, we joyously sing her name.
The ocean sings you can hear the mighty roar.
The oceansong wings, into the sky it soars.

It was after returning from Oceansong that I began to feel in earnest what I can only describe as a spiritual dilemma. Driving through Ananda Village was always a pleasant experience. Swamiji has often mentioned how he could feel Ananda before even arriving. There is an aura of peace that pervades the property. No place on earth feels more like home to me than Ananda Village, yet at that time, when I arrived in the monastery parking area I found that I had trouble getting out of the car.

It was a truly unique experience for me. It wasn't that I didn't like anyone or I was angry with someone. Even the fact that I didn't attend the group meditations as regularly as Nitai would have preferred wasn't a contested issue. No one made me live there. I had chosen to be a monk and built a great place to live. Everything should have been perfect, but there was something inside me that was at odds with my circumstances.

For about a month I would arrive in the parking area, sit in my car for twenty minutes to an hour and struggle with whether or not I should get out of the car. Often I would start the car back up and drive away, feeling a relief as soon as I left, but knowing that I had to go back. Sometimes I went back two or three times before I could get out of the car. Once I got to my cabin I was fine. I wasn't depressed or unusually restless. As I said, it was unique in my life experience.

It was also at this time that I took a job at Ananda's Earthsong health food store and café. I worked at stocking shelves and checking people out at the register. This was at the original store next to the SPD supermarket in Nevada City. I had always loved the variety of things that we got to do at Ananda. We never identified ourselves by what we did, but by how we lived our discipleship. While I didn't see myself as a career grocery man, I did enjoy working there.

Between my time commuting from the village to the store – about thirty minutes each way – and the time that I spent sitting in the parking lot at the monastery, I had a fair amount of time to think. Eventually I accepted what should have been obvious for a long time, I didn't belong at the monastery. So I wrote to Swamiji and explained my circumstances.

Swamiji totally accepted my feelings, he never made any attempt to change my view. He also never made me feel that I had in any way failed. It was probably the belief that I might be failing in my spiritual life that kept me from seeing the writing on the wall for so long. The Ananda culture at that time, which I mentioned earlier, was very much one of complete dedication to God through the monastic life. Even though the community was created to spiritually support those who had chosen the householder path, there was, on an unspoken level, the belief that family life was only done if you couldn't handle the true monastic life. In our youthful exuberance we had a tendency to see the spiritual life in the form that we idealized – being monastic, as an all or nothing proposition that only had the label of monk or nun.

I don't think I have ever met anyone more accepting of other people's right and need to make their own choices in life than Swamiji. His supportive attitude made all the difference to me. So with Swamiji's blessing I ended my time as a monk, but kept the cabin!

As it happened, my home was on the opposite side of Swamiji's dome from the rest of the monks. And it was totally invisible from the road, so it didn't bother anyone that I was living there.

My new designation as a non monk didn't really change my life outwardly. It isn't like I started partying and living what might be called the *worldly high* life. Life at Ananda was what I generally considered the real *high* life and I didn't feel in any way less committed to that. But I no longer felt a compelling need to sit in my car in the parking lot. It was like a flashing light that goes off on an answering machine because the message has been received. Of course, I didn't realize at the time that I hadn't yet received the *whole* message!

I have sometimes been tempted to think that life is easier for those people who know from an early age what they want to be when they grow up. This sense of strong personal direction strikes me as a kind of rudder that can keep one's life on an even keel. Of course I know that all people have personal struggles in their lives, so it is also true that it doesn't matter what you do, but how you live that makes the real difference in life. I had found my spiritual path at the age of seventeen. The active seeking to know God and serve God was my chosen vocation. Yet my life didn't consist of sitting in a cave and meditating all of the time as my fantasy impression of the spiritual life would have led me to believe.

The Ananda Community wasn't a place where everyone threw their money into a communal hat when they arrived and then was supported by the group. Everyone had to pay monthly rent, which left full financial responsibility on the shoulders of each member. Traditionally, monks and nuns are supported by their order and sequestered to some degree from society, but at Ananda everyone had to pull their own financial weight and interact with the world as the demands of their work required.

We are each born into a life track that we can't see clearly from the beginning. Even as we begin to live more consciously and think that we are making independent decisions, we will be powerfully driven by the momentum of our karmic past and the Divine plan for our future – if we choose to cooperate with it. Even though Swamiji's original intent when starting the meditation retreat was to create a place where people could fully commit themselves to the inner life without the distractions of society, he quickly began to see that this was his opportunity to create a "world–brotherhood colony" as envisioned by Yogananda. It was so clearly part of the story that God wanted to live through his life that even as a teenager Swamiji had written about the creation of a utopian community.

Swamiji's life had taken twists and turns that he never could have predicted. Who would have thought that after fourteen years of dedicated service he would be thrown out of SRF and the monastic lifestyle that had become his home. Or that he would not only have to come to grips with the shock and hurt of the way his fellow disciples treated him, but also come up with some kind of plan for the rest of his life. What would he do? How would he live?

It would be so easy to think all these years later, after the countless successes that have been accomplished through Swamiji's life, that it was all divinely planned out and that because it was destined to happen it therefore wasn't very difficult to do. But that would be a misunderstanding about how life works. All of the great deeds throughout history, even though they have been powered by the Divine, have been manifest through the blood, sweat and tears of the participants. Swamiji has had to find his course through the uncharted waters of his own life with the compass of his personal attunement to God/Guru and his own life's potential. In observing how Swamiji navigated his own life we each, in our own way, sought to emulate his approach to balancing inner perception with practical outward actions.

Of course the desire to attune one's actions to the Divine Will for our lives is easier said than done. It isn't like having a GPS system in your car that tells you which way to turn before you get to the corner. The key is to remember that while we do our best to inwardly seek and perceive guidance, we are also, through the attunement of that process, drawing and aligning ourselves with the invisible efforts of the Guru on our behalf. I say invisible because most of us can't see God's hand in our lives before something dramatic happens. Once something unanticipated does happen, the invisible becomes quite visible. And even then we may be tempted to doubt God's unseen participation by attributing all of life to coincidence.

I was now twenty–nine years old and full of energy and enthusiasm. My lifestyle was uninvolved with the mainstream of society. When not working at Earthsong I spent most of my time by myself. Before coming to Ananda I certainly had an ardent interest in women. Since my arrival at Ananda I had married and then been unexpectedly divorced after three years. I describe my experiences with my wife Mukti at length in my book *Traveling with Swamiji.* I then became a monk for two years and now I was no longer a monk. I spent time with a couple of women who were friends, but I didn't have what I would describe as a serious relationship. I was certainly open to change in my life, I just didn't know exactly what that new direction might be.

I stayed in touch with a few of my friends in Sacramento since leaving the center at the beginning of the year. I had spoken to Toni a number of times. She had taken the next step in her own life and had separated from her husband. I even visited her house in Roseville a couple of times and once I was no longer a monk we joked that it was too bad we weren't more compatible as a couple, since we felt so much the same spiritually.

If you had asked me at the time what made Toni and me incompatible, I would have said that she is a city girl at heart and I am a country boy at heart. She is neat, I am messy. She drinks coffee, I don't. I like movies, she doesn't. These obvious outward differences helped us to be relaxed together without any worry about defining our relationship beyond spiritual friendship.

There had never been any physical chemistry between us since I met Toni. Certainly I had noticed she was good looking, but beyond that I can say that we were purely and simply friends. Her interest in the spiritual life was truly the root of our relationship. I had no reason to think or even want that to change. The Universe apparently knew more about the situation than I did.

I remember it clearly because it was Thanksgiving Day. I called Toni to see how she was doing because I knew that it was her first big holiday since divorcing from her husband. Her children would be with their father for the day. I was concerned that she might be a little depressed.

When I reached Toni on the phone I found that she was feeling down, but she had an unexpected reason. She explained that the water heater had for some unknown reason gushed hot water all over the floor and the carpeting had gotten soaked. This had never happened before and she wasn't sure what to do. What could I say? I couldn't in good conscience do anything on Thanksgiving Day but go to help her.

Of course the Divine trickster was on duty. When I arrived in Roseville we could find no reason for the water heater's Thanksgiving release – and it never did it again. Even as we laughed at the absurdity of it we didn't yet see its true purpose. Only as the evening progressed and we began to share one of those special moments in life when the veils of separateness are pulled aside and we became one in body, mind and spirit, did we realize the truth of what was taking place.

I can only say that I believe God did hold a veil of distance between us when I first met Toni because it wasn't yet time for us to be together. On that Thanksgiving day the veil was lifted. It was such a dramatic inner experience that I have no doubt of its truth. Suddenly all of the little differences were as nothing compared to a larger overwhelming rightness. Though I couldn't see the path we would walk together, I knew that God's hand had drawn us to this moment and I fully accepted that this unexpected turn of events was God's Will for our lives.

Chapter 8

Momentous Changes

"A true yogi may remain dutifully in the world; there he is like butter on water, and not like the easily–diluted milk of unchurned and undisciplined humanity. To fulfill one's earthly responsibilities is indeed the higher path, provided the yogi, maintaining a mental uninvolvement with egotistical desires, plays his part as a willing instrument of God." –Paramhansa Yogananda

Like the early signs in nature that the season is changing, if we are inwardly attentive we may notice hints that our lives will be moving forward in new ways. I had experienced that period where I couldn't get out of my car at the monastery and finally got the message. What I didn't realize was that the message wasn't only for me, that it was part of a dramatic change that would sweep across the Ananda community with just as much challenge and change as the fire of 1976 (described in *Traveling with Swamiji*).

It was years later that I found out another one of the monks had been spending time in the parking lot as well. He was having almost exactly the same experience as myself. In fact, we had seen each other sitting in our cars one time in the parking area, but hadn't discussed the true import of its meaning. Even had we talked at that time we never could have anticipated the scale of the coming changes that would affect all of Ananda.

I didn't over think the ramifications of my transformed relationship with Toni. I just entered wholeheartedly into life as it unfolded before me. I had discovered from my life thus far that I couldn't possibly know the details of what would happen in the future, what I did know is that whenever I had followed my best understanding of how to proceed, no matter how rocky the road got, I always arrived safely at a next destination.

It is common for people to equate divorce with failure. When I considered my previous marriage to Mukti I never saw it as a failure, I saw it as having gone through an unexpected outward change. Isn't unexpected change one of Life's most prominent qualities? So success isn't about there being no changes, but that those changes be met with equanimity of mind and an open, honest and caring heart. I never stopped loving Mukti, I just didn't live with her anymore. I supported her need to seek her own truth. Certainly I was disappointed that that truth didn't include us staying together, but should I be so selfish as to hold her back? When people try to force their round relationship into a square hole does that ever lead to happiness?

Was Toni's marriage to Richard a failure? No. Did she stop caring about him? No. What happened is that he actively pushed against her spiritual life. Had he not done that they may have stayed married. When she had to choose between her marriage and deepening her relationship with God, she chose God.

While some might say that Toni could have quietly kept company with God on her own, the truth is that few people are prepared to grow to their spiritual potential on their own. We need teachings, techniques, spiritual fellowship and a good teacher. Most importantly, we need a guru and anything that will help us to attune ourselves to our guru. Toni recognized these truths in her own life and had the courage to step forward into the unknown.

Had Toni and I become in any way romantically involved before her conscious and communicated separation from Dick – which we didn't – it would have been a different situation karmicly. Had Dick not consciously tried to hinder Toni's spiritual aspirations she would have been dharmicly bound to honor the marriage in spite of it being a potential impediment to her spiritual opportunities.

The scriptures say, "A lower dharma (right action) is superseded by a higher dharma." If you are driving over the speed limit just for fun it is different than if you are taking an injured passenger to the hospital for urgent care. The biblical conscription, "Thou shalt not kill" may be superseded in some cases if it is necessary for the strong to protect the weak. Knowing what action in any given situation is attuned to the highest truth takes not just intellectual understanding, but an intuitive connection to Universal Truth.

It wasn't long after Thanksgiving that I took up residence with Toni. I moved out of my palace at Ayodyha and moved into suburban Roseville. I had no idea what I would do or how things would proceed, I just knew in my heart that it was right. We didn't tell anyone or ask for permission, we just did it. Of course, the Ananda grapevine spread the news quickly enough; by Christmastime we were old news.

Once again the all day meditation at Ananda worked its magic on my soul. And then a mixture of Christmas at Ananda and Christmas in Roseville with Toni and her children, Dan and Cristi, made for a beautiful blend of Spirit and family. Since I had known Toni and her children for about three years already, there was no awkwardness, just happiness.

On New Year's Day Swamiji had an open house at his dome. Toni and I attended. We were greeted by many of our friends with congratulations. Just being there to share my joy with my spiritual family was sufficient, but God had even more in store for us.

There was a point at which Swamiji was sitting near the large window that overlooks the Yuba River and to the left side of a beautifully decorated Christmas tree. We approached him and then knelt at his feet. He smiled at us so sweetly; filled with the divine presence of the season and the joy of our joy. Then he reached out with each hand and touched us both at the spiritual eye and blessed us. It was in that moment that we felt that our relationship had been bonded and sanctified. So that when we had an official ceremony later that spring, I felt that it was beautiful, but mostly a formality.

Not far into the new year I attended a meeting of *The Yoga Fellowship,* which at the time was the official name of the Ananda church. These meetings were always special because it was a gathering of close dear friends where we could relax and talk as a family. Swamiji was always in good form and we all savored his inwardly powered love, joy and wisdom. We also knew that there would be a good session of laughing involved!

One of the common items of business for the group by this time was the appointment of new ministers. Sometimes people would make suggestions, but the final decision was always Swamiji's. At that time every minister had lived at Ananda Village and was a member of the Yoga Fellowship. On that day Swamiji broke that tradition and approved as a minister a person who had never lived at Ananda: It was Toni.

The story of our wedding contained much more than our own small story, it was an expression of the turning tides in Ananda's future. Ananda as a culture is not a place of rules, but it is a place of traditions. The most important tradition after dedicating our lives to God and Gurus was that we cherished Swamiji's role in our lives. Though we considered Paramhansa Yogananda our Guru, we saw Swamiji as his personal representative, and as such, afforded him the importance in our lives as if he were Yogananda. Certainly this line was blurred for many people, and each in their own way found the resolution of this issue for themselves. In fact, this is also an important tradition at Ananda: people are always free and responsible for making their own life decisions.

Swamiji would never interpose himself between a disciple and Yogananda or God. There were plenty of people in the community that would have been very happy if he would be more commanding, but he staunchly refused. Still, most people would consult Swamiji before making any decision of import. If they didn't, Swamiji was not offended.

In the case of marriage many members would first ask his opinion. If it was in the positive they would request that he marry them in the temple at Ananda. Afterwards there would be snacks and chit chat. This was standard operating procedure at Ananda. I had followed that path when marrying Mukti, so I knew from personal experience that convention alone, while being valid and wise, was no guarantee of a long and happy marriage. When it came time to plan our wedding Toni and I did none of those things.

Well that is not exactly correct. We had already sought and received Swamiji's blessing. Having done so we felt we had satisfied the most important tradition. After that I felt that there was more to be considered.

At that time there were momentous changes taking place, not just in our lives, but with all of Ananda. In the beginning Ananda was an ideal in Swamiji's mind based on one of Master's published aims and ideals: To aid in establishing, in many countries, self–sustaining world–brotherhood colonies for *plain living and high thinking*. As a result of Swamiji's commitment to this goal he had purchased the Meditation Retreat property in 1967 and the Village property in 1969. This wasn't something that he could do by himself.

Swamiji needed fellow disciples; souls who were dedicated to living the path of Self–Realization as he lived and shared it. As a direct disciple of Yogananda he had been trained and empowered to carry on after Master's passing. Yogananda said to him one day, "You have a great work to do." Swamiji had been born with the skills of body, mind and spirit to do this work, but the instruction manual of his training had been on how to work with life as it presents itself and not how to assemble a spiritual community by the numbers.

Swamiji's example of discipleship, the energy and magnetism of his life, had led the budding Ananda spiritual family through the ups and down of infancy and childhood. Ananda was now fully in the transition from adolescence to adulthood. We were all, under his leadership, discovering how to use the skills of daily spiritual living to reach out and share this way of life that we treasure.

The work was growing way beyond the original property that we called Ananda Village. During my two years in the Sacramento center Swamiji traveled extensively across America on two separate tours, sharing his music, Master's teachings and the Ananda approach to life.

During a period of seclusion Swamiji wrote a new course called, *Superconscious Living*. In the course he condensed Yogananda's teachings into language and exercises that he felt would make them more accessible to the general public. The grand launch of the course took place at the *Palace of Fine Arts* Theatre in San Francisco.

Another feature of the *Superconscious Living* launch was sprung on a group of us unexpectedly. Just as the program was about to begin all of the ministers and teachers present were unexpectedly gathered to walk in as a group and sit in the front row, where seats had been saved for this purpose. When we were asked to line up I had no idea why. As we walked into the theater the audience instinctively hushed, as they did it inwardly came to me what was taking place. God through Swamiji was asking us to officially take up the mantel of responsibility that Swamiji had worn alone. We were being asked to commit ourselves personally to taking on sacred duties that we had thought were only Swamiji's. The ministers and the community in general always preferred Swamiji to be present. And who could fault anyone for feeling that way? I certainly felt that way! Now we were being asked to consciously share Swamiji's responsibilities so that we could grow spiritually and more people could be served.

The practical truth was that it simply wasn't going to be possible for Swamiji to physically be everywhere for everything. I had personally been present when Swamiji had grumbled without grumbling on this issue. So as Toni and I began to plan our wedding we decided that Haridas would be our main minister and Santosh with Prahlad would be supporting ministers. We had the ceremony at our home in Roseville, on the spacious lawn next to the house. We didn't send out private invitations to anyone at Ananda, including Swamiji – which I later regretted because it just didn't seem right, but at the time I couldn't see that truth. Of course, he never said a word about it. We put an announcement in the Village Newsletter that everyone was invited and welcome.

For a few moments, I am ashamed to admit, I doubted that Swamiji would come. Certainly I thought he would come and I desperately wanted him to come, but I also had doubts as to whether I deserved him to come – not that I had a specific reason for this thought other than the fact that we hadn't sent him a personal invitation. It would serve me right if he didn't come! But of course, he came, and in that we were all most appreciative.

I believe that in many groups of people and with most leaders, there would have been an undercurrent of gossip about what a scandal it was that Swamiji wasn't the minister and that the wedding wasn't at Ananda. But to the best of my knowledge that never took place. Everyone was just simply happy for us. There was nothing more complex than that. And there was more than just good food at the wedding, there was also a lot of food for thought.

Swamiji had arrived, not in his ochre swami robes, but in the blue suit that had been custom tailored for him when we were in India. Certainly we had all seen him in western clothes many times, but to be at an Ananda wedding and not be the minister and in a blue suit, well, it had never happened before!

We also did something else that had never happened at an Ananda wedding, we had dancing. This got me into a bit of trouble in several ways and it was totally my fault. You see we wanted to have dancing, but we weren't sure if we should, so we seesawed about it until the last minute. Then we weren't sure about how to do it in the best way. As the musician of the family it was my responsibility. In the end we used a cheap record player with minuscule speakers and some miscellaneous records – yes, vinyl! – that came from my new mother–in–law, Yolanda.

It started off pretty well, very ballroom. We had our first dance – I have no recollection of the song – and then everyone joined in. The next thing we knew Swamiji had taken over the dance floor and was waltzing up a storm. We had no idea that Swamiji would or could do such a thing. It was amazing and startling at the same time. I was totally surprised when later

Swamiji pulled me aside and told me that I should have arranged for a better quality sound system; which of course bent my brain and made me laugh.

Things got even more exciting and out of control when someone found a record with some rock and roll. Since we didn't even own a record or record player, I had no idea how the situation had gotten to this point, it certainly wouldn't have been my personal choice, but I had forfeit the situation through lack of involvement. I remember seeing Madava, who was a very big guy, letting loose with some smooth moves and at that I withdrew all preconception and let nature take its course.

Well, Nature – Life, God, the Universe – decided that the festivities needed more spice. When I found myself slow dancing with a woman friend that I had seen socially after I left the monastery things took a very unexpected direction. We weren't serious, but just good friends. At least that is what I thought until that night, while we danced, she burst into tears and said, "This should have been my wedding!"

It was a sobering experience and very unusual for an Ananda member to express personal disappointment in such a way. Yogis are trained to internalize their feelings, offering them up to the Divine. I wasn't sorry that she shared her feelings with me, but I didn't think it was really the right time and place for it – to say nothing of being too late. Though, the fact that it happened meant that there was something that I could learn from it.

How easily we can forget that on the outside, life is always full of ups and downs. Even at this time of celebration the Divine was reminding me that next to all the roses of life's outward involvements there are thorns of disappointment. It is only on the inside, through communion with eternal Spirit that we can find lasting equanimity.

There was nothing that I could say that would really help her in that moment. The truth was that I had not myself made a choice in the traditional sense about who to be with. To the best of my understanding, God had made that choice and I – more than willingly! – went along with it. Though, it did make me feel a bit like a pawn in the game of my own karma. At the same time, I had learned to trust God and Guru's guidance of my life and in this case my trust was well served: though maybe in a bumpier way than I would have preferred, except that I have become a better person because of the bumps. So there it is again, as Yogananda taught: All life circumstances are neutral, it is what we do with them that determines a positive or negative outcome.

As amazed as we were at Swamiji's dancing, hindsight would tell us that the year 1981 had many more surprises in store for us. Monks and nuns leaving the monastery and then marrying had begun not all that long after the monastery started. In the very early years the monks and nuns used the same tipi temple. It isn't hard to imagine how meditation together could lead to an attraction. Once the monks and nuns were separated it helped. But the truth is that at Ananda, underneath our storybook images about the way the spiritual life should look – seclusion in a cave or forest ashram with minimal interaction with society – we were simply dedicated to loving and serving God, outward labels were totally secondary. In any case, where Swamiji led, we would follow.

When we live in attunement to Spirit we learn to expect the unexpected. It wasn't too long after our wedding that Swamiji called for a satsang at his home. The following is part of a transcription of what he said. I have shortened his narrative because he shared more information than we need for our current purpose. This incredible view into Swamiji's personal spiritual process at the time is a sacred glimpse into the breath and depth of his discipleship and spiritual life purpose. It provides a template that many at Ananda have sought to emulate in determining their own life choices. I have changed a few words for clarity's sake, but have endeavored to change nothing of substance.

Swami Kriyananda's Announcement

Those of you who've known me for a long time know that I don't like to talk about myself in public. Or for that matter, that much in private. But these last few months I've talked quite a bit about myself and the reason is its been a time of trying to change my directions and knowing that whatever change in my own life I went through would affect you. I felt that it would be of some benefit to you for me to discuss the things that I have had to go through in my own mind.

I came to Master with two desires. One was to find God. The other was to help get this work established. I read the *Autobiography of a Yogi* in New York and thought, "Why doesn't anybody know about this stuff?" I had an intense desire to share it with people. I've always been the kind of person who wanted to share.

I know I said to Daya Mata at one time, "I don't have any desire for what you give me to do. I'll be happy to do anything at all, you can put me to cleaning toilets at Mt. Washington, and that's fine. I would be perfectly content doing that, as long as you want me to. The only thing I have to add to that is that if you give me such a job, within a week everybody at Mt. Washington will consider it the most important job to do."

It's just the way I've always been, I get so enthusiastic for it that I get involved in the deeper meanings of it and in this case, for example, the lesson in humility and how wonderful it is to be the servant of all and so on. And people would get so caught up in this idea that they'd all want to clean toilets.

So I have that kind of nature. Master, seeing that, pushed me in that direction and told me, "You have a great work to do." When he told me my life work he said, "Your life is one of intense activity and meditation." I sort of shuddered when he put meditation second. I would rather have him say intense meditation and some activity. But I had to admit that this was my nature.

In fact, all my life I've been pulled in opposite directions because nothing that I have done has really mattered to me. I've not had any desire for it. I don't see great gains in it, except that – yes, it helps people. But I'm thinking of it from the standpoint of what's really important, which is that this is all a dream and we're trying to find our way out of that dream and merge in the Infinite, and realize that it all didn't even happen. That's where my mind is. So that I've always felt very, in a sense, out of it, free from it, yet at the same time I've had this volcano inside me that's driven me to do things and it's been a pull in opposite directions.

On one hand this has made me want to be a hermit and be away from everybody. I know the times that I have spent in the Himalayas completely alone and not speaking to anybody except God, Master and Babaji, I felt so blissful that I know I could stay that way the rest of my life, very, very happily.

And yet, the other side of me, my duty, said yes, but there are all these suffering people. Many times in my own mind I've made the choice between salvation and service. I've always chosen service. I always felt that, well, if I don't get salvation this time, at least I've helped a lot of people and I'll have served my guru. It's been a conscious and deliberate choice that I've made anytime that I've come to this conflict, until finally I woke up one morning and realized that there had never been a conflict, except in my own mind. That by serving Master I would become free. That in doing his work and bringing other people to it, I was becoming more and more joyful in myself and I was given the same benefits as though I had been off there in the mountains, because I realized more and more there was just nothing that tied me in anyway. So I went on this way for quite some time.

About two years ago I began to feel there was a change coming and I told my close friends that God wants something new for me. I didn't know what it was, but I was starting to look, and a year ago I went to the Caribbean. I had reached a point where I felt, I saw rather, that I had done all the things that I set out to do and to do more would only be doing the same thing. As the French say, "Plus ça change, plus c'est la même chose." ("The more things change, the more they keep going the same anyway."). That's the way I was beginning to feel.

I see a lot of people as they go through life, they've done one good thing and then they don't have the courage to do anything else. So they keep going in that direction and keep getting boxed in more and more until finally they just don't have anything to offer. It would have been just as well if they died. In fact, I was wondering quite seriously, if it wasn't my time to go. I felt that I could either die or I could go into seclusion and leave everything, go to the Himalayas and live in a cave, or be with Anandamoyee Ma. I just didn't know, but somehow something inside me said, no, that's not what God wants. Your life is dedicated to service; you have to find a new way of serving.

So I tried to cast about for a new way. It's not easy to change one's whole approach. The new way that I wanted was to get out completely under this drive, this will to finish what I've set out to do, this very rational mind that is always looking for the right solution to this, looking for the flaw in that, so that I could find what the right answer is. It's always pulling things apart so that I can see it more clearly, so that I can explain these teachings in such a way that people would say, "Sure, of course, even a child could understand that."

How do you change something you've been born with? It isn't easy. I've felt an almost kind of despair in the very project, but I didn't want to go on in the same way. My life has always been to try to break new ground, discover new ways and once it's done then leave it. In fact, that song of mine, *Go On Alone*, its really been my way: Once the seed is sown, seek freedom, don't linger, go on alone. I had this very strong longing to – I've talked about it, haven't I? – leave Ananda, go off and live alone with God.

I knew that I couldn't do it and I almost resented the fact, but of course, I didn't. It was also a joy that I had started the community and made a place for so many people, hundreds of people to find inspiration, peace and harmony. It was a responsibility that I couldn't turn back on, so I regretted the fact that I couldn't turn my back on it, I rejoiced on the fact that it was there, not to be turned back on, if you can understand that.

What I really wanted to do was know what God wants of me and give me the strength to do that. And so I did not in any way want to leave you all when I thought of you as people. When I thought of Ananda as a project, that's what made me want to run away. But when I thought of you as people, my heart's love went out to you. I knew that there was simply no choice. I had given my heart and my life to you.

So what was the answer? I went to the Caribbean to find neutral gear: And found it. [laughter] Nothing on that ship was interesting to a devotee. I mean, if I was interested in eating wonderful meat dishes and seeing lovely Broadway–styled shows it would have been fine. I just stayed in my room and read. Yet somehow, when I came back I found that I no longer felt bound by my old ways.

After returning from that trip good old Shivani came and said, "We need a new book on marriage, we need a new book on money, we need a new book on Women in the New Age, and we need this thing and that." And then others were talking,

"What about the program at the retreat? What about teachers in Sacramento?"

Shivani hadn't gotten a rise out of me sufficiently, so she sent me transcripts of lectures and classes on marriage, money and so on. She said, "Are these alright?" Well, you know what I'm going to think of my spoken word, when I saw them on paper. They were horrible. So I had to write those books. [laughter] And I began to get a little desperate and I thought, "Am I never going to get out of this trap?"

Shivani was not only my problem, but became my solution. Because what happened was this: She said she was going to Hawaii with Arjuna and wouldn't I like to go to. At first I turned away with a light yawn, but I finally thought, well, why not? God maybe even worked though Shivani, making me desperate enough to go.

So I went to Hawaii and I looked at the beautiful scenery and I thought: What else is new? It was lovely alright, but I wouldn't go just for that. I remember I was sitting down one morning and praying to Divine Mother. I said, "Divine Mother, I just need help. I need guidance. I know that there's something you're trying to show me, but what is it? It's time I find out. This has been going on a year and a half and that's quite long enough!" I just knew that She was there whispering some kind of guidance in my ear, but I never got it.

About two hours after I got up from my meditation, Annie (Uma – a form of Divine Mother) and I went into a shop. I had pictures that I had taken in August of Kauai and they were beautiful photographs, and so I wanted to see if any of the shops in the area might be interested in carrying them. A young lady got up to look at them and the moment we laid eyes on each other it was like a soul recognition. It was something very, very deep. It was extraordinary.

I told her just two or three days later, that "You really are my ideal person." I was wondering what made me say that, because although she's certainly beautiful in a physical way, I couldn't even remember what she looked like. Her reality was something inside myself. I know, moreover, although she's beautiful, that there are many more beautiful women in the world. Her personality is very nice – I love it. On the other hand, there are other people with equally nice personalities and it's not as if her personality was perfect. But there was something on a deeper soul level that made me say that and that makes me feel it today.

There is something that happened between us that suddenly made me realize that this is what I have been looking for – not a person but a state of consciousness. It was that in her presence I began to find that I was developing automatically, without even trying, those qualities that I've been longing for. I was becoming the kind of person, and finding that I'm moving at last in the direction that I knew intuitively that I had to move, if I was to keep on growing spiritually and to be able to hear people.

The other choice would be to go into myself, withdraw from the world and only think of God. If I was to go on serving people it simply had to be in this new way. The old way was finished. It was as if I had died and I no longer felt any attraction to it. But I was now in limbo, I knew the direction I had to go, but I didn't yet have the understanding to do it. It was so new, so different – not really foreign to me, otherwise I wouldn't have wanted it – but so outside the realm of my own experience I was unsure how to proceed.

In her presence I would feel a joy welling up inside my heart and coming up to the Christ center. This was the entire reality of my experience of her, despite all the times we had talking. We had lots of fun talking about philosophy and spiritual things. In fact, I discovered she had just ordered *The Path*. And so she was very intrigued to meet me, as the author of this book that she wanted to read. She was very, very ripe and ready for the spiritual teachings that we have. I knew instantly that this is where she belonged and that she belonged working with me. In fact I saw the whole thing completely, clearly, as it has unfolded since then.

The question came, "Now what do I do? Should I accept that this is the way that God sent me and therefore, this is the way that He wants me to go in?" She seemed to come, unless you believe that it is a pure coincidence, in answer to that prayer. In fact that prayer was only the culmination of many prayers before it. But this is when it was particularly intense. So what should I do?

Should I just say, "Well, okay, now that I've got it, goodbye? I've got to go on in my own?" Or should I say, "No, God has come in this channel. Therefore He means for me to work with her in some way." It seemed very clear that I had to work with her and that this was our destiny.

I prayed deeply to Master and asked him. I put every thought out of my mind. For instance the thought came into my mind two or three times, "If he should tell you that this has been wrong, won't it make me look ridiculous, having committed yourself this far already?" And I said, "I don't care what I look like. I want to know what you know, because the only thing that I want is what you want, because the only thing that wins in the long run is Truth. And I want to spare myself all the pain of finding it out after a long time. I'd rather know now. It just doesn't matter to me how foolish I look or how wrong I might have been, I have to absolutely know whether this is your will or not."

I felt very strongly his guidance on the matter – which was that you have already fulfilled your monastic calling because it has given you those qualities a monastic calling is intended to give one – freedom, inner joy, realization that nothing belongs to me, and that everything is God and the wish only to serve him. I feel really amazingly free in myself on all these things. So I said to Master, or rather Master said to me, mind you, he did not appear in vision, but these were the thoughts that were imprinted strongly on my mind and that's how my intuition has always come to me, how it's always worked for me.

What he was saying in this sense was if I was to continue to follow the path of monasticism, then I would have his blessings. He would be perfectly happy with me for doing so. But in that case the only way I could develop these monastic qualities more would be to go more and more within myself, to become more and more in tune inwardly. That would mean withdrawing from the work and no longer be willing to serve in a relevant way to save his work.

So this was a very heavy thought for me: the realization that "You're not doing something just for you. You're doing something for a lot of people. And you're not just doing it for a lot of people, you're the only person doing it at all as far as Master's work is concerned."

Now that's the point I hope I will not be judged too harshly if I'm wrong. Maybe there are many others doing it. It's just the way it looks to me, as if their whole energy, the energy of all the other disciples goes towards preserving what he left behind and I'm the only one out there breaking the new trails and building new roads, so that many different kinds of people coming from many different directions will recognize this as a meaningful way for them. And anyway, whether that extended thought, which of course makes it ten times heavier, is valid or not, whether it's simply a question of my life, that's heavy enough in itself.

I prayed very earnestly and what I felt was, he was saying that if you want to go that way, then that's fine. I know that that's your calling. I know that you are perfectly happy in that way. I know that you love being a monk. I know that you feel really basically more contented living alone, because you've done it all your life. And you won't be, in your work, relevant to what millions of people are now. People are suffering; they're confused. They need something relevant to their own actual lives.

When Buddha lived all his disciples were monks and nuns. And it was a time when the family life was secure and safe, stable. But now there's no stability in the family life and how can you go that one step further from here. Everything is so rotten. This is the place where the work is needed. The greatest thing that people bring to me in interviews is most frequently questions having to do with male/female relationships or with marriage. That's the greatest issue in the country today where at least 50% of the couples that marry get divorced – people don't even understand what marriage is all about. They've lost contact with it.

We have a few beautiful models that have been given to us in history, but somehow it doesn't apply to a marriage in 1981. There's something missing and you see the disciples of a few of Indian masters who emphasize marriage. You see them going in a way that doesn't relate to American life. How to bring it about in a way that Americans can then say, "Oh that's what it's all about."

That is a very, very important question. Something that is perhaps more important than any other on the spiritual path: to teach people how to have a spiritual marriage. True I wrote a book on the subject, but that's words. Much more is needed. And although my book on spiritualizing marriage has a lot of insights in it, nevertheless it's not come from direct personal experience. It has come more from meditation and the intuition that's born in meditation.

So I asked Master and he said, "If you really want to do this then this is what you should do." I said, "Well Master, I must know, not on the normal intuitive level, I've got to feel your blessings on this step." As soon as I asked him for that I felt this bursting joy, more intense than I ever felt in guidance before. It convinced me it was what I had to do, that I was not acting out of personal desire. I was acting out of a sense of duty, out of sense of mission, out of a sense that this is what people need.

Chapter 9

Roots of Purpose

"You must not let your life run in the ordinary way; do something that nobody else has done, something that will dazzle the world. Show that God's creative principle works in you." –Paramhansa Yogananda

Swamiji's informal heartfelt sharing about his current state of body, mind and spirit was a wellspring of insight into him as a person and the forces that are at work behind the scenes of our lives. The very act of revealing his own internal struggle was a hallmark of his openness and humility. That Swamiji would share his process and not just announce what he had decided to do – especially since in this case he himself didn't know exactly what to do – well, it was his way, a sacred trust and commitment to the spiritual family. This wasn't something that he was doing just for himself, he was doing it for and with all of us – including those who will come in the future. While every Anandite has their own personal journey, it was clear that we were simultaneously having an ever growing and evolving spiritual family experience.

Had Swamiji proclaimed that he had a vision of Yogananda in which he had been instructed to do so and so, we would have been thrilled and thought, of course he did, he is Swamiji! His intuitive guidance and actions over the years had proved so consistently insightful and reliable that some believed he was all knowing. Although, as I have said, Swamiji denied that and never that I am aware of presented himself that way.

The intensity and clarity of the description that Swamiji gave of his inner turmoil and how he dealt with it is in itself a handbook of discipleship instruction for the ages. He wasn't just telling us what happened to him, we were being guided in how to approach our own life challenges. We had all imagined various views of what it might be like inside Swamiji's awareness, well here we had it and it was well worth emulating.

This current sharing loomed large because of the scope of what he was proposing to do, and the uncertainty of what it would look like and how it would be received. He was diving into the roots of his and our self-definition as monastic yogis and reminding us that we were living not just for ourselves, but also for the future of Master's service to the world.

In order to experience and deepen an inner awareness of Spirit it is necessary to withdraw from personality identification and experience more Spirit identification – the Universal Self. Spirit in its cosmic, untouched by the Creation form, is impersonal because there is only one Infinite Consciousness of ever-new bliss: When fully immersed in Universal

Christ/Krishna Consciousness there is no duality, no one to be personal with!

The Creation itself is the splitting up of that one Universal consciousness into individualized consciousnesses: souls becoming identified with limited parts of the Creation and losing the ability to perceive the oneness of all life. Souls don't actually become separate from Spirit, they just think they are because their consciousness is identified with the outward Creation. When we decide to retrace our awareness to its inner source we must diminish our identification and attachment to life through the senses/personality and experience on ever-deeper levels that we are in truth, Spirit.

In order to develop interiorization yogis have commonly preferred to live apart from society and its many distractions. For the past three or four thousand years this has been the trend. Why this would be true is explained by Sri Yukteswar's presentation of the Yugas – the rise and fall of consciousness on planet Earth during 24,000 year cycles of time – in his book *The Holy Science* and in *The Yugas: Keys to Understanding Our Hidden Past, Emerging Present and Future Enlightenment* by Joseph Selbie (Purushotama), and David Steinmetz (Byassa). For our purpose at this time, further explanation is not necessary.

Swamiji had grown up spiritually in this lifetime as a monk in a monastery which was well insulated from the mainstream of society. His way of expressing monasticism was molded by 14 years in that environment. It fit well with his most dominate sense of Self. When he was separated from Self–Realization Fellowship he carried that pattern into an uncertain future.

Through the practice of Kriya Yoga and the other techniques of yoga that Yogananda taught, along with the monastic lifestyle, Swamiji had developed strong inner attunement and a powerful magnetism for drawing new creative ideas. In fact it was his prowess in that area that caused so much tension with the SRF leadership. They had all grown up in the monastery with Master. They didn't need to think creatively, that was Master's job. They were happy to keep things the way they were, while Swamiji was bursting with fresh ideas to bring the message of Self–Realization to the world.

During the five years between separation from SRF and the beginning of the Ananda Meditation Retreat Swamiji had to get his bearings and redefine his way of serving. He took on sole responsibility for his actions – in inner attunement to God and Guru – instead of being restrained and second guessed by his organizational superiors. This was such a dramatic shift in his life that it again took him some time to digest and adjust to his new circumstances.

Swamiji's reinvention of self to become a monk when he first met Yogananda and then again as a monk outside of the SRF monastery can be seen as preparation for another metamorphosis, to become a monk householder. It was so unexpected and outside of past public definitions of Swamiji that certainly there were people who thought that he had fallen prey to personal desires. Some people even left the community because of Swamiji's decision.

Something that isn't always taken into account is that God synchronizes the fulfillment of one soul's past desires not just in terms of their own karmic flow, but also with the flow of others. In this way we can see that the individual, family/group and societal karma were all in play simultaneously. Swamiji admitted that some of the situation was tied to personal preferences, but emphasized that by itself his personal interest wasn't the tipping factor in moving forward, it was the value that could be gained for others that swayed his choice. Swamiji's life thus far had been a beacon of hope for thousands of people. There were a lot more reasons to trust Swamiji than not.

Certainly there were some who claimed that in this instance *helping others* was simply a justification for indulgence. If you put this into the context of Swamiji's life, dedication to service and commitment to living in his best understanding of inner guidance, regardless of the exact percentage of personal or serviceful motivation, it was a great example of a devotee living intensely committed to Spirit. And even if it was more personal fulfillment than service, so what? Swamiji's life had been dedicated to service and continued to be so. The only ones that continued to be interested in judging Swamiji over this new direction were people who, as my narrative will reveal, had their own personal axes to grind.

What Swamiji was presenting wasn't a new teaching, in ancient India the way to be a householder had always been based on yogic training side by side with academic and vocational education. The first of the Vedic four Ashrams (Stages of life – each lasting approximately 24 years) was called Brahmacharya (In this usage: student of dharmic life skills). So that by the time you came to the second ashram, Gṛhastha (householder), you had years of spiritual training. In the third stage, Vanaprastha (Forest path) yogis serve the world from outside of the hubbub of daily life; educating, mentoring and guiding as inspired by their intuition. The final stage is Sannyasa (Renunciation), withdrawing from all worldly activity and focusing completely on Spirit within. This model for life isn't a time-clock into which every life should fit in the same way and schedule, but a life flow guideline that offers a harmonious spiritual life template.

Unlike Swamiji – who was ahead of his generation in understanding society – most of the Ananda community at that time grew up through the 1960's which had in a large scale rejected the confining and hypocritical values of American society. We were ready for something new, you could say we were born for it. But Swamiji, he was a fascinating blend of old and new. He deeply valued his vow of monasticism and the lifestyle that went with it. He had given his word, which he held sacrosanct. He wasn't going to leave all that he currently understood on a whim. Yet to fulfill his commitment of service to Master, Ananda and the world, he was willing and able to wrestle with momentous changes and experiment with new possibilities.

I personally found it incredibly courageous. How many leaders of a business or organization that they had labored for years to create, and especially spiritual leaders who run the risk of being ostracized by a larger organization or their followers, would take the chance of looking a fool if things didn't work out. Clearly Swamiji was *all in.*

What Swamiji was proposing to explore was much deeper than saying, "Okay everybody, we are now all going to get married and be yogi householders!" Swamiji had dedicated his life to knowing God and serving God. In order to achieve this dual goal it is necessary to unify them. The path to doing this is rooted in understanding the way the soul journeys through the Creation and interacts with the ego/personality. We have touched on this already, but going a little deeper into it will help us to see other aspects of our circumstances.

The Creation is a projection outward from God's unmanifested infinite bliss consciousness. It starts as the Causal Plane which has no outward form, it is the ideational foundation of the Creation. Souls who inhabit this invisible realm are visualizing and animating the Creation through conscious will as God's instruments. Causal thought projections are then manifested as the energy and light of the Astral Universe. It is the causal body covered by an astral body that conveys the soul from lifetime to lifetime. In these subtle bodies are carried the samskars (Vortices of karmic entanglements.) that define the soul's current level of spiritual advancement and past life baggage (Karmic attachments) which are the substructure in the Physical Plane body that we now inhabit. It is our karmic baggage from almost countless incarnations that keeps us rolling down the seemingly endless hall of reincarnation on the wheel of karma, keeping us from remembering our true Self: Spirit.

In order to become manifest the Infinite One had to become dual. God is unmanifested beyond the Creation and manifest as the Creation: Alfa and Omega, light and dark, pain and pleasure, positive and negative. The dual human forms (male and female) represent reason and feeling. As a broad generality, it is understood that males tend to hold reason uppermost and females tend to hold feeling uppermost. The reason that this doesn't tell the whole story is because there are more factors involved.

Yogananda described the soul as individualized Spirit. The soul is neither male nor female. Through the process of reincarnation the soul travels through the Creation in forms with extremely limited consciousness potential all the way to the human form, which is most capable of remembering its infinite Divine origin.

Evolution Through Kingdoms of Consciousness Potential

(As described by Paramhansa Yogananda.)

Mineral Kingdom: In the mineral kingdom, consciousness exists in a state of unconsciousness, responding to external forces without self–awareness.

Plant Kingdom: In the plant kingdom, consciousness begins to manifest as a rudimentary form of life, with feelings and sensitivity, but lacking self–awareness and intellect.

Animal Kingdom: In the animal kingdom, consciousness develops further, with instincts, emotions, and sense perception, but still lacking the capacity for reason and higher thought.

Human Kingdom: The human form is seen as a stage where consciousness can develop intellect, reason, and the ability to choose and evolve spiritually.

When the soul advances to the human form it is born into both male and female bodies. So the evolving consciousness spends time in both reason uppermost and feeling uppermost environments.

Karmic tendencies (Attachments of feeling reactions to every life experience.) are carried in the astral body to each succeeding incarnation. It is the magnetic qualities of our personal karma interacting with the karmic cogs of all life that draw us to the specific conditions of a new lifetime and the experiences of that incarnation. They may lay dormant until a feeling connected experience presents itself unexpectedly, or they may sprout easily through the fertile ground of a compatible environment. As they interact through the filter of DNA and the environmental conditions of our lives they can cause both comfortable and uncomfortable effects.

Highly developed talents at a young age and relatively easy successes in any area of life come from past life development. On the other side, so do consistent difficulties in life and even mental instability, various unhealthy addictions and early death. Another complication can manifest as gender confusion. It is easy to understand how someone who had incarnated as one gender over numerous lives in a row could reincarnate in a body of the opposite gender while maintaining identification with the past life gender.

Remember, the soul has no gender, it has become hypnotized by the power of Maya (Cosmic delusion) into thinking that it is, and only is, the body/personality that it now inhabits. The path of Self–realization is the journey to free ourselves from identifying with the idea that the body/ego/personality that we now inhabit is our sole reality by experiencing more and more awareness of our Divinity.

The ego/personality though activated by higher powers sees its perceptions of reason and feelings as being tied to the body, the results of biological/chemical processes. Human limits of intellect and emotions (ego based feelings) are for most people held in harness by the powerful forces of ego identification. But sitting in the background are the powers of intuitive soul perception which include soul feeling perception and wisdom that are rooted in the calm stillness of Universal consciousness or superconsciousness, not the agitated restlessness of ego consciousness.

It is the restlessness of ego consciousnesses that keeps us from perceiving the superconscious potential that is always present. What we want to do is live inwardly connected to intuitive spiritual perception while we outwardly express through the imperfect body/personality that we have been given to use. This means that we don't need to become perfect outwardly, but inwardly. Outwardly we just don't want the ego/personality to do things that might drastically hinder us from that inner purpose.

I am not saying that we shouldn't seek to perfect our expression of Spirit into outward life. The better that we get at expressing Spirit in daily life, the happier we will be along the way. It is just that outward success is not itself the goal. Sometimes we learn more from our losses than our victories. The goal is to realize that God is trying to shine through our lives and the ego/personality is often in the habit of limiting that light. When we live as conscious instruments of God, outward success and failure are secondary, attunement to God is primary.

It made me smile and feel a little better about my own life when I realized that even avatars make mistakes. The meaning of the word avatar has become confused in modern language because of the movie Avatar and the word's use as an online identity. It is now common to describe an online personality as an avatar, basically the opposite of its original meaning. Avatars are souls that have successfully graduated from the school of life and are no longer forced to reincarnate. They have released all past samskars/karmas and have merged their individualized soul back into the cosmic sea of bliss. Out of compassion they return voluntarily to serve mankind as God's instruments of upliftment.

In order to stay in the physical realm Siddhas (Completely free souls.) must identify sufficiently with an ego/personality in order to maintain a physical form so they can fulfill their serviceful intention. This is one of the reasons that for the purpose of our education we read in *Autobiography of a Yogi* that Lahiri Mahasaya, had a misunderstanding with his guru Babaji, Sri Yukteswar had a misunderstanding with Babaji, and Yogananda had misunderstandings with his guru Sri Yukteswar – all of whom were avatars.

History is filled with stories of saints who have idiosyncrasies that seem incompatible with sainthood. Saint Francis was the life of the party before his spiritual transformation. The sage Valmiki, who lived about three thousand years ago, and wrote one of the greatest Indian spiritual epics of all time, the *Ramayana,* was a successful thief before he came to the spiritual life. St. Augustine, who was born in 354 AD, was known to have led a hedonistic life in his teens. After coming to the Roman Catholic church his writings and sermons helped shape Christian thought. Milarepa, a great saint in Tibet was a trained assassin as a youth and then turned successfully to the spiritual life.

No one is required to be outwardly perfect all of the time. The stain of regret and shame is removed by the realization of God's love. When Yogananda pointed out an error by one of his disciples, the disciple asked, "Will you forgive me?" and Yogananda responded, "What else can I do?" No matter what mistake we make in life, God's love is always present.

If my personality is a trumpet I don't have to become a violin, I just need to become an ever-more spiritualized trumpet. You don't need to be the best trumpet, just keep improving. If you can, join a group of musicians playing spiritual music and try not to get kicked out of the band! Although, as we can see in Swamiji's life, that doesn't have to be a bad thing if we do something good with it.

Once a soul consciously comes onto the spiritual path it will help to take into account that soul's nature and find a path and teacher that can harmonize with it's nature and not against it. This is why there are so many paths offered in life and why claiming that one path is better than another should be seen in terms of its usefulness to its members rather than on its place on the scale of higher or lower paths, or its general popularity. The best classroom for a first grader is first grade not graduate school; all graduate students were in first grade when that is what they needed. So in this way success as a student shouldn't be seen by what grade we are in, but how we are utilizing the learning opportunities that are presented.

When I was growing up my father and many of my teachers in school were overbearing and I couldn't wait to get away. When I arrived at Ananda and met Swami Kriyananda I encouraged him to tell me what to do, yet he rarely did. At the time I didn't realize that had he force fed me, I would have eventually gagged. It is in the nature of the personality that I live through that if I am told that I have to do something or I can't do something, I have instantly the urge to do the opposite of what I am told. Over the years I have learned to redirect that reaction when it is beneficial to do so, but not always!

It is also helpful to understand that the journey of higher Self-discovery is one that must be chosen, it can not be forced. The body and mind can be molded from the outside in, but for Self-realization we must awaken our awareness of Spirit from the inside out. As I mentioned briefly in the Introduction, Patanjali, ancient exponent of the yoga science, presents this inner journey in his Eight-Fold Path.

The Eight-Fold Path is a description of the qualities that are expressed through the human form when the soul is fully identified with Spirit. It is also the prescription for the spiritual aspirant to advance towards complete enlightenment. These are universal principles and not sectarian beliefs. We are all living our own version of these concepts whether we realize it or not. Although there is some overlap, Patanjali's Eight-Fold path is not the same as the Eight-Fold path attributed to the Buddha.

Patanjali's Eight-fold Path

1. **Yama** (Control) The soul will naturally restrain these qualities.

    Ahimsa: Non-violence or harmlessness. Never having the urge to hurt anyone or anything physically, mentally or spiritually.

    Satya: Non-lying or truthfulness. Always representing the highest truth in words and deeds. Speaking factual truth in such a way that it isn't unnecessarily hurtful to others.

    Asteya: Non-covetousness. Not desiring more than what you need or what others have.

    Brahmacharya: Restraint in living through the senses and sexuality.

    Aparigraha: Non-possessiveness. Not being attached to that which you have: body, possessions, position, money, relationship or any other thing.

2. **Niyama** (Non–control) The soul will naturally allow these qualities to flow freely.

    Saucha: Cleanliness of the body, mind and heart.

    Santosha: Contentment. Described as the supreme quality. Resting at all times in the superconscious Self.

    Tapasya: Austerity or self-control. The practice of energetically challenging yourself to improve in the direction of your goal while at the same time not injuring yourself.

Swadhyaya: Self-study or introspection. The practice of honest non–attached inner observation and self-awareness.

Ishwarapranidhana: Worship of the Supreme Self. Universal Love flowing through the ego/personality back to Universal Love.

3. **Asana – Posture**

   The ability to sit absolutely still for extended periods of time. The practice of hatha yoga can help to achieve this goal, but is not by itself the definition of asana.

4. **Pranayama – Life force control**

   Pranayama means control over prana (life force) in the body. The conscious ability to tap into and control inner life force is key to inner and outer success.

5. **Pratyahara – Interiorization**

   The interiorization of one's attention and thoughts.

6. **Dharana – Inner absorption**

   The withdrawal from the restless mind.

7. **Dhyana – Single-pointed concentration**

   Through the use of a meditation technique or focus on an attribute of God/Universal Consciousness.

8. **Samadhi – Oneness**.

   The soul withdrawing consciously from the body/personality and experiencing Cosmic Consciousness.

The Eight-Fold Path is both linear and non–linear at the same time, a set of practices and descriptions of the goal of yoga all at the same time. Like a guide map it points out the goal and a way to get there. We can start at the beginning and work our way to the state of samadhi, but at the same time we need to work on all aspects simultaneously, each person adjusting their training to their current state of consciousness. To complicate things, we can't perfect any stage until we reach samadhi and we can't achieve samadhi until all the other stages are perfected. Well, this isn't exactly true and here is why.

As I said previously, we don't have to be perfect outwardly, we just can't be so imperfect that it gets in the way of becoming inwardly perfect. One of the reasons this is true is because there is a wild card in the whole situation: Grace (Universally based support).

Yogananda taught that Self-realization is 25% the effort of the devotee, 25% the effort of the Guru on the disciples behalf and 50% the grace of God. This is good news! No...this is the ultimate great news!

Life/God/The Universe is going to provide us with everything we need, all we have to do is draw that grace into our lives. How do we draw God's grace? We live the Eight-Fold Path, utilizing the techniques and teachings of Yoga which will create an energy flow through our consciousness, increasing and uplifting the magnetic qualities that we radiate, causing the Universe to respond accordingly: Grace.

One of the great tipping points in the soul's long journey through the Creation is when the yearning of the soul becomes so energized that it magnetically draws a guru. All souls tread uniquely similar steps along the way, according to their individual journey. This is why even though maps like the Eight –Fold Path are readily available, when one climbs the highest peaks, a guide is still required for the greatest chance of a successful summiting. The guru is God's guide or personal ambassador to the soul when it is ready to seriously apply itself to remembering its Divinity.

Swamiji's way of guiding us was to represent what he had learned from Yogananda. He believed that he could serve us best as a friend or elder disciple rather than a figurehead with a grand title. For him, being the disciple of a great master was title enough.

Swamiji didn't tell us what we had to do, he shared with us suggestions that he thought, or knew from personal experience, would be helpful; we were on our own as to what we would do with his offerings. Those who couldn't digest his ideas eventually got unhappiness indigestion and moved on. Those who stayed, banqueted on the gourmet vibrations and guidance that his life offered.

When we live through a consistently Spirit guided ego/personality, no matter what we do, it can turn out to be beneficial. If we make a mistake the Universe will adjust in some way to make that mistake a positive instead of a negative. When we link our intentions and actions to knowing God and serving God, they become one and the same thing. Swamiji was giving us a behind the scenes view of how this works and inviting us to join the journey on a deeper level. As we will see, Swamiji's leap of faith into the swirling waters of redefining marriage in a yogic community was filled with ups and downs as is par for life on planet Earth. In Roseville I was coming to grips with my own leap of faith.

Along with the joy of our new designation as a couple, I had to land on my feet and support a family. Family? Yes, Dan and Cristi lived in a constantly shifting schedule between their father's house – just two blocks away – and our house. So now I was instantly a stepfather. To make it even more interesting, Dick wanted to come over and talk to Toni occasionally, but his presence was so disturbing to Toni that I had to – with her appreciation – keep Dick outside of the house and mediate the current issue at hand.

Dick's attempts to get through me to Toni were not successful. Fortunately we didn't come to blows. In fact it wasn't long before we were sitting down on the front porch together and having longer than I would have preferred conversations. Dick was what you might call a regular guy who had boxed himself into a corner and couldn't quite see how it all had happened. I didn't dislike him, in fact, I felt for him. I tried to help him come to grips with the situation as I would with anyone that life presented me to serve. Since he came more than once, I believe that our conversations did help.

The large garage in our house inspired me to reawaken my piano tuning and repairing skills. I bought a couple of used pianos from the classified ads and put in an ad of my own to offer tuning and repairing services. I already had an enclosed trailer for moving pianos so I was up and running very quickly.

It was my enclosed trailer that got Haridas and I invited to move a grand piano. We drove to Swamiji's parents home in Atherton, California, to pick it up. Mrs. Walters greeted us with warmth and a beautifully animated smile. She radiated a calm purity and sincerity that was immediately embracing. Mr. Walters was more reserved but genuinely friendly, it was a joy to meet Swamiji's earthly parents. To see Swamiji's demeanor as their son was touching. He had grown up in a home of harmony and clearly there were no edges underneath the surface, only love and appreciation. After we had installed the piano in Swamiji's dome at Ananda, as usual, Haridas once again teased me about choosing pianos over violins, since violins would be so much easier to move!

One day when I was in Swamiji's dome he brought me over to the piano and showed me where a tuning pin was broken. He asked me if I could fix it. I immediately said: "Yes." I should have added: "I think I can." It was a procedure that I knew in theory but had never personally performed.

When I arrived some days later to do the repair I was calm on the outside and a little concerned on the inside. As I remember it, Swamiji was in silence at the time. Since we weren't in the habit of making *chit chat* with Swamiji anyway, with a smile of greeting I just sat down on the piano bench and got to it. Taking out a broken tuning pin takes a bit of finesse because you don't want to damage anything nearby with your tools – which was equally concerning to me as actually getting the pin out. The pin had broken off below the surface of the beautifully golden surrounding metal plate, so getting it out was not going to be a leisurely walk in the park.

While I got prepared Swamiji was distantly puttering around the room and I was feeling comfortable. With impeccable instincts, just as I was about to begin the operation,

Swamiji walked over and then bent at the waist to lean in and get a good look at what I was doing. He came right up to the limit of the polite personal space line. He didn't say a word, he just peered in with calm interest. My comfort level took a steep dive to below the basement.

I had watched many people work their art over the years with the same inquisitiveness that Swamiji was exhibiting. I wanted to give him a show, but I couldn't handle it, I began to do my own puttering. No words were said, I just stalled until Swamiji got the message and bent upward at the waist to wander off. This interaction can be used to understand more clearly the subtle shift that was trying to take place at Ananda, which is key to understanding a yogi householder.

Oh... before I move on, I am happy to report that the operation was a complete success! The patient was repaired and still lives happily to this day.

It was both typically male and yogic of us not to speak. The practice of consciously not speaking for the purpose of calming the mind in order to achieve and maintain an inner connection to Spirit is classic yoga practice. Disciples at the ashram with Yogananda were discouraged from speaking with him unless spoken to. This was not to protect Master, but to train the disciples in developing inner stillness and intuitive perception.

So for Swamiji and I not to speak was yogicly normal. Even though Swamiji was in silence at the time, he could have written a note if he wanted to communicate. We had done that many times in the past. I could have spoken up and explained that I was happy for him to watch, but that I was a little nervous about doing a good job. It wasn't that I thought Swamiji would be offended in any way or that he would think less of me. It was certainly to some degree my male conditioning: don't show weakness, don't communicate feelings.

Male energy yogis can easily live this way and not realize that female, Divine Mother, energy is also necessary for balance. It is not unyogic to embrace and have emotional feelings, it just isn't as clear how to do that because much monastic training emphasizes male energy: spiritual accomplishment and pulling away from the world, rather than female embracing life with expressions of love and compassion.

Yogananda's personality expression was powerfully male and female: equally Divine. Many people have looked at pictures of him and thought that he was a woman. He cried when Sister Gyanamata – Yogananda's foremost woman disciple – passed from this world, even though he said he had watched her entering into the infinite bliss state. Pictures and video of Yogananda's face at Sri Yukteswar's burial are a study in yogic agony. Master was wonderfully balanced in his expression of humanity at its best and powerful loving Divinity.

God the father is beyond the Creation; Divine Mother is the Creation. We say mother nature, it is instinctive. Compassion and dispassion live side by side when balance is achieved. At this time in history male energy is uppermost, what is needed is a correction in the direction of female energy. Not greater ego based emotionalism, but the recognition that outward works without love, caring and inclusion are empty and a path to unhappiness, which we can see so prevalent in the world today.

The male drive for *doing*, accomplishment, needs to manifest in balance with the female qualities of *being*, nurturing, drawing people together. Remember, this isn't about whether we are in a male or female body, it is about qualities of consciousness flowing through both. No matter which form we currently inhabit, we are already expressing a mixture of the two, through inner attunement we can gradually balance out these qualities.

Paramhansa Yogananda taught that this balancing is both microscopic (taking place in each individual) and macroscopic (taking place in the whole world). We need to apply this understanding for our own benefit, which will automatically help the world to do the same. As civilization advances science and technology, it is essential that we evolve our expression of their uses in a balanced way. Otherwise, instead of taking us to new heights of well-being they will doom us to greater loneliness and suffering at best and extinction at worst.

It isn't that Swamiji hadn't addressed this subject previously, the very idea of having a community necessitated having families and a society that would support raising children. We were already successful, but now, Swamiji was saying that we need to take this to a whole new level. In order to continue raising the vibration and balance of the Ananda culture, he was going to help by diving into the waters himself. Helping us all to discover what living the ancient yoga teachings looks like in the beginning of Dwapara Yuga – the age of energy.

In Roseville I was completely caught up in my new lifestyle. Along with piano projects I began to remodel a large room above the garage that had previously gone unused. It was perfect for a combination yoga studio and recording studio. I also somehow inherited Swamiji's first computer which had 64 kb of ram and large floppy discs for memory storage. It used the very first version of Wordstar for word processing. I was so full of creative energy that I started writing and even wrote a musical with words and music called *Conversations with a Christmas Mystery*.

The musical was about a joyful family that lived in a rural cabin. During their Christmas celebration an older fellow with a smiling bearded face and a large bag over his shoulder shows up and fun ensues. I used some of Swamiji's songs and also some that I wrote myself. There was even a little dance at one point. It was a story of unexpected blessings and the appreciation one feels when the Universe responds to unspoken and sometimes even unrecognized needs.

It was also around this time that I wrote another song:

Can you hear? by Vijay Girard

Can you hear? He is calling your name.
Will you follow, His whispering flame.
He is reaching to us from high above.
From a temple of golden love.
He is rising from the clouds of a glorious heaven.
In such sweetness He lifts us to His side.

Do we perceive His presence all around.
Are we willing to touch His sound.
Its a world that we can not see,

With these eyes of mortal man we are not free.
We can rise to me the challenge of His name,
in the mystical eye of Spirit are all the same.

If we care, we can be with Him,
As we share everything within.
Its in giving that we become free,
Then the world will respond as we need
And we will live in the rightness of His story,
So the power of God finds its glory.

Toni and I were also getting creative in a very traditional and down to earth way, soon we were expecting a child by the end of the year. Little did we know how bountiful our good fortune would be.

Chapter 10

More Truth about the Truth

"To develop pure and unconditional love between husband and wife, parent and child, friend and friend, self and all, is the lesson we have come on earth to learn."

–Paramhansa Yogananda

It wasn't so much the details of what Swamiji did once he was with Parameshwari (Supreme Goddess) that created a dramatic change in Ananda's inner atmosphere, it was more that he had opened a door that we hadn't realized was closed. Thus far, even though families were part of Ananda we all had practiced or at least valued highly an ascetic's approach to life. Now a veil had been removed and we could see a little more clearly what Master was asking us to embrace.

Yogananda's description of World-brotherhood colonies was that they were for "plain living and high thinking." Simple might be a better word than plain. It wasn't a call to live in poverty or visual dullness and ignore the beauties of this world, but a proclamation that the energies of the age that we are now living in are freeing us from that old – the spiritual life is about suffering for God – view and inviting us to bring our inner life joyfully into everyday manifestation.

There was one change in the community that I had mixed feelings about: hugging. It wasn't that I was against hugging in general, it was two particular aspects of hugging that concerned me. The first had to do with hugging anyone/everyone. Maybe it is because I didn't get a lot of hugs when I was growing up so I see hugging as very meaningful. But it is also an issue of sincerity, which is connected to truthfulness. I am not a fan of meaningless handshaking or hugging.

According to Vedic tradition the exchange of vibrations through these kinds of contact can be very powerful, both positively and negatively, depending on the qualities of energy flowing through the people involved. So the traditional hello and goodbye in India is a pronam – palms joined in front of the heart with fingers pointed up – with a spoken or unspoken n*amaste or namaskhar,* which means: Spirit in me bows to Spirit in you. When done properly those who practice pronam are not just greeting each other on the surface but inwardly communing with them in the oneness of Universal love and joy. When I first came to Ananda and practiced this it opened up a whole new level of communication for me. I found it very meaningful. I wasn't in a hurry to give this up by lots of outward hugging.

My second personal issue was hugging Swamiji. Up until that time I would describe Swamiji as an occasional huger with only a few of the people that he had known for years. As an occasional recipient of some of those hugs I found them to be, "super-duper unbelievable fantastic!" I didn't want to lose the value of those hugs by too great a volume.

It isn't that I didn't want to share Swamiji, I had seen over the years that those close to Swamiji rather than being jealous of Swamiji's attention to others, were able to appreciate his blessings to others. I was thinking more on the lines of the famous quote, *Familiarity breeds contempt*. Too much of a good thing can sometimes lessen our ability to appreciate its value.

Over the ensuing months I observed Swamiji "the hugger" and my thoughts on the subject changed. I can't tell you how often Swamiji's thoughts and actions were larger than my concept of what could be understood. This was another case of him taking things to a higher level. Swamiji was an incredible mix of relaxed, spontaneous, completely present, slightly withdrawn, inclusive, dignified, childlike, sensitive, calm, heartfelt, joyful and incredibly kind. As I watched him hug people I noticed that he was equally fully present with each person. I never saw him hug someone proforma. Anyone who has greeted a long line of people knows that it takes tremendous energy to do so.

Swamiji wrote in Chapter 24 of T*he New Path*:

> Sometime in February or March 1949, Master instructed me to stand outside the Hollywood church after the Sunday morning services and shake hands with people as they left. In his lessons he states that people exchange magnetism when they shake hands. Thus, what Master wanted me to do was not merely greet

> people, but act as his channel of blessings to others. The first time I tried it, I felt so drained of energy afterward that I actually became dizzy. I suppose what happened was that people unconsciously drew from me, in the thought that I was there as Master's representative.
>
> "Master," I said later, "I don't believe I'm ready for this job." I explained what had happened.
>
> "That is because you are thinking of yourself," he replied. "Think of God, and you will find *His* energy flowing through you."
>
> His suggestion worked. By holding to the thought of God, I discovered that I actually felt more uplifted, after shaking hands with congregation members, than beforehand.
>
> "When this 'I' shall die," Master once wrote in a rhymed couplet, "then shall I know who am I."

Swamiji was practicing what Master had trained him to do, it looked a little different on the outside but it was the same on the inside: a hug pronam. It appeared to me that Swamiji already had the male/female balance available, he just didn't yet feel the complete freedom to express it because of his monastic training and because we, and future generations of disciples, needed to watch and learn from his discipleship's evolution of expression, so that we could understand and allow that to happen in our own lives.

Once I had absorbed more layers of what was taking place my concern about hugging dissolved. Since that time I have tried, when called to hug, to do it on ever higher levels. This was a key part of the message at that time. Even when things are going well, don't stop evolving forward, because as long as we are on planet earth there is always something new to observe and understand. Once we have learned a lesson, life will change so that we can learn a new one. This is certainly what happened with Parameshwari.

While Swamiji and the community were embracing this new understanding for the future, Parameshwari was coming to grips with the enormous changes in her own life. Being around Swamiji was wonderful but also very intense, she had to be on her "A" game 24/7, for a newcomer to our way of life that was a lot to ask. Add to that hundreds of people watching your every move and the responsibility of potential future leadership: it is not unreasonable that she would occasionally need some time on her own to let off steam and process.

What was surprising, was that by the end of the year Parameshwari had taken a break and wasn't coming back. The practical truth is that not every good potential in life will be realized in the way that we would prefer or expect. When Swamiji had spoken of their relationship he even said he didn't know how long it would last in its current form, though clearly he thought it would last longer than it did.

While Swamiji was digesting this turn of events in his relationship with Parameshwari my life in Roseville was also evolving. There was no question that we had entered a phase of nesting. We discovered that Toni was pregnant and I was over the moon happy with the news. Because I have shared our birth story extensively in my book, *Positive Flow Childbirth* – originally titled *Doorway to a New Lifetime: Childbirth from a Spiritual View,* I won't go into all of the details here, but there are some thoughts that I do want to share.

One day Toni was out working in the yard and became inwardly aware that conception had just taken place. Having previously experienced this occurrence twice before when Dan and Cristi were born she said she felt the same but different. The difference she couldn't quite put her finger on wasn't understood until six months later when a visit to the midwife revealed two heartbeats: Twins!

The yoga teachings and techniques are so central to the way that life is made that through them virtually every life experience can be better understood and addressed with greater practicality and spirituality. Dan and Cristi had been born in the hospital with the protocols of the then current mainstream medicine guiding the proceedings. This time Toni wanted to do things more in line with her greater understanding of how life works from the inside out.

We decided that the twins would be born at home using natural birthing modalities and three midwives. I once again found that I was thinking too small when I discussed breathing exercises for the birth with Toni. The student became the teacher when she responded to my query by saying, "Why should I learn birthing exercises? I already practice Kriya Yoga and hatha yoga."

Kriya Yoga is a pranayama (lifeforce control) technique which uses the internalized control of the breath to move energy up and down the spine. One of the results of successful practice is to withdraw the yogi's awareness from the physical body to commune inwardly with Universally rooted well-being. For those who are sufficiently practiced in the technique it is a powerful natural alternative to medically induced pain reduction.

The story is told that Master's father, Bhagabati Charan Ghosh, who practiced Kriya Yoga his whole adult life, needed abdominal surgery later in life. At that time chloroform was the only anesthesia available and its use was considered too dangerous to use in Bhagabati's case. Bhagabati responded to the situation by saying that he would just practice Kriya Yoga and consciously withdraw from the pain. He did so successfully and the operation was completed without complication.

It is a time honored practice in India to read holy scriptures to the unborn child during the pregnancy. So while Toni rested her head on my lap I read the Bhagavad Gita to her and the twins. The Bhagavad Gita is one of India's most beloved scriptures and is a discourse between Arjuna – who represents all devotees/disciples – and Krishna – who represents God/Guru. We were uncertain about what the long term effects might be, but we certainly enjoyed that time of uplifted sharing. Many years later we discovered that one of the twins had a strong inner affinity with Krishna.

Just before Christmas the time for the birth arrived and we began the process of inner withdrawal together. Soon Toni was deeply withdrawn. After some time the midwife wanted to know what was going on, she had never seen anyone do this. I communicated what was necessary so that Toni could stay inwardly concentrated. Eventually it was time to push and I encouraged Toni to come out of her withdrawn state. It took her a few minutes, she had gone very deep, but soon she was fully present and took charge of her efforts. There was never any of the yelling and screaming like you see on television or in the movies. Toni was amazing.

Theresa Sabari (A woman saint from ancient India) arrived first and then twenty-five minutes later Francis Kaivalya (The state of absolute oneness with God - Kai for short.) was born. Watching a newborn arrive and take that first breath presents the miracle of life like nothing else. I was awed by the power of the moment. Once the midwives announced that mother and twins were well I could fully embrace the elation that was flowing through me.

Some weeks later we drove up to the original meditation retreat at Ananda to have a christening ceremony in the temple. Haridas was once again our minister and our dear friends Santosh and Valerie were blessed as God parents. These first months with the twins were so fulfilling and inspiring to me that I wrote a song for the ceremony.

Welcome Home by Vijay Girard

Chorus
Welcome home we're so glad you've come.
We are here to welcome you for everyone.
Verse
We bow before the spirit of our Lord
and give to Him all that we are.

And with His grace we will share a holy place,
with you our friends we gently embrace.

You've always been dear and in our hearts so near
and now we can share this life together.
Let us remember why we are here this way
and live our lives the way we pray.

Now that you're here we hope our love is clear.
We offer to you all that we have to give.
And if we fail in even some small way,
We trust the Lord to smooth your way.

It was being able to work out of the house with piano tuning that allowed me to spend so much time with Kai and Sabari when they were infants. Toni was very tired after the birth – for good reason! - and because of this breast feeding became impractical. At first I was disappointed, because mother's milk is known to be best for the child. But as it turned out, bottle feeding allowed me to get up in the middle of the night to feed the twins and Toni could get a full night's rest. Those middle of the night feedings were incredibly nourishing to my heart.

Our home life in Roseville was everything that my own upbringing was not. What I mean is that with Toni and the twins there was an aura of calm happiness. I had grown up in a home with turmoil underneath a public facade of good grooming. Sure, we had some good times over the years, but there was never what I would describe as a deep closeness. I lived at a distance from my parents and siblings: I felt very alone. With the birth of the twins and my life with Toni, I experienced a release from that lack in my life. It was like an invisible thorn had been removed from my heart.

One of the features of the spiritual life is the realization that we are all one in Spirit. Through the practice of meditation we learn to inwardly commune not only with Spirit underneath the surface of life, but with Spirit as all life. The family environment is the place we are supposed experience Divine Love manifested as Divine human love. I didn't begin to understand this until I came to Ananda.

My early years at Ananda, which I would describe as my spiritual adolescence, was where I first experienced a group of people who loved each other in the love of God. This is the setting aside of ego/personality preferences and seeing yourself and all people as expressions of Spirit. In the beginning Swamiji was my father/mother and the other members my spiritual siblings. It was the first time in my life that I felt I was with my own people. It was for me not just a group of devotees, but truly a spiritual family. As time went by we could better be described as friends in God, because in a way family can create a consciousness of obligation, where friendship can be as deep as family but completely voluntary.

In fact, the original name of the Ananda Church was *The Friends of God*. And letters – before email! – were often signed: In Divine Friendship. When we pray we include God as Friend. Over time my relationship with Swamiji, with its both personal and impersonal components, certainly included Divine Friendship and guided the way I relate to all of life.

Our training at that time had necessitated that we deeply internalize our consciousness so that we could develop the skills of inner communion which we had not developed before coming to Ananda. Now, as a group, each in their own way, we were being encouraged to express our inner communion outwardly while holding on to the yogi's natural disinclination to be overly drawn into physical and mental/emotional restlessness: which causes the loss of the inner calmness, thus diminishing awareness of Spirit.

With twins everything is more: more time, more effort, more attention, more food and more diaper changing. I once did seven diaper changes in an hour! Of course there is also more bonding, more hugging, more smiling, more laughing and more loving.

When people make the claim that the spiritual life isn't practical it makes me shake my head in wonder. Life doesn't get more down to earth than parenting. The skills of the yogi are centrally applicable to every life circumstance. Swamiji had trained us to inwardly reach out and feel the truth of the moment. This skill is a huge help when trying to understand the needs of infants who have limited tools for communication and also for staying calm while you try to figure things out.

Learning to come up with creative harmonious solutions at every stage of parenting and life in general is a skill that is central to living superconsciously. By watching Swamiji spiritually parent all of the people who lived at and traveled through Ananda we could see how the central approach of the yogi can help us dance gracefully to all of the movements in the symphony of our lives.

After the birth of Kaivalya and Sabari I became very aware that they had arrived with their own uniqueness. Separate from being a boy and a girl was a vibration of consciousness that each radiated: a soul emanation which was underneath the little bodies and gradually appearing personalities. This reminded me that they were not mine in the way that most people think of their children. In the English language we say, "This is *my* child." My means mine. Mine means for many a kind of ownership. I was keenly aware that this was not how I felt.

Life isn't about ownership of things outside ourselves, but stewardship for that which you feel a responsibility. This includes children and spouses. In years past – and currently still for some people – children and spouses were treated more like the property of the *man* of the house. My father was certainly of that era. I never felt that way with Toni or the kids. I felt blessed to be with them and honored to serve them, to love them, and support their efforts for success in life. Along the way I got to simply enjoy their company, which I did very much. But from the very beginning I realized that they were their own souls, on their own journey through the Creation and while I felt a very personal connection with them, I also realized that the imposition of my will on them should be kept at a minimum.

The younger the child the more control and/or guiding energy is required of the parent. But as the child grows it is essential that they take more and more responsibility for their own actions. Since most of Swamiji's spiritual children arrived as adults he deeply honored their need to be self-directed. So he focused on providing an environment of magnetic spiritual opportunity for deeper inner attunement and very rarely on telling people what to do.

It was around this time that Swamiji was inspired with the possibility that Ananda should incorporate as a city. The idea of presenting Ananda to the world as a city – Ananda, California – showing how the ancient tradition of dharma could help modern life to be more harmonious was very exciting. It was a massive undertaking which had not only the many economic and governmental components, but even more challenging, the political ramifications.

For years we had wrestled with Nevada County, both Planning Department and general officialdom. It was certainly a hopeful perk of incorporation that we would be less under their thumb. However, it was on the political front that we faced the greatest opposition. Ananda's neighbors on the San Juan Ridge, inflamed by former Ananda residents, and even influenced by the leadership in SRF, banded together to oppose us.

It all came to a head at a LAFCO (Local Agency Formation Commission) hearing, where unlawful testimony against our religious beliefs was allowed. There were no meaningful arguments against us. Yet in the end our application was denied. And of course, it was all playing out not only in the local media, but had reached national attention as well.

This whole process had taken herculean efforts over many months. It was clear that we had grounds for appeal. Yet even with all of this energy committed to the goal, when after the denial Swamiji inwardly asked Master if we should continue the fight, the answer came back: No. And so Swamiji let it go. He had no attachment to his previous efforts, only a willingness to move forward according to his best understanding of inner guidance.

This was a beautiful example of Karma Yoga. Nishkam Karma is desireless action. Action without the desire for the fruits of our actions. This isn't about not caring or having a lackadaisical attitude. It is about serving Truth in all things to the best of our ability and then being detached from the results. If we live for elation when we succeed and disappointment when we fail, we will live disconnected from the Universal spring of soul joy that is always available to us.

The worldly mind would see this episode as a loss, but history tells us that loss can be a stepping stone to greater success if we respond with the right attitude. Through the devotee's eye we see God's hand in all life experiences. In this instance we were given a preview of the future and training in the skills that would be needed for the epic battle to come. SRF's involvement and former Ananda members acting against Swamiji and Ananda in this case was just an appetizer for a banquet of conflict that had been simmering for years.

Swamiji's continued practice of inwardly seeking guidance was a reminder that no matter how strong an inspiration may be, we should always continue to inwardly listen along the way. It is through this practice that we minimize the chances of getting off course and then wondering where we went wrong.

When Kaivalya and Sabari were seven months old we took advantage of Toni's mother's offer to watch the twins so we could attend the SRF convocation at the Biltmore hotel in Los Angeles, California. I had been to the convocation before, but

Toni had not. It is a week long series of classes and meditations that is highlighted at the end of the week with a Kriya Yoga Initiation ceremony. In the past there had been difficulties with the way SRF treated Ananda members, Swamiji had withdrawn his recommendation that people attend convocation because of this. He didn't say we couldn't go, only that he just no longer could promote Anandites going to a program where they may be subject to mistreatment.

Disciples of Paramhansa Yogananda come from all over the world to attend this yearly event. Meditations were held in the ballroom where Master, after reading his poem *My India,* entered into mahasamadhi – a yogi's final conscious exit from the body.

Swamiji wrote in chapter eight of *The New Path*:

> The following day, March 7, he came downstairs to go out. He was scheduled to attend a banquet that evening at the Biltmore Hotel in honor of the Indian Ambassador. "Imagine!" he said, "I've taken a room at the Biltmore. That's where I first started in this city!"
>
> Then again he repeated, "Wish me luck."
>
> Master had asked me to attend the banquet with Dick Haymes, the popular singer and movie actor. Dick had recently become a disciple, and had taken Kriya initiation from me.
>
> Years ago Master had said, "When I leave this earth, I want to go speaking of my America

and my India." And in a song about India that he had written, to the tune of the popular song "My California," he paraphrased the original ending with the words, "I know when I die, in joy I will sigh for my sunny, grand old India!" Once, too, in a lecture he had stated, "A heart attack is the easiest way to die. That is how I choose to die." This evening, all these predictions were to prove true.

Master was scheduled to speak after the banquet. His brief talk was so sweet, so almost tender, that I think everyone present felt embraced in the gossamer net of his love. Warmly he spoke of India and America, and of their respective contributions to world peace and true human progress. He talked of their future cooperation. Finally he read his beautiful poem, "My India."

Throughout his speech I was busy recording his words, keeping my eyes on my notebook. He came to the last lines of the poem:

Where Ganges, woods, Himalayan caves and men dream God.

I am hallowed; my body touched that sod!

"Sod" became a long-drawn-out sigh. Suddenly from all sides of the room there came a loud cry. I looked up.

"What is it?" I demanded of Dick Haymes, seated beside me. "What happened?"

"Master fainted," he replied.

> *Oh, no, Master! You wouldn't faint. You've left us. You've left us!* the forgotten playwright in me cried silently. *This is too perfect a way for you to go for it to mean anything else!* I hastened to where Master lay. A look of bliss was on his face.

The room has powerful vibrations in spite of its generally worldly use. The very still and silent meditators, in attunement to the power and blessings of Yogananda's life, and legacy, radiate the continuation of Master's living presence. The Convocation classes were given by SRF Monks and the room of books and gifts was hosted by the Nuns. Daya Mata (Compassionate Mother), the Sangha Mata (Fellowship Mother) gave an inspiring presentation, sharing her experiences at Mt. Washington with Yogananda.

We stayed in the Biltmore Hotel for the whole week, experiencing a kind of seclusion. There were current and former Ananda members there as well and we enjoyed sharing the inspiration with them. Fortunately political overtones were minimal that year and we were able to comfortably commune with a large spiritual family of gurubais (fellow disciples). By the end of the week we were spiritually recharged and eager to get back to life in Roseville.

We spent the next year in Roseville, focusing on Dan, Cristi and the twins. The life changes for us were just as big for Dan and Cristi. Their parents had divorced, their mother had a new husband and now they had a twin brother and sister! We all needed to take a breath and get familiar with our new circumstances.

As I mentioned, Toni's former husband Richard lived two blocks away and her mother Yolanda was one block farther. Her sister Jeannine with her husband Dan and daughter Monica lived in nearby Granite Bay, so I too had a new extended family!

Being a step parent is one of those roles in life that takes extra sensitivity. Since my parents divorced when I was fourteen I had some experience on that side of it. I was also still young enough to remember how I felt when I was younger! Additionally it was a big plus knowing Dan and Cristi for some years before I joined their family.

Cristi is one of those people who's nature is to like everyone. I can't remember a single time that we ever locked horns over anything. When the twins were born she jumped right in as elder sister and shared with delight our familial bounty. If she ever felt any difficulty in adjusting to me as a part of her family I am unaware of it.

Dan was a little more challenging at first. As a boy entering manhood he felt both a strong loyalty to his father and a disinclination to be bossed by anyone. At the same time he was so good-natured as a person that he wasn't really sure how to act, so occasionally he brooded. I felt keenly for his point of view and gave him the space to work it out at his own pace.

The early 1980's was the beginning of the golden video arcade era; Pac Man and Donkey Kong were well into their ascendance as video game powerhouses. In an effort to do a little male bonding I invited Dan to come to a video arcade with me. I could see him calculating in his mind how to react. On one hand was the distance between us, on the other hand was playing video games. I hid my smile when video games won.

We spent about an hour and a half at the arcade. I gave him a good chunk of change when we arrived and then we went our separate ways. I don't think we said more than a few words to each other the whole time. Between games I would occasionally walk over and watch him play for a few minutes, but I didn't intrude on his concentration. It was a very old school manly outing. I can't say for sure what results our time together produced, but I think I noticed a slight easing in his chest. We did it more than once, so just as with his father, I think it did help.

Toni's mother, my new mother-in-law, Yolanda, was a force to be reckoned with in the best sense of the word. She was a classic New York Italian, welcoming with open arms, nonstop conversation and an incredible cook. I must admit that at first I found it a little overwhelming. Over time I saw all the genuinely caring energy that she brought to every situation and it reminded me that my ways are not the only good ways.

During this time Toni continued to teach yoga classes both in the local recreation center and at home in the studio above the garage. We would go up to Ananda Village as often as possible. Eventually we began to talk about moving up to the village and Toni discussed this idea with Dan and Cristi. Of course it was a shock at first, but wonderfully, Dan and Cristi were able to see why this was so important to their mother. They had watched Toni's dedication to the spiritual life grow and while they desperately didn't want her to go, they also saw that it was right for her.

Toni felt deep anguish over the situation. Her Italian heritage held family above all else. But she had given her life to

God and married someone who was dedicated to Ananda. So just as she had given herself into God's hands when she got divorced, she gave herself fully to our life together. We made plans to sell the house in Roseville and build one at Ananda Village. I had seen in the past that when my life was on the right track everything lined up and things moved quickly. Little did I know that moving quickly was about to become an ongoing theme.

Chapter 11

A Momentous Year

Jesus said, "I give you a new commandment: Love one another. Just as I have loved you, you must also love one another." (John 13:34)

In the fall of 1983 the Roseville house had been sold, tears of departure had been shed with Dan and Cristi, and we moved into a home near Ananda Village. It should be mentioned that we now lived only a one hour drive from Roseville, so it wasn't the other side of the world.

We rented a mobile home near the village because at the time there was no housing on the property that would meet our needs. Toni started life in the new residence with a humorous episode. I don't remember why it happened this way, but for some reason she spent the first day and night there alone. Having grown up as a city girl and then a suburban housewife she loved opportunities to go out in nature but was unfamiliar with living in a forest. When I arrived back from wherever I had been she had a concerned look on her face.

I asked her, "What's wrong?"

She replied, "There has been a bird chirping loudly on and off since I got here. It was so loud it sounded like it was inside. It seemed so insistent that I looked through the windows to find it, but never had success."

I couldn't imagine what kind of bird would be hanging around making enough noise to disturb her. I assured her not to worry about it. A little later we were in the living room and we heard a loud chirping sound.

"There it is!" Toni exclaimed.

Not long after it started I began to laugh and Toni looked at me with more confusion. Now I knew why she hadn't answered the phone when I tried to call her! The chirping was the sound of the ringer on the land line phone. She thought it was a bird outside so she didn't answer it!

During this time Swamiji was continuing to broaden his horizons. Ananda had established centers in Sacramento – which eventually grew into a community, San Francisco – 1979 to 1988, Seattle – which also grew into a community, and Menlo Park (which became a community in Palo Alto), and a community in Sonoma county, California, called Oceansong (1979 to 1986). In 1979 teachers were sent to Italy and those early efforts now started to bear fruit. Expansion both inward and outward was picking up steam.

At the Village there was a lot of construction taking place. In order to better serve the increasing stream of visitors a new retreat facility was under construction. It's original *World*

Brotherhood Retreat name was later changed to *The Expanding Light*. In 1976 a fire (described in *Traveling with Swamiji*) destroyed most of the homes in the village. By this time many had been replaced and new areas on the land were opening up for use. Instead of homes being scattered helter-skelter all over the property the way it had been before the fire, they were now built in clusters to consolidate infrastructure and minimize disturbing the natural environment.

The cluster concept also represented the communities social shift from a kind of monastic pioneering *each on their own energy* to a *we are all doing this together* communitarian energy. It was planned that each cluster would have a small temple so that the residents could meditate together and develop closer personal relationships. With the increasing number of residents it was important that people have – each according to their nature – circles of friends so that they didn't feel too isolated and could take spiritual advantage of the group energy. Toni and I dove into life at the Village with full enthusiasm. Along with attending spiritual activities and introducing Kaivalya and Sabari to the community – who of course embraced them with open arms – I had a house to build!

There were a lot of hoops to jump through before I could actually start building. First I had to get approval from the village council and Ananda planning department. We chose a site on a ridge in a newly available southwestern part of the village. Our timing couldn't have been more perfect. The dirt road to that area with power and water had only recently been put in so ours would be the first house. The cluster had not yet been named; it was my honor to do so. I found the name in the

Bhagavad Gita: Chapter Ten. Krishna is telling Arjuna some of the ways the Divine manifests in the Creation and in verse 23 He says:

> Of all the Rudras (Deities) I am Lord Siva (Dissolver of the Creation back into Spirit); of the Yakshas (benevolent nature spirits) and Rakshasas (malevolent nature spirits); I am the lord of wealth Kuvera; of the Vasus (deities of fire and light) I am fire, Agni; and of the mountains I am Meru.

Meru is said to be the abode of Shiva who is also described as the destroyer of ignorance. I prayed that all who lived here would become purified; free of all delusions.

Through the years I had taken advantage of my elementary school shop classes. We had been taught: If you can draw it, you can build it. So I drew up plans for the new house and submitted them to the Nevada County Building Department. As an owner builder I could legally do all aspects of the construction. The project was inspected at each stage by the county inspector to confirm that I had followed all of the building codes. While I did most of the construction myself, I had help at several stages: both human and Divine.

Ananda has a long tradition of helping each other with large projects. We called them work days, but they were really "service and spend time with your friends" days. We all took pleasure in doing things for each other in any way that we could. One fellow came to help me move large planks that were used in creating the forms for the foundation. Then a group of guys showed up when the cement truck arrived to pour the foundation. Sheetrock for the interior and shingles on the roof were also blessed with help.

Starting the project during the winter presented additional challenges, some of which I had anticipated and others that caught me by surprise. I planned to use plywood on the floor, but I was concerned it would be damaged by rain and dirt before the roof was up to protect it. So before any of the walls were up I stained, sealed and covered the floor with thick plastic. It later put a smile on my face when after the interior walls had been painted I cut away the plastic covering and all the floor needed was some light mopping.

On my first day of framing walls I decided to assemble a twelve foot section that had a window. It then occurred to me that since it was an exterior wall about six feet above the ground level I should make things easier by putting the window in before raising the wall. By the time I had the header for the window, the window and all the 2 x 6 framing nailed together on the floor it weighed a ton!

The first time I tried to pick up one side I knew I was in trouble. But that didn't stop me from pushing forward. I finally got one side up about a foot and dropped it. Surprisingly the window didn't break. I tried and dropped it again; still the window was okay. By now my muscles were complaining pretty convincingly: I wasn't sure they had another attempt in them. I tried relaxing my arms and then energizing them with one of Yogananda's recharging exercises. I gathered my will and made a supreme effort, just barely getting the wall up to my shoulders where I rested for a moment. Then with a final burst of will I got it up all the way. Now I was standing next to the wall with exhausted arms and it still needed to be slid into position on the very edge of the floor. After some laughing, side to side head turning and resting, I eventually got the framing in the proper position. That was when the wind started to occasionally gust and the window to act as a sail.

Adding to my dilemma was the unfortunate fact that I had not properly prepared a board to hold the wall in place. I tried to nail the wall to the floor, but I had to let go of it to do that. Each time I tried, the wind would decide to blow and I would have to stand up grasping quickly to keep it from flying out into space. When I eventually realized that this just wasn't going to work, I took a deep breath and pulled out my most powerful tool: Prayer.

I stood there hugging the wall with occasional sways while I prayed for help. It seemed pretty far fetched. I was way out at the end of a muddy dead end road that was so new that very few people even knew it was there. Maybe the wind would stop? While I was inviting Divine Mother to lend a helping hand I looked out over the surrounding trees and hills, communing with nature. The day was comfortable, the sun was shining, birds were singing, bugs were buzzing, life was beautiful. After some time I began to hear a sound in the distance, it gradually got louder and closer, I smiled when I recognized what it was: a small truck!

We had seen this happen at Ananda many times over the years, but each time was always sweet and special. Not only was help on the way, but clearly it had been sent before I even realized I would be in need. God's representative that day was

Dwayne: Durga and Vidura's son. As a recent graduate of a vocational electronics school Dwayne and I had talked about starting a small business called *Electrotech* for repairing electronic equipment. I hadn't seen him for a couple of weeks and he had never visited the construction site. After helping me secure the wall, he told me that he had *on the spur of the moment* decided to come out and talk to me. When I told him what had happened he was amazed.

I ordered trusses for the roof and one day they arrived on a large truck with a crane. I had the operator unload the large trusses right onto the waiting walls. The next day I began to slowly maneuver them into their proper positions. In the afternoon the Universe decided that we weren't yet having enough fun. As I worked, the wind began to blow and then after some time rain began to fall. The next thing I knew I was in one of those man vs nature moments. I was concerned that the unsecured trusses might fly off in the wind so I was determined to get them solidly in place. I spent about two hours in the storm doing what needed to be done. When I walked off the job that day I felt appropriately manly and inwardly grateful that it had all worked out.

It took me six months to complete the house. It was 1,400 sq. ft. with three bedrooms, meditation room, full bath, cathedral ceiling living room and kitchen with breakfast nook. Some time after we moved in I sat in the living room one day and looked around. As my eyes roved the walls and windows for a moment I felt pleased and appreciative of how nice it was, it had been a very challenging endeavor; I had emerged victorious with both satisfaction and relief. I also realized that I didn't feel any *this house is mine*. I had no idea at the time that this truth would be tested.

Before I share Toni's experience at Ananda Village while I was building the house we need to return to a subject that I touched on in Chapter One: Simultaneous Truth. The Universal view of life is very different than the ego's view. The ego sees life as *I am doing this to you* and *You are doing that to me*. In actuality the Universe is doing everything to itself – there is only one Life/ God/ the Universe. So in essence all of life is God loving, serving, playing with God. If this is true than why does life not look and feel like sensitive caring, helping and having fun all of the time? In order to answer this we go back to the basic yoga teachings.

There are four root aspects to human consciousness: mon, buddhi, ahankara, and chitta: mind, intellect, ego, and feeling (emotion based feeling). This is the system through which the power of Maya (Cosmic delusion) ties the soul to limited consciousness.

Swami Kriyananda explains this succinctly in Chapter 34 of *The New Path:*

> Likes, dislikes, and their resultant attractions and aversions, all of which induce desires and repulsions, are the root cause of our bondage. The progressive stages of involvement with maya may be traced through the progressive functions of human consciousness: mon, buddhi, ahankara, and chitta: mind, intellect, ego, and feeling.

> Paramhansa Yogananda illustrated these basic functions by a horse, seen in a mirror. The mirror is the
>
> **Mon** (mind), which shows us the image as it appears to us through the senses; the mind alone, however, cannot qualify or define that image.
>
> **Buddhi** (intellect) then defines what is seen, informing our consciousness, 'That is a horse.'
>
> **Ahankara** (ego) then appears, declaring, 'That is my horse.' Up to this point we are not necessarily yet bound by the thought of ownership; the identification, though personal, may still remain more or less abstract.
>
> If, then, chitta (feeling) comes onto the scene, saying, 'How happy I am to see my horse!' true ego-bondage begins.
>
> **Chitta** (feeling) is our emotional reaction, including likes and dislikes, desires and aversions. It is the true source of ego-bondage, and the essence of all delusion.
>
> Thus, the ancient classical exponent of the yoga science, Patanjali, defined yoga itself as 'the neutralization of the vortices (vrittis) of chitta.'

So it is our emotional actions/reactions to every life experience that ties us to ego/personality consciousness. As yogis we are consciously attempting to live in such a way as to not create new vortices of attachment and release ourselves from all attachments/identifications of the past.

Every person is individualized Spirit (Soul) identified with the body/personality, but not everyone is at the same degree of identification. A saint is minimally tied to this world and a soul just advancing to the human stage of evolution has full immersion in this outward world as the only reality. Strangely, because of the uniqueness of each soul's journey, sometimes animals seem more spiritual than humans and advanced souls do things that we wouldn't associate with their high spiritual stature.

Each of us is the sum total of all our actions (A reaction is also an action) since we entered the Creation. Every action in life is connected to a chain of actions/reactions that can be called the flow of Karma through the world. It is so complex that the only way to grasp it is not through the mind but through intuition. One of the key ways to develop intuition is to open the heart, because as I mentioned previously, the heart is our portal to Universal awareness.

All actions in life are measured on the one scale of Truth. The way they are valued on that scale is simple: That which brings you closer to God is Truth (dharma/right action) for your life and that which takes you further from God is untruth (adharma/against right action).

Everything in life represents a guna (quality or attribute of consciousness) and there are three gunas: Sattwic (elevating/expanding), Rajasic (activating/energizing) and Tamasic (downward pulling/contracting). When we live in a sattvic flow of energy we are expanding our consciousness and in a tamasic flow we are contracting. Rajasic energy represents the activating power that takes us toward expansion or contraction.

Here are some examples from Paramhansa Yogananda's Psychological Chart.

Psychological Chart (1925)

Sattvic - Elevating

- Brahmacharya (self-discipline)
- Love towards neighbors.
- Love towards animals.
- Love for good qualities.
- Love of bliss and calmness.
- Practical sympathy for others.
- Amiable.
- Benevolent tendency towards the needy.
- Love for great people.
- Truthfulness – spontaneous (i.e., habitual) – irrespective of consequences.
- Dutifulness – out of love – out of respect.
- Reforming spirit.
- Moral reason – sense of "ought."
- Sense of self-respect.
- Quiet.
- Reserved.
- Tender.
- Faithful.
- Obliging.
- Patient.
- Forgiving.
- Acting in accordance with the suggestions of superior minds.
- Outspoken.
- Having sense of propriety.
- Simple, frank.
- Calm or balanced.
- Having devotional feeling – habitual or short-lasting.
- Contented.
- Love for mental and physical cleanliness.

- Modest.
- Having philanthropic tendency.
- Gratitude towards benefactors.
- Impartial.

Rajasic - Activating

- Occasional truthfulness with selfish motive.
- Fickle.
- Adroit.
- Over-serious.
- Smart.
- Impulsive.
- Demonstrative.
- Meddling.
- Sanguine.
- Fastidious.
- Lively.
- Having tendency to equip himself with information about environment.

Tamasic – Downward Pulling

- Attachment to objects of senses.
- Hypocritical sympathy.
- Moral reason – undeveloped sense of "ought."
- Want of self-respect.
- Quiet (inactive).
- Stupid.
- Dull and shy.
- Impervious to reason.
- Callous.
- Dependent through want to capacity.
- Procrastinatory.
- Morose.
- Deceiving.
- Careless.
- Negligent.
- Getting strong feelings of obstinacy and anger when chastised for faults, but careless when not chastised and simply asked to mend faults.
- Crooked – finding out undesirable meaning in

things.
- Showing duplicity.
- Intellectual bent but heartless.
- Lustful.
- Covetous.
- Having stealing propensity.
- Having begging nature.
- Superstitious.
- Treacherous.
- Untruthful – habitual.
- Shrinking attitude (lack of self-confidence).

It is a positive use of discrimination to recognize these qualities being expressed, but it is not beneficial to judge yourself or others when you do. When we evaluate every life experience according to its qualities of consciousness we can understand how to make spiritually beneficial decisions. The more energy that is in an action, the greater the effect will be produced in the direction of its qualities.

Every karma is comprised of both the act and the motivating consciousness behind the act. Certainly it is different if we unintentionally injure someone than if we do so intentionally. This old saying is also true: The road to hell is paved with good intentions. We are responsible for the repercussions of our actions, but not the reactions of others to our actions: those are theirs. We can't hide the truth from Truth. We are responsible for the Truth of everything that flows through us.

Over the years I have occasionally seen hurtful actions being excused by people saying, "It was your karma to have this experience." Which implies that it was God's Will and so the delivery person is excused from responsibility. While it is true that all experiences come from God, that doesn't mean the channel that dishes out the karma is immune from consequences. A free soul can act without accruing karma, all else are subject to the law of karma according to their current state of consciousness no matter what their intended purpose.

The recipient of karma becomes a doer by their reaction to that karma. When someone accrues negative karma by mistreating us we don't want to respond by mistreating them in thought or deed. As Jesus taught, "Love your enemies." Additionally: Is your enemy really your enemy if they give you the chance to pay a past karmic debt and help you to grow spiritually through your right response?

We have already talked about how seemingly wrong actions or situations can lead to beneficial opportunities. It is up to the receiver of karma to be aware and react in helpful ways. Every situation in life in which we don't feel comfortable is an opportunity to grow: the tougher it is the greater the opportunity for growth. As previously stated, "All life circumstances are neutral." It is what we do with them that determines their benefit or harm.

In the beginning many devotees are concerned about their "good and bad" karma. They want to increase the good (This is pleasant!) and get rid of the bad (This is uncomfortable!) karma. Over time the focus shifts from concern about karma being good or bad to, as Sri Yukteswar described it, "Awakening the natural love of the heart." It is communion with God (The Universal Heart.) that will ultimately free us from all karma. When we live in Universal Love and Joy – Swamiji described Divine Joy as Love in action – we will be much less concerned about karma. When we live in the joy of

God's Presence outward experiences lose their power to control our inner well-being.

In the larger scheme of things karmic responsibility is quite complex and can only become fully resolved in the final stages of Self-realization. One of the things that we can be sure of is that we don't know all of what is going on at any given moment. Everyone has their own set of karmic blinders on that keeps them from seeing the things that they can not yet see.

Good news! It is not against the rules to try and improve things. The whole purpose of spiritual community is to provide a supportive environment for growing spiritually. This includes the individual needs of its members and serving the world as well. When we live superconsciously everyone is benefited whether they realize it or not.

Given that almost all of us are here in the school of life because we haven't yet graduated, we should expect that almost everyone will make mistakes. And since we are all in the same boat it seems wise to not rock the boat unnecessarily by poking at each other when discomforts present themselves. At the same time, some mistakes in life should not be ignored no matter how messy they are. Knowing when to speak up and when to hold one's tongue is the path of the wise. Unfortunately we can't become wise unless we learn from our mistakes, so mistakes can become our friend, not something to hide in the closet. Just like everywhere else on planet Earth life at Ananda is not perfect, many mistakes have been made. I can put myself at the head of the pack...well, certainly up front somewhere! I have been loved in spite of these mistakes and I love all of my Ananda family in the same spirit.

When mistakes are made by truly well intentioned people it is often not an issue of fault, but one of understanding. When we misunderstand a situation we make decisions followed by actions that we wouldn't have made had we clearly perceived the actual truth of the moment. The making of mistakes is not really the issue. Even if we are successful in a task, as devotees striving to improve ourselves we will want to know how we can do even better in the future. So the goal of ever-new improvement in the way we live and serve God and Gurus is our purpose: In that spirit, let us continue.

For the rest of this chapter, because this is not being shared for the purpose of blame, I won't be using names. The caveat for this is that Swamiji, as he has always been for us, will be Swamiji.

While I was building the house, Toni was both with the twins and reaching out into the community for service opportunities. She consulted with Swamiji about how to proceed. His response was, "Carve out a niche for yourself!"

When we moved to the village Toni had been teaching yoga for ten years and was certified by Swamiji as an Ananda Yoga Teacher. She had become a kriyaban (Practitioner of Kriya Yoga) in 1979 and was an ordained Ananda Minister, so it was natural that she would gravitate to the retreat.

Toni's level of positive anticipation for life at Ananda was very high. She had walked away from her first marriage and now moved away from Dan and Cristi for spiritual reasons. She was fully invested in her spiritual life. Having established a strong spiritual practice as a disciple of Paramhansa Yogananda on her own, now she would have the benefits of living in a whole community of gurubais (fellow disciples). She had visited the village numerous times and already knew many in the community, so it wasn't like she was arriving at an unknown place not knowing anyone.

Temperamentally Toni had a good mix of yogi Italian: generally calm, not easily over excitable, joyful, embracing of others, easy to get along with, not quick to assert herself over others and sensitive to the underlying energy of life. She was quite capable and willing to do whatever was needed to be done. Another quality that she had I didn't pick up on as soon as it would have been helpful: Toni held things in. As a person who was quick to blurt out what I thought or felt and then let it go, I didn't really understand people holding it in. I thought women were the sharers and men where the hold-it-iners! It wasn't until the house was completed and we had moved in that Toni finally shared with me that life at Ananda was not going the way she had expected.

When Toni arrived at the retreat and volunteered to lead sadhana her reception was lukewarm. Eventually she was allowed to lead a mid-morning sadhana for community residents. At that time the facility was still under construction and the temple was a multi-purpose space. On some days she arrived at 10 am to lead the session and was informed that the space was being used for something else.

The unexpected canceling of a class by itself could be easily classified simply as an inconvenience; however there was more. Over the next few months she had interactions with several *old timers* who criticized her teaching style and spoke to her in a way as to belittle her value and competence as a teacher, and thusly as a devotee. One person even said to her, "What gives you the right to teach here?"

It is understandable that people wouldn't know Toni's history with Ananda. She was the first of her kind and in some ways the *only* of her kind. At that time most of the teachers and sadhana leaders had learned the teachings from Swamiji directly and the yoga postures in sessions at the original meditation retreat with Satya. There was a strong similarity of style in the group. Toni was a little different. The thing that really devastated her was that she had arrived as a member of the Ananda spiritual family, but it felt like the family didn't want her.

Once Toni unburdened herself to me I spoke to a few people and requested Swamiji convene a meeting of what seemed the appropriate group. Toni reluctantly agreed to attend. Once we were all sitting in a circle in Swamiji's dome at Ayodhya he looked around the group to see who would start. He knew the meeting had something to do with Toni, but nothing more than that.

Swamiji invited Toni to speak, but she had nothing to say. He looked at me and I could see that I would have to start things off. I managed to communicate that there was a problem having to do with Toni. There was a long silence while Swamiji looked around the group for more information. Eventually several people in the group reluctantly agreed that there was a problem. A description of exactly what the problem was, no one was either able or willing to express. Swamiji was perplexed by the whole thing. He did his best to draw out conversation, but it just never happened.

The meeting itself was both proof of and a description of the situation: insufficient open heartfelt communication between family members. It was simultaneously the current level of understanding that the Universe made available to a group of great souls that were doing their best to know and serve God. While there was no group revelation of higher understanding during the meeting, there was also zero ill intent present.

I believe this is an essential component of the whole shift of the community from monastic – keep everything to yourself consciousness – to householder – reach out and share even when it gets a little messy consciousness. It is a subject that becomes more and more vital as a group grows. Those who might be quick to condemn everything from the individuals present at the meeting to communities and religion in general should remember what Jesus said, "Judge not, lest thee be judged." We will be diving more deeply into this subject in future chapters.

That summer the new retreat was officially opened and all guest programs moved down from the old meditation retreat. The question of how to use the original facility presented itself. Six miles from the village and isolated down a three mile dirt road it was a great place to withdraw from the world. It was decided that a residential training program for new village members should be started. Toni and I were invited to lead the program.

So we moved out of the home that I had just spent six months building and into a small cabin in the woods at the original meditation retreat. This had been a family tradition since the early years of Ananda: sudden moving, doing new and unexpected jobs, and various forms of house swapping. It made me laugh!

In a classic turn of karmic circumstance, it was now our job to welcome newcomers to residency at the village and the Ananda way of life. We dove in wholeheartedly. It was a diverse group. Some had come through Ananda satellite groups as Toni did and they already had a good grasp on the teachings. Others needed much more attention because of having been totally on their own.

The program included a review of all the basic yoga teachings and techniques that are at the foundation of the Ananda way of life. Along with daily group practice there were many discussions about how to integrate the teachings into life as a whole, as well as, life at Ananda in particular.

One of the most important signs of a successful program like this is that a strong heartfelt bonding takes place among the participants. It can take only one fly in the ointment to diminish that potential. And wouldn't you know it, God gave us a huge horsefly! I don't mean to be disrespectful, but this person was more than a handful. Both Toni and I could see that she had potential, but her personality was so overbearing that she, like the proverbial bull in a china shop, wreaked havoc wherever she went. I could see shades of my own life experience in her, I felt determined to help her, but it wasn't in any way easy. Effort after effort was sloughed off by her inability to hear and act on caring suggestions.

One day it all came to a head. I remember standing in the kitchen dome with her about two thirds of the way through the program. We were once again at loggerheads and a clarity of truth came out of my mouth unbidden, "If you don't change your ways you won't be at Ananda much longer." What I hadn't taken into account before speaking was simultaneous truth: She was soon gone of her own volition and so were Toni and I.

Once our prickly friend had moved on harmony reigned supreme over the group and we eventually received the best compliment that a group leader can receive: No one wanted to leave! Another sign of good things having happened is that several of the participants in the group became lifelong residents of Ananda.

In spite of the success of the program Toni still felt unsettled, the sour taste of Toni's feeling of community rejection persisted. To her credit, she wasn't at all angry about the way things had turned out. Her main feeling was anguishing disappointment and she couldn't shake it. Staying at the isolated Meditation Retreat and living in a small cabin with two toddlers didn't make things easier for her. And of course, who wants to stay where they feel unwanted?

Another factor in this equation was the lack of sufficiently meaningful communication on both sides, which we touched on in the meeting with Swamiji. Yogis sometimes feel that it is negative to share problems. In a small community, being outspoken can easily become a liability, of which I was well aware. And as I mentioned, Toni's current practice was to keep her own counsel in most situations.

This turn of events was a big deja vu for me. My first wife Mukti had divorced me and then shifted her loyalty to SRF. About six months after our separation she contacted me to say that she wanted to reunite with me and live in Encinitas. Well, I had no intention of withdrawing my loyalty from Swami and Ananda so it wasn't a difficult decision for me.

Toni felt that she needed to leave the village, not dedication to the Ananda Spiritual family and path. She just didn't see how she could keep living in a place where she didn't feel welcome. Interestingly, most of the people at the meeting about Toni with Swamiji were in the not too distant future moved out of the village by the Universe to other Ananda service opportunities.

Having been at this junction before I didn't feel excessively bothered or overstressed about the situation. Yes, it was disappointing. Did I want to leave? No. But I couldn't blame any of the people that I love for being who they are. I just needed to be clear in my mind and heart about how to proceed. Of course, my marriage and the kids were huge factors, I really wanted Kaivalya and Sabari to grow up at Ananda Village. My main concern was dharma, what would God prefer that I did? I prayed for guidance.

I had learned in Sacramento that Master, Swamiji and Ananda were etched in my heart, no physical change could effect that. Through the years my life had not been static, it was always moving forward. Change is not uncomfortable to me because I am not attached to most of the details of my life. From surfing big waves in my youth I had learned to paddle into the scary unknown. It became inwardly clear to me that Toni and I would go on an adventure together. Added to that was a silent pledge to God: I would do everything I could to bring Toni and the twins back to the village.

It is a natural question at this junction to wonder why some people have smooth sailing when they arrive to life at an Ananda Community and others do not. The teachings tell us that every life experience is rooted in the Universal law of Karma. One of the ways Yogananda described Karma is as a learning tool: "Trials do not come to destroy you, but to help you appreciate God better".

As we shift our nomenclature from "good and bad" karma to "comfortable and uncomfortable" or again as Yogananda said, "Objective conditions are always neutral. It is how you react to them that makes them appear sad or happy". This shift of definition frees us from the old solid view of karma that says that discomforts that we don't prefer are always bad. When we respond to life's challenges with a positive solution-oriented attitude we can redirect the intensity of the karmic conditions from hurt feelings and mental agitation to a greater experience of inner joy and outward accomplishment.

We learned that this wasn't just a good idea but a practical tool available to all by watching Swamiji react to the countless ups and downs that presented themselves year after year. What we saw was that no matter what happened he didn't overreact. He took the circumstances into his center, offered it up the spine to the spiritual eye and opened himself up to Universally rooted intuitive inspiration. We often watched him do this in everyday situations. You could see in his eyes and the energy of his presence that he was inwardly connecting more deeply.

Does this always work equally well? No. We may know the technique but we probably won't be able to apply it equally in all situations. Sometimes it is like doing a computer search and you don't yet have sufficient security clearance to get the answer you want. We may also be too disturbed by the situation to calmly focus our inner attention. It can also happen that the timing for a proper solution hasn't yet arrived and we don't need to know the answer until we need to know the answer. It can also happen that we never quite know why things worked out the way they did, but they did work out. Doing what we can do and calmly waiting for solutions to present themselves is also an essential part of this process.

There are certainly many practical outward and inner issues involved when we embrace full time residence in a spiritual community, many we will discuss as we go along, but it has been my observation of others and my personal experience that the tipping point is when we are so bothered by the situation or the actions/attitudes of others that we arrive at: I can't handle this any more! It is then that we may need to remove ourselves permanently or for an indeterminate period of time during which our inner feelings can adjust and/or the outward situation that caused us to feel the need to remove ourselves changes in a way that helps us to reenter the previously unbearable situation.

Commonly, when disharmony presents itself, participants in that challenge will assign fault to those that they consider to be the offending party(s). I never saw this assigning of blame to others in Swamiji's response to life's difficulties. The yogic tradition is to seek the truth underneath outward circumstances. This Truth doesn't cast the negative aura of blame, but presents a clarity of the situation that takes into account all karmic circumstances. In the presence of Universally rooted truth we can see karmic responsibility floating on waves of Universal peace, love and wisdom. In this view God is not vengeful but ultimately caring. Allowing us to fulfill our part in the play of life: to pay our debts and reap our rewards (pleasant and unpleasant) along the path to spiritual freedom.

Swamiji's attitude toward blame was expressed in Yogananda's words, "Praise cannot make me any better. Blame cannot make me any worse. I am what I am before my own conscience and God." When we have shifted our internal compass from the ego's view and common negative reactions like blame, to God's impersonal view of Truth it completely changes the our state of consciousness. The heart stays open. It doesn't clamp up and harden. Swamiji was able able to maintain sincere caring for others even in the most trying situations. I never saw him react to the negative energy of others by pulling out a sword of words or actions to cut down others.

In Swamiji I found a person that was completely willing to be wrong. He never assumed or presented that he was always right. He often revealed in private or small group conversations that that he was constantly trying to deepen his understanding and improve his ability to help others.

As a growing community with diverse backgrounds and at different levels of spiritual understanding we all integrated Swamiji's example into our lives with varying levels of success. Newcomers to this dynamic environment also had to process the sometimes unexpected energies that are a part of more and deeper spiritual practice. Like a big family stew the pot is often stirred up, heated up, cooled down and generally kept in a state of flux that offers ever-new opportunities for coming closer to God.

Chapter 12

Riding the Wave of Life

"This life is not man's own show; if he becomes personally and emotionally involved in the very complicated cosmic drama, he reaps inevitable suffering for having distorted the divine 'plot.'" –Paramahansa Yogananda

Life can easily be seen as a flow of energy like waves in the ocean. Sometimes the ocean is calm and relaxing while at other times there is a storm and large waves crash left and right. Understanding the dual pleasure/pain nature of the Creation helps us to come to grips with the ups and downs of our lives. If we were never challenged we would be bored, and more importantly, we wouldn't be motivated to grow. At the same time, it isn't necessary to live with a *happiness is always out of reach* feeling: we don't need to wait for samadhi (Oneness with God) to be happy.

When I lived in *worldly society* before arriving at Ananda, I loved nature and had a low opinion of modern civilization.

After I arrived at Ananda I thought "This is how mankind is supposed to live, all else is folly." I'm not suggesting that everyone move to Ananda Village. I mean that living with a positive life purpose among harmonious people and an expanding awareness of God's joyful presence is possible.

Often when the spiritual life is discussed more focus is put on the end goal of Self-realization and less on the benefits along the way. Before coming to this path I lived on ups and downs. When life was proceeding as I preferred I experienced a temporary state of *my personality is happy*. When life turned against my desires, I suffered.

One of the most important things I learned from Swamiji in my early years with him was how to be happy on a soul level no matter how my personality was feeling. His example of even-mindedness and cheerfulness in all circumstances proved that it could be done. When I was with him his presence had a transforming effect on my consciousness and gradually I realized that I too could live that way. Eventually my meditation practice helped me to feel this way even when I wasn't with him.

The ability to live day to day with a positive, energetic and enthusiastic soul awareness is by itself worthy of our spiritual efforts. I don't mean that we have to be outwardly bubbly and grinning all the time. We will each express outwardly our inner well-being according to the filter of our personality. The key is that we live not only for God, but with God, and even more deeply, in God.

It is important that we remember when making decisions in life that God will be with us equally no matter what we do.

The real question is: How will this decision effect our ability to be with God? As we discussed previously, this is the measuring stick for valuing all actions: Will this expand my consciousness or contract it? Will this bring me closer to Universally rooted happiness, or tie me more firmly to the limitations of ego/personality? And not: Will it be easy? Will I be comfortable?

As soon as I accepted that it was right to move forward with Toni we shifted to figuring out where to go. We decided that going to the beach was a good idea and took a trip along the California coast to go city hunting. Since it was key that we be in a place that would be healing for Toni I was careful to have an opinion but not force my personal preference. Fortunately we had very similar tastes in the feeling of our environment and decided that of all the places we visited the one we felt the best in was Santa Barbara, California.

It was fall, the off season for tourism, so we were able to find an apartment right on the beach in Carpenteria, just south of Santa Barbara. While we didn't have an ocean view because of the landscaping, we did have the sound and smell of the beach which was just outside our door. Even though we would have to move when the rents went up for the next summer season, we felt it would be worth it to spend some months by the ocean.

It didn't take long for the yin and yang of life to present itself. The peace of living at the beach was one day invaded by a loud scream coming from a nearby apartment. A woman's voice could then be heard calling for help. I asked Toni to call 911 and went out to investigate. I soon found an open door where inside I could see a man hitting a woman who was crouched down against a wall with her arms covering her head in defense. Domestic abuse is shocking and fraught with energy that is clearly out of control. Once again I found myself, like when the assailant came into the music store, unsure about how to proceed.

I stepped up to the threshold of the apartment and announced my presence. The man turned toward me and told me to mind my own business and go away. He was still standing over the woman but had stopped hitting her. I informed him that the police had been notified. His curse filled response was unpleasant, and his glare toward me could have been his mental process of deciding to shift his anger toward me.

Once again I felt inadequate to face male aggression. I had learned to center myself in the spine through meditation, but I still had physiological auto responses of fear of being hit from my youth. I had no practical mental or physical self-defense skills. Well, I could talk, and I tried to keep up a non threatening conversation that would fill the time until help arrived. My words of distraction allowed the cloud of violence to gradually dispel. When the sounds of police arrival reached our ears the fellow stepped away from his victim and I backed out of the situation to let nature take its course without me.

While looking through the job listings in the newspaper I gravitated towards sales positions. The next thing I knew I was a photocopier salesman! Had you told me when I was a teenager that one day I would sell copy machines I would have laughed at you. Now I laughed at myself! I had never in my life thought about having any kind of career to make money.

Having done various jobs through the years, I didn't think of myself as being any of them. I defined myself as a devotee, loving and serving God, everything else was transitory.

Something that I had not realized at the time was that my experiences as a copier salesman would help me as a sharer of the spiritual life. It gave me "real world" experiences that I could share with others on how a relationship with Life/God/The Universe can be of practical use even in business. Years later I would put some of these stories in a book called *Flowing in the Workplace: A guide to Personal and Professional Success.*

Living in the Santa Barbara area wasn't new to me. Not only had I surfed many times in the area but I had lived in Montecito (neighboring Santa Barbara) for some months when I was nineteen. In fact, I considered Rincon Point, which is eight miles south of Carpenteria to be my favorite surf spot in California. Now that I was living nearby I could and did visit my old surf spot friend.

One day when I was surfing at Rincon, waiting for a wave to greet me and dance with me, I watched cars traveling on Hwy 101. I remembered doing the same thing about fifteen years previously. At that time I had thought, "Look at those poor people traveling on the highway when they could be surfing!" Now I was one of those people! I traveled that highway on my way to work and only occasionally went surfing. Yet, I was happier in my life now than I had ever been as a surfer. While I knew I still had far to go, it was encouraging to be reminded that progress had been made.

Shortly after starting my job selling copiers the company announced a three month long contest. The salesman who sold the most of a particular model machine would win a trip to St. Martin in the Caribbean. I applied myself to the task and the Universe supported my efforts. Grandma Yolanda once again watched the kids while Toni and I took off for our five day all expenses paid vacation.

When we returned from St. Martin it was time to find a new place to live because the coming summer rates were way too high for us. After renting a home in Santa Barbara proper we started an Ananda Meditation Group. We held satsangs in a local church and taught yoga postures and raja yoga. Some of the people we met at that time are still connected to Ananda.

One day we had a big surprise. Swamiji and the Joy Singers arrived in town on one of their tours. Some of the singers came to our house and we had a great visit. Swamiji with a few others were staying at a private residence and we had a chance to visit with them. After arriving we were ushered into the main gathering area in the house – in classic Italian style – the kitchen. There we found Rosanna, her parents, her sister Juliana and our brother from Ananda, Prahlad (excess of joy). Everyone was talking, embracing, smiling and just being happy. Soon Swamiji had joined the group and joyousness raised to an even higher level.

I could feel from Swamiji a calm yet powerful radiation of bliss. It was clear that he was more than comfortable with the continental flavor of his companions. Swamiji had met Rosanna in Italy two years previously. She was part of a group called PEKI (community of peace) which is a charismatic Catholic group. The group had all read the *Autobiography of a Yogi* and taken discipleship, and later Kriya Yoga initiation from Swamiji;

now Swamiji and Rosanna were a couple. Toni and I had briefly met Rosanna at Ananda Village before coming to Santa Barbara and there was a quick and natural feeling of family.

The next day I had a chance to drive Swamiji on an errand. While we rode silently in the car I was reminded of another time I had driven Swamiji. It was fall and he wanted to take some pictures of the colorful trees in Nevada City. We spent about an hour without talking while he took pictures out of the open car window. When he finally signaled that we could head home he said as a kind of afterthought, "Next time drive a little more slowly." It was so like Swamiji to not complain that he didn't think to ask me to drive more slowly sooner. Who would have thought that just sitting in the car with a person would feel like a great blessing?

Toni had hoped to get a spiritual name from Swamiji but at the time he wasn't giving spiritual names. So she asked me to come up with a name and I chose Bhavani (Bhava is a devotion state consciousness, Bhavani is also the giver of life, mother of the three worlds). During Swamiji's visit, Toni had a chance to talk with him about it. After presenting the name Bhavani, Swamiji said,"When I was in SRF there was a nun with that name and it has a bit of a bad taste for me. But it is not a bad name." Toni then requested that if Swamiji had any further thoughts on the subject to let her know. Inwardly she decided that she would wait until her next birthday, which was some months away, before making a final decision.

Coinciding with our move to a new rental house was me changing jobs. While I could successfully sell photocopiers, it didn't feel like home to me. I remembered the time I got a job in

Sacramento as a piano salesman and decided that I might try that again. There was a music store in Goleta, just north of Santa Barbara, and I decided I would check in with them.

When I walked into Castle Music it felt natural to me. The store was two large rooms, one with pianos, accessories counter and guitars on the wall. The other room was filled with drums and all of the most modern electronic instruments and equipment. There was a desk in the back of the piano room and I was ushered in that direction.

The man at the desk was on the phone so I didn't intrude, but when he hung up I moved towards him. He stood up and we shook hands. I then explained that I was looking for a job. He invited me to sit and he shared that he was the owner of the store. I told him of my qualifications as a piano technician and my experience selling pianos and organs. As I spoke his eyes seemed to get a little bigger and then a lot bigger. When I was done sharing he started to move his head left and right with a look of unbelieving. He then explained, "The call that I was just on was to the newspaper. I was placing an ad for a piano salesman." We both smiled: He because because of the synchronicity and that he could save the cost of an ad, and I because I knew God was with me. What I didn't know at that time was that God had even more musical instrument fun for me in the future.

I enjoy learning about new things and musical instruments have always interested me, so Castle Music was a great fit. What I hadn't known upon arrival was that the store was very popular with musicians from Los Angeles and Hollywood. They would come up to Santa Barbara on vacation or maybe even own a home there. For musicians, a good music store is a natural attraction. So I soon discovered that this was a *happening* music store. Along with a good selection of traditional instruments they had all of the latest music technology, including Atari computers which were the first computer at that time with built in MIDI (Musical instrument digital interface) allowing the computer to control synthesized instrument sounds.

It didn't take me long to wander out of the piano department and dive into everything else. It was like I had entered Musical Instrument Store University. I soaked it all up and within a month I was selling the latest synthesizers, guitars, drums, band instruments, amplifiers, speakers, and oh yes, pianos. I was a kid in a candy store! We worked on salary plus commission, so I had to be careful with the non piano salesmen. If I got too many deals from their department they started to feel like I was taking money out of their pockets.

When I heard that the owner of the store played racquetball I offered to play with him. We had some good games. Interestingly, he always beat me. He felt that he could impose his racquetball will on me and he did. It was challenging for me, so I really didn't mind losing. But one day I spontaneously decided that today I was going to win. Towards the end of the game, when he exerted his will to win, it didn't work and I could feel him getting hot under the collar. I then thought, "Maybe beating the boss isn't such a good idea! Oh well..." He never acted like it bothered him that I won, but from that day forward I somehow knew that my time at Castle Music was coming to a close.

Our time in Santa Barbara was nice, but once again Toni surprised me. This time it was, "I miss Daniel and Cristi. So the next thing I knew we were on our way back to Roseville. I had left Ananda with the determination to bring Toni back to Ananda and Roseville was much closer to that goal than Santa Barbara, so I didn't complain.

We had an unexpected adventure on the trip to Roseville. We had more stuff leaving Santa Barbara than when we arrived so I rented a small trailer and connected it to the back of Toni's car. I had my piano trailer connected to my car. I planned to drive behind Toni and the kids to keep an eye on them. It is a good thing I did!

We hadn't even gotten out of Santa Barbara when her car started to sway back and forth. Then the trailer started to tilt and there in the middle of the highway it tipped over on its side causing a huge traffic jam. Her car stayed upright and was fine. Amazingly, the rental trailer was not in any way damaged. But clearly her car couldn't pull it. So we had it towed to a place it could safely be stored and after driving my trailer to Roseville I drove straight back 400 miles and picked up the second trailer. Lots of driving! But no harm, no foul! After that we would tease Toni about it. I would ask the kids, "How does mom drive the trailer?" And they would respond with, "Like this!" and they would put their palms together and then wiggle their hands frantically in a snaking like action, eventually laying them over to the side to show the final result.

We rented a home on Lou Place in Granite Bay, just east of Roseville and next to Folsom Lake. The lake and the trail next to the lake was almost an extension of our back yard. We were able to take advantage of the lake without needing to get into the car.

Once I had returned from Santa Barbara with the second trailer my mind turned towards employment. I started by remembering how much I enjoyed working at Castle Music. One of the reasons I liked it was because people came in for things that they wanted but didn't need. When I sold photocopiers I had to convince people to buy our copiers which they didn't really want but needed. I felt positively useful in both situations in that I was helping people make decisions according to their interests or needs, but people really wanting what you are selling is a lot more fun.

As I was trying to feel how to proceed a crazy idea came into my mind: Why don't you open your own store! I had almost opened a piano store in Nevada City some years previously. At the time Swamiji didn't think it was a very good idea, so I didn't proceed. The idea persisted in my mind so I decided to look at it logically. It really wasn't complicated. I didn't have any money to open a store!

Strangely, the idea wouldn't give up. I decided to do an experiment. I would go to the bank and ask for a loan to open the store. If I got a loan I would take it as a sign that there was Universal support for the project. I started at a branch of a nationwide bank that I had used for many years. The loan officer shut me down in about 3 minutes. Being a person that is not very good at giving up I decided that a local bank might be a better possibility. I was right. After I explained my piano and sales history, along with the importance of music in the education of youth, the local bank representative showed an encouraging amount of enthusiasm and gave me some paperwork to fill out. I left the bank with a pleasant sense of possibility.

While filling out the loan forms I began to realize how ridiculous it was that I was even trying. They wanted me to submit a business plan and personal financial statement. When I got to the line for listing assets, I put down the credit limit of my credit card...it was certainly an asset that I had a credit card! I wasn't trying to mislead them, at the time I genuinely thought of it that way. For the business plan, I just dreamed a dream. I had no actual basis for the projections that I presented. I did at least know that I should show a profit in the not too distant future!

I was then treated again to a slight pulling back of the curtain so that I could see some of the mechanisms that work unseen behind the scenes of life. Only after the loan was approved did I get the full story. As it happened, the loan officer's mother was a local supporter of the arts. When he told her that I wanted to open a full line music store with pianos, orchestra/band instruments and everything else she got very excited. When he told her my name she burst out, "I know him, he tuned my piano!"

It was a reminder that we leave footprints (karma) wherever we go. In this case it was that positive interaction that made its way through the "coincidences" of life to help me in a time of need. Once the bank had given me a line of credit all of the necessary suppliers lined up to do so as well. Incredibly, I went from the idea to open a store to actually opening the *Roseville Music Exchange* in six weeks.

Swamiji and life at Ananda had taught me how to attune to Universal potential. When we get into the positive flow for our lives the seemingly impossible can become possible. The basic building blocks for success in outward and inward life are the same: we need energy, concentration to focus that energy and we need to not give up until the goal is achieved or we receive guidance to redirect our energy in a new direction. The yoga teachings offer specific techniques for connecting our efforts to greater Universal potential rather than if we only think of ourselves alone as the doer.

Paramhansa Yogananda developed a series of exercises called the *Energization Exercises* that train the practitioner to consciously access Universal life force and direct it through will power to vitalize body, mind and spirit. Once this technique is applied successfully in our body the same principles can be applied to success in any part of life. Getting the music store up and running so quickly was for me another example of this happening in my own life.

The next sign of Universal support was customers coming into the store and buying things. It didn't hurt that the store was on a very busy street with a good sized sign! Toni spent a fair amount of time in the store the first year. One weekend I left her, with some trepidation, in charge of the store while I went to a music industry trade show. When I returned, she proudly announced that she had sold a baby grand piano! It got a little hectic at times, but for the most part things went smoothly.

While I was playing...I mean working...well, I really mean serving, you see I had stopped thinking that I worked for myself or an employer, I served God. It didn't matter what it looked like on the outside, serving Life/God/the Universe had become my reference point. So, while I was serving in the music store life moved forward at home. The kids started attending a Montessori preschool and Toni began to volunteer there, which led to them hiring her. We attended the Ananda Center in Sacramento, which at that time was led by Shraddha (faith) and Nagarjuna (a Buddhist saint), as often as possible.

In September we traveled up to Ananda for a very special occasion, Swamiji's wedding to Rosanna. The celebration of their marriage was the convergence of a number of substantial flows of energy in the community.

The wedding was held at the Crystal Hermitage which had originally been Swamiji's dome home at Ayodhya. The dome floor was a platform on stilts overlooking an expansive forested valley with the Yuba River far below. The dome itself was subject to expansion and contraction from the heat of the sun, and eventually leaking became a problem. Vidura covered the dome with a waterproof mastic but even still a large crack appeared. Since I had been a surfer, and surfers use fiberglass and resin to make surfboards which are waterproof, I was enlisted to apply a strip of fiberglass over the offending crack in the dome. A couple of weeks after completing the job Swamiji told me that he had heard a horrifically loud tearing sound coming from the roof. That was the last time the Universe requested me to apply fiberglass.

I had also been invited to assemble an above ground swimming pool next to the dome. After it was complete others built a deck next to the pool and it was enjoyed until the construction of the Crystal Hermitage began. The pool and deck were then moved to the village and became the Ananda Swim Club.

The final solution to the leaking dome was the building of a new roof over the whole dome along with creating a kitchen and dinning room wing, a staff and recording room wing, as well as an office and residence for Swamiji wing. This expanded construction with inground pool, gardens, chapel and museum/gift shop became the Crystal Hermitage. The construction took place over several years and was sufficiently complete to make a beautiful setting for the wedding.

Swamiji wasn't a person that did things half way. Having decided now to embrace a wedding ceremony he wrote original music and a completely new ceremony and vows for the occasion. At one point the couple makes this vow in unison:

> Beloved Lord,
>
> We dedicate to Thee our lives, our service, and the love we share.
>
> May the communion we find with one another lead us to inner communion with Thee.
>
> May the service we render one another perfect in us our service of Thee.
>
> May we behold Thee always enshrined in one another's forms.
>
> In every test of love, may we see Thy loving hand.

In any disagreement, may we seek Thy hidden guidance.

May our love not be confined by selfish needs, but give us strength ever to expand our hearts until we see all human beings, all creatures as our own.

Teach us to love all beings equally, in Thee.

This vow captures the spirit that Swamiji was encouraging the whole community to embrace. We were being reminded to bring these attitudes into every human interaction, and in fact, to all life experiences. The beauty of the setting, the music and the united loving presence of about 700 well-wishers created an atmosphere of heavenliness. Not only were Swamiji and Rosanna properly blessed, but everyone in attendance communed with that blessing as well. That was Swamiji's way: to not just talk about being uplifted, but to share with us an experience of it.

The Roseville Music Exchange was so successful that by the end of the first year I was ready to expand. I rented a completely unfinished space in a brand new shopping center and started building the necessary improvements before and after hours of the existing store. There wasn't even electricity in the new building yet, so I started framing the interior by using a chain saw.

I saved many thousands of dollars by doing the construction myself, but I paid a different kind of price by doing so. Once again I was lifting wall framing by myself and on the third day I started to feel back pain. Instead of stopping to heal I began wearing a back support belt and kept working. By the end of a week my back was literally twisted, when my shoulders faced front, my hips faced forty-five degrees to the right. I certainly didn't have time to go to the doctor so I just kept on building.

One day the Universe spontaneously responded to my unspoken need. A young man entered the new store and we had the following conversation.

"Hello?" called a young man in his mid-twenties while peeking through the door.

I put my tools down and faced him, happy to relax my back for a moment. "Hi, can I help you?" I responded.

He was a little shy and looked down at the ground for a moment, then looking up again he asked, "Do you need some help?"

I smiled as I responded, "Well, yes I could use some help, but I don't really have the budget for it."

"Oh, I don't mean that you have to pay me!" he said with surprise, "I just want to help."

I inwardly bowed, I was touched and deeply thankful for this God sent help.

My new friend, Dennis, pitched in with enthusiasm and soon there were four rooms for instrument lessons with storage area above, a long counter for accessories, band instruments and harmonicas, and the wall behind was filled with hanging electric and acoustic guitars. The main floor held sheet music, drums, guitar amplifiers, synthesizers, and both upright and grand pianos. It was quite a sight!

As I got to know Dennis I found that he was reliable, friendly, honest and hardworking. He also played guitar, so I offered him a job in the store he voluntarily helped to build. The grand opening of the new store was in September 1986. It didn't take long for customers to come in and for sales to increase. Soon there were six instrument teachers, a bookkeeper/cashier and two salesmen.

I didn't feel uncomfortable living in Roseville, Yogananda taught that Spirit is center everywhere and circumference nowhere. Which means that God is everywhere, but it doesn't mean that everyone agrees on God being present and they want to talk about it. I didn't feel that it would be helpful to advertise the ways that I look at life differently than others, so I kept it to myself unless there was a specific reason not to. Occasionally the distance between my spiritual culture and language would cause challenges. I had spent years using Indian spiritual words in everyday conversation, but now I was Larry in Roseville, no one knew of my spiritual background.

One day I was talking with one of the music instructors and he gave me some good news. At Ananda I would have said, "Hari Bol!" Which means: Say God! And is often used in India as a general positive exclamation. I reflexively started to say Hari ... and while it was coming out of my mouth I decided I shouldn't say Bol because that would be weird...but what could I say instead?...I didn't have much time to think...there was a slight pause...and then I continued with "Har har har!" The instructor looked at me, blinked like there had been a break in the space time continuum and then went on with the conversation as if nothing strange had happened.

This occasionally happened in reverse as well. At the time the word *bad* had become a very popular slang word. When used as slang it meant the opposite of its original meaning. So *bad* became good. Sometimes when it was used it would be clear to me how it was being used and at other times it was not clear, so I would have to ask, "Do you mean good bad or bad bad? My question usually caused people to laugh, so either way the question about bad was good.

My journey into Roseville society went farther than intended when Kai decided to join the cub scouts. I had attended a pack meeting with him a couple of times when it was announced that the current pack leader was retiring and they were looking for a volunteer to lead the pack for the next year. In Ananda culture volunteerism is way of life. According to the teachings, all things being equal, the more unpleasant the task you volunteer for the better it will be for you spiritually if you can do it with a positive attitude. When Sister Gyanamata, Yogananda's most advanced woman disciple, gave advice on the proper response to a request to serve, she said, "Just say yes and make it snappy!"

Well, this group had definitely not heard that advice. There was a prolonged period of silence that stretched on into the very uncomfortable. I had been in cub scouts and boy scouts as a youth, so I knew it had a positive purpose. I began to wrestle internally with "Why not?" on one shoulder and "Are you insane?" on the other. There was an audible group sigh of relief followed by an enthusiastic amount of applause when without having made a firm decision in my mind I heard myself say, "I'll do it."

So for the next year I was a cub scout pack leader. I was informed that my duties included getting trained and leading monthly meetings. What I had not been told up front was that I would need to lead a group prayer at each meeting and that I would have to judge the annual Soap Box Derby.

I wasn't concerned about the group prayer. I had led groups in prayer many times at Ananda. But I did have to make a couple of adjustments for prayer at scouts. At Ananda we repeat the leaders words in a back and forth style. In most Christian groups the leader orates a prayer ending with *in the name of Jesus Christ* or *in Jesus's name* and the group says, "Amen." Since scouts is supposed to be a non-denominational group I started with a generally accepted Heavenly Father – which we also use – but left out the Jesus reference at the end and went straight to Amen.

It isn't that I felt uncomfortable with Jesus, Jesus is one of the Masters of Self-Realization, we use his name in all our prayers. It was because there might be people of other faiths who would not feel comfortable and I didn't feel it should be imposed on them. Since I received no complaints on the subject it appeared that offense had been avoided. Swamiji had often reminded us about the importance of not imposing our beliefs on others. He wrote in *The Way of the Sanghis*: We seek never to convert anyone to our specific *cause* except, in love, to inspire all with the desire to reclaim the bliss of their own being.

As for the Soap Box derby, that was a whole different story!

As you might imagine, the parents took the race much more seriously than the boys. I knew this would be the case and

I arrived at the competition with some misgivings. Kai and I had built a small black batmobile. It looked pretty good, but it was too light. We added some metal washers for weight, but that didn't do the job and we were very quickly eliminated.

About half way through the competition the energy in the room shifted. I had turned my head away just for a moment and missed the start of one of the races. The next thing I knew there were shouts of protest. One of the men was complaining that there had been a problem with the start and that his son's car had not had a fair chance to compete.

Since I was the referee and I had not seen what happened – which I saw no reason to inform anyone – I first listened to the boy's father and then canvased the group for corroboration. There were more people in support of the father's claim than against, so I called for a rerun. When the rerun ended with the same result as the original race, it was generally accepted that justice had prevailed: Whoo! Crisis averted.

My career as a scout leader was limited to that one year. When I informed them that I would not be signing up for another year there were no protests. I took that as a relief and not an insult for I did not feel a calling to the scouting clergy.

Toni's forty-second birthday was special not only because it was her birthday, it was also the day that she officially started using her spiritual name: Bhavani. She didn't do it half way, she used the name all of the time and eventually legally changed it to Bhavani.

Not everyone at Ananda takes a spiritual name, it is a personal choice. For those who do, it is a conscious act of helping to redefine one's self identity and life purpose. If the name is sensitively chosen it will resonate with a person's vibration and be an affirmation of their spiritual aspirations. When people use our spiritual name they are honoring our spiritual life and whether they realize it or not, blessing our spiritual path.

Our lives in Roseville were busy with raising the twins. We enrolled them in the Roseville Sugar Bears swimming program which is known for being the home pool of the Olympic Gold Medalist Summer Sanders. Soon Kai and Sabari were enthusiastically competing. Sabari also attended ballet classes and Kai was on a T-ball team.

I also served Kai's soccer team as coach for two seasons. At the first practice one of the boys got knocked down and soon his eyes were rolling up into his head and he had passed out. Needless to say I had no idea what to do. Fortunately he soon came back to consciousness and all was well. When I later explained what had happened to his parents they said, "Oh, don't worry about that, it happens with him all the time." I just barely was able to hold my next thought in: I could have used that information before the practice!

As mentioned, the kids were enrolled at the local Montessori School. We found that the Montessori approach to education was very in tune with our own life philosophy. They were particularly adept at positively keeping the attention of the students and teaching them how to research their own interests independently.

Bhavani and I also broadened our horizons with new hobbies. Bhavani chose to learn the Japanese tea ceremony and found an instructor who specialized in that art. I chose a much more active skill: Tae Kwon Do. It seemed like a good opportunity to develop some self-defense skills. I found that there was a very qualified training center in Roseville with a Martial Arts Master that had come to America in the 1950's with his teacher as a part of the Korean Demonstration Team. His master settled in Sacramento and Master Lee in Roseville.

At first I was a little uncomfortable calling him Master Lee, since I had only ever used that word when referring to my guru Paramhansa Yogananda. I didn't want to be disloyal to my guru. Master Lee was certainly qualified as a martial arts instructor, but he was not a Self-realized master. Yogananda had released all of the little self identification as being separate from God. He lived as a blessing to the world with full access to God Presence/Potential. Eventually it became like knowing two people with the same name. Only the name is the same, the people are different.

Master Lee's teaching style was attentive and in no way abrasive. Had he been one of those teachers that yell at their students I probably wouldn't have kept going. He also promoted the philosophy that training is for self-development and not for fighting. He taught that one of the goals of training is that you don't feel the need to fight, but you are capable if it is necessary.

Having grown up with a father that imposed himself both vocally and physically, along with an elder brother who was bigger and stronger than me, I had always felt physically intimidated by men in general. Through surfing I had developed physical and mental confidence in many ways, but it seemed to me that learning self-defense would be good for me.

It also struck me as being good exercise and, even more important, just plain fun!

As a young man, Yogananda enjoyed going to the gymnasium and watch wrestlers in the ring. He would sometimes yell out suggestions to the combatants and if they followed his advice that person would often win. After coming to America he would sometimes wrestle with his first American disciple, Dr. Lewis.

All of the students wore white uniforms and a belt color – starting with white – according to their rank. In ancient times there were no colored belts. The uniform would stay white because it would be washed after each use, but the belt would not be washed and eventually it would turn black from years of training: that is the origination of the black belt. In modern times each style of martial arts has its own color system for ranking and time frame for progression.

At Master Lee's the fastest a student could progress with regular attendance was two years from white belt to red belt with two stripes, after which a minimum of one year at that rank was required before testing for first degree black belt. To advance the student would need to be invited to test. The instructors would invite a student to test when they had shown during class the needed skill requirements for their next level.

Another feature of the training was the inclusion of humility, respect and helping others. On my first day of training Master Lee taught me individually, on my second day of training a 10 year old who had started two weeks before me was my instructor. Once I had understood the most basic moves I was allowed to join group classes. I appreciated that being a student and a sharer of what you had learned was part of the training. I remember Swamiji saying, "If you can't explain it to others you don't yet understand it."

In the beginning of my training I was so caught up in the physical details that I didn't fully grasp the implications of what I was doing. In Asia, the word Chi is used to describe life force. In the yoga tradition life force is prana. As I mentioned, Yogananda's Energization Exercises are specifically designed to learn how to become aware of life force and consciously draw it into the body through conscious direction of will. Gradually it began to dawn on me that Tae Kwon Do was just a different form of energization exercises. This brought my practice to a whole new level.

I had started training not long after arriving back in Roseville but had to take a break when my back rebelled during the new store construction. The twist in my spine eventually returned to normal, but my lower spine was in spasm and when I moved the wrong way the pain was severe. I consulted with Santosh who had dealt with his own back problems successfully. He recommended walking and swimming. So I found a place where I could start swimming. The first day was very difficult, I needed to use a paddle board to stay above water because it was too painful to kick. Gradually my body loosened up and I began move my legs more freely. After about two weeks I could actually swim slowly and in a month I was doing laps.

The good news was that swimming brought me back to full mobility, the not so good news was that every time I rolled over in bed at night I would wake up from pain. During the day

I walked around normally, so I began to experiment with going to Tae Kwon Do class and found that nothing that I did there had any effect on my back. Even being thrown to the mat had no negative result. So I started training again in earnest even though every time I rolled over while sleeping I woke up in pain.

The store was doing well and the staff could get along without me so we decided to take a summer camping vacation. Bhavani's enthusiasm for camping was very low but she loved being out in nature; so I asked her why? She explained that her previous camping experience was mostly cooking without the convenience of a nice kitchen and not much else. So I assured her that I would do all the cooking.

We went west to Clear Lake where we rented a jet ski for the first time. Then we drove out to Highway One and headed north. We camped on the beach and the kids tried boogie boarding in the cold water. Then we played for hours in the sand. The beach had been home for me as a teenager so I really enjoyed it.

Being with the kids all day every day and doing the cooking was great fun, but it was also exhausting. Bhavani and I would trade off getting some alone time. At one point I had planned for a moment of personal space by purchasing a candy bar and keeping it with me so when the time was right I could wander off into the quiet and enjoy a peaceful treat. When the moment came I found a private place, opened the wrapper and with what I thought was the appropriate level of anticipation I moved the candy in the direction of my mouth. In that moment I had no idea that I was about to experience a Divine pop quiz.

As if a magician had waved a magic wand, Kai suddenly appeared from behind a bush and I was caught in the act. I lowered the sacred candy bar, knowing what was about to come and dreading it. When he asked me to share the chocolate manna I knew instantly and clearly the proper response. I struggled internally, knowing that I love my son and that a moment of revealing my actions to the world would come some day in the future; I would have to speak the truth. And the truth is that I said, "No." Kai watched me eat the candy. To Kai's credit he didn't turn against me in any way that I could see, he passed his side of the test with flying colors.

Certainly in the larger scheme of things this was not an insurmountable failure on my part, but its so disappointing to live for dharma, to commit oneself to right action in life and then to selfishly fail in such a petty way. Over the years I have had to remind myself more often than I would prefer that we are only defined by our faults if we give up improving ourselves.

In Chapter Three of the *Essence of the Bhagavad Gita,* Yogananda's interpretations edited by Swami Kriyananda, it says:

> (5:14) It is not God, the sovereign Self, who creates in mankind the consciousness of acting in this world. God neither causes people to act, nor entangles them in the (karmic) consequences of their actions. It is maya, the cosmic illusion, which acts through them.
>
> This stanza might seem mere casuistry: God might be taken as trying to shift the blame

elsewhere by saying, "He did it!" In fact, however, it can be a great aid to the spiritual aspirant to realize how much a puppet of delusion he is. God created the delusion, true. Yet God Himself remains unaffected by it, for in His Supreme Spirit He is beyond all vibration. The yogi must feel, at his center within, that he, too, is immovable and at peace. Maya (cosmic delusion) acts through him, but cannot define him.

There is another "angle" on this teaching, however, which seems to contradict what has been taught above. Yogananda used to say, "It is better, if you do commit an error—whether slight or great—to tell yourself, 'God did it through me.'" He continued, "God likes that! For you will find it easier, if you do, to release the feeling of guilt which makes people beat themselves, with thoughts like, 'I did that! Oh, how weak I am! How wrong of me! How sinful!'"

My Guru used to say, "The greatest 'sin' is to call yourself a sinner." Instead, if you don't want to blame God (which Yogananda insisted, however, is perfectly fine with God!), tell yourself, "Maya (cosmic delusion) committed this deed through me. I dissociate myself from everything connected with it. In my true Self, I am untainted and ever free!"

> "Of course," my Guru added, "you must then act in such a way as not to commit that error again!"
>
> Every time you slip, instead of moaning, "I've failed! I'm a fallen soul!" tell yourself, "I haven't yet succeeded!" If you do that, your words, instead of affirming negativity, will be an affirmation of eventual success.
>
> "The best time for sowing the seeds of success," Paramhansa Yogananda used to say, "is the season of failure!"

Once again we are reminded that both successes and failures are able to bring us closer to God or further from God according to what we do with them. It is a very powerful shift in life perspective when we realize that God is doing everything. That we are all channels for God. And that our happiness is ultimately tied to how we represent that Truth.

Southwind

Roseville
MUSIC EXCHANGE
MUSICAL INSTRUMENTS
PIANOS·GUITARS·BAND
OPEN

Music Exchange

Chapter 13

Fulfillment of a Vow

"The happiness of one's own heart alone cannot satisfy the soul; one must try to include, as necessary to one's own happiness, the happiness of others."–Paramahansa Yogananda

Our family road trip that summer continued north from the beach to where we drove through a huge Redwood tree, to Lake Shasta where we took a boat ride to incredible underground caverns, to Mt. Shasta where Kai and I hiked up to an ice field that we could slide down on our butts, to Lassen Volcanic National Park where we saw hot bubbling pools of liquid earth and finally back to our home in Granite Bay. All in all it was a fine adventure and it highlighted the general harmony of our family. In spite of a few challenging moments we all enjoyed each other's company.

As parents, Bhavani and I emphasized participation rather than observation alone. We didn't have a television in the house at that time, when the kids were some years older we got one for watching an occasional video and the Olympics. We didn't want TV to become a forbidden fruit, so they were allowed to watch an hour of television at Grandma Yolanda's when they visited there. Occasionally we went to the movies, making it a special event rather than a regular activity.

As the owner of a music store it might seem strange that my own children didn't play an instrument, but we didn't feel that they should be forced to play. We started them both on piano lessons, but after a few months they announced they didn't want to continue. Years later they told me why they quit. It was because the teacher had stinky body odor! I see it as my failure to not know this. Years later I asked them if I should have forced them to continue and they both said, "Yes."

I enjoyed being with the kids at bedtime. In the beginning I would read books, but gradually I switched to telling stories that I made up on the spot. Sometimes I would ask them who the main character in the story should be and they would call out the name of an animal. I would then tease them a little by starting the story this way:

"Once upon a time", I would say with wonder in my voice and they would look at me with anticipation. "There was...(pause)...the end!"

Then they would giggle and say, "Come on Dad!"

After repeating this once or twice more, depending on their mood of the moment, we would move on to the narrative which would end with a proper: The End.

Occasionally I would ask them questions about the main character and adjust my story to their comments. Gradually this evolved into them telling a story or each of us telling a line of the story and we would go in a circle to see how the story evolved.

Both Kai and Sabari learned to read at a fairly young age and developed a lifelong enjoyment of reading. Even at the age of twelve and thirteen I would read a book to them. By then they were reading adult books. I read them, *Kongo Kitabu* by Jean-Pierre Hallet and *Rogue Warrior* by Richard Marcinko: both are real life adventure stories of different kinds. When I came upon swear words I would say bleep. When I look back at this part of our lives together I think it was very bonding and was a powerful counterbalance to the times when life was more difficult.

It also established a level of commonality that allowed them to talk to me about more subjects than your average parent. Although that wasn't always the case. One afternoon I found Kai and Sabari sitting about ten or twelve feet above the ground in a tree.

One of the advantages of twins is that they always have a companion to play with. They were about six years old at the time, Kai was sitting with legs on either side of a branch, but Sabari was sitting on two boards that she had placed between two branches at the same height. The boards were just barely long enough to reach between the branches. I pointed out to her that it was an unsafe situation and she assured me she understood and would be careful.

After consulting my inner *what should I do?*, I decided to let it go and made my way back into the house. About ten years later I found out that no sooner had I disappeared from view,

Sabari had shifted her position and fallen out of the tree. The good news is that she wasn't injured and she learned a valuable lesson.

Of course, lessons with the kids could also backfire. We had shared the traditional learning to ride a bike experience together and now the kids were quite comfortable on a bicycle. One day they were riding their bikes and it occurred to me that they were ready to take it to the next level and go off a small jump. So I placed a little ramp in the driveway and encouraged them to try it.

They looked at the jump with skepticism. I tried to convince them that it would be okay. They weren't biting, so I finally said the infamous Dad words, "Okay, I will show you how its done!"

They both became quite animated in trying to discourage me, but I wouldn't listen. I got up on my suburban trail bike that I had used successfully riding next to Folsom lake. I lined things up and off the little ramp I went...instantly over the handlebars into a very short superman flight that landed in a good dose of road rash on my hands and forearms but no major injuries.

It was such a classic disaster that I couldn't stop laughing. The kids came over to make sure I was okay, so I thought that was nice. The stream of "I told you so'," that they kept going, for what they considered an entertaining amount of time, also made me laugh. Swamiji had taught us to be able to laugh at our own foibles, so I laughed at myself as well.

I also managed to get in trouble with Bhavani around this time. One day when I was attending Tae Kwon Do class I came upon a young brother and sister in front of the training center. They were sitting on the sidewalk next to a large box in which a litter of puppies were huddled in the corner. The next thing I knew two of the cuddly little puppies were in my arms – I couldn't take just one, it would be lonely!

When I arrived at home with the big surprise Bhavani wasn't too pleased. She felt that I should have consulted her first, and of course she was right. Oops! I offered to take them back, but she wasn't upset enough for that. The kids were thrilled and soon they were welcoming and naming Daisy and Clara to their new home. When the dogs were old enough we took some training classes and they learned to heel, sit and come. Eventually I could take them to the lake and they wouldn't go in the water without permission.

One of the skills that comes from calming the mind in meditation is the awakening of one's awareness of harmony and disharmony in life. We have talked about the three gunas and how these qualities of consciousness underpin all of the Creation. The restless mind is only aware of the froth on the surface of human experience, and believes that good tasting froth is the best part of life, and bad tasting froth should be avoided as much as possible. This way of living bases awareness and reaction to life on ego-rooted emotional likes and dislikes.

The devotee is attempting to live on a *connected to Universal consciousness* soul level. Soul perception is not tied to the ego/personality but to intuition. Yogananda described intuition as "the soul's power of knowing." What will intuition reveal to us? The Truth of the moment, that which we can use to understand and act in ways that best represent that Truth, leading us ultimately to spiritual freedom and lasting happiness.

As we develop spiritually our inner perception reveals things about life that we could not previously perceive. Anandites as a group have developed what I would describe as a very sensitive harmony meter. When we are in harmony we are in tune. When we are not in harmony we are out of tune. This is true for both individuals and groups.

It is natural that an orchestra or choir would want to be in tune all of the time. Certainly all devotees are seeking to live in harmony with themselves and with life. Yet, it is also true that good music often includes a certain amount of dissonance, which when resolved into harmony makes the whole experience richer. This is akin to the discussion we had about mistakes, sometimes mistakes or experiences that we would not prefer, lead to positive results that would not have been present otherwise.

In this way it is possible to be in tune through dissonance: doing what you are supposed to be doing in spite of its outward appearance of dissonance. Being a channel for harmony producing dissonance is a risky business. Jesus chasing the money changers out of the temple would be an example of this. He was able to maintain inner calm while performing that task, not everyone would be able to do that. The act itself was an uncomfortable expression of Truth.

In order to play well with others the best musicians are able to inwardly reach out and attune themselves to those that they are performing with. Swamiji would inwardly reach out and attune himself to the audience when he was lecturing. This inner listening is an essential skill for the disciple. Attunement is the ability to perceive, absorb and express the inspirations and understandings of our higher Self. Swamiji taught, "Attunement is the essence of discipleship. The deeper the disciple's attunement, the more perfect an instrument he becomes for the guru's grace."

Attunement to the guru, along with the practice of Kriya Yoga and devotion, are the most powerful tools of the spiritual aspirant. Along with this comes satsang, service and fellowship with others that are going the same way you are going. The group vibration is like a boat with many rowers. If everyone rowing is in sync it is a great benefit, if everyone is doing their own thing in the same boat full speed ahead won't go so well.

Finding balance between individual and group effort in the spiritual life is a very challenging issue. Some students need extra attention and interaction, others require greater levels of independence, most groups are benefited by high levels of group participation, and yet there are those that need to avoid becoming rigid by insisting that others participate. Understanding the individual needs of each student, as well as the needs of the group, is one of the great skills of spiritual leadership. Swamiji was very sensitively aware of these sometimes competing needs and supported both sides as each situation presented itself.

My own harmony meter began to twitch in 1988. The store was going well, but it was very challenging. In spite of the fact that my personal income was the highest it had ever been to that point in my life, every month there was potential anxiety about paying all the bills. The new store was more expensive in almost every way and the increased sales went to pay more and higher bills instead of increasing profits. Cash flow was often tight, so even though the sales were higher than ever, it started to feel like I was working for the bank, creditors and the landlord; they kept wanting more and more. At home I also began to feel that something was amiss, but I couldn't quite put my finger on it until Bhavani and I went on a vacation together to the beach in Mendocino. We shared a beautiful weekend, but on the drive home we had the biggest argument we had ever had.

The main area of discussion was money. It wasn't just about the tightness of cash flow, Bhavani felt uncomfortable with my approach to money. The details of our differences weren't really the main issue. The issue was internal unease. When we become upset that life isn't exactly the way we want it to be, we are the one's who have caused ourselves to be unhappy, not the circumstances. When Sister Gyanamata faced this in her own life, she resolved it by offering this prayer: Lord, change no circumstance in my life, change me.

It is not wrong to recognize that there is a problem and to try and improve our lives, but it is mistaken to blame others for our unhappiness. We need to separate *there is a problem,* from our awareness of well-being. Even in a righteous war where a soldier is required to do their duty and kill the enemy, they are not required to hate and/or act dishonorably. Jesus went so far as to say: Love your enemies. Can we learn to love our discomforts in life as well? Yogananda said, "There is no such thing as obstacles, only opportunities." For people who are rooted in ego consciousness this can be a very difficult teaching.

We have touched on the subject of karma already. Every life experience comes from our karmic past, when people say, *that person didn't deserve* an unpleasant experience, they usually don't know what they are talking about. While it is a simultaneous truth that some experiences fall into the *they didn't **have** to have* the experience, they also didn't *have **not to have*** the experience. The Universal law of karma is at the foundation of cosmic justice which drives all life experiences.

If we react poorly to our challenges we will not only create new negative karma by those reactions, but in some cases we will have to repeat that unpleasant experience again and again until we can positively release the energy of that karma. One of the great gifts of the practice of Kriya Yoga is that it helps us to release past karma in bulk, thus dramatically speeding up the process.

We are ultimately the gatekeepers of our happiness. The yoga practices train us to gain control over the reactive process so that we can maintain our connection to Universal peace in all circumstances and avoid the creation of new karma that may require additional incarnations to resolve. Until we perfect our control we will have some successful days and some not so successful days.

Yogis, as a generality, direct most of their communication inwardly to Life/God/the Universe and sometimes develop a disinclination to communicate outwardly because it can easily turn disharmonious. I heard Swamiji say numerous times that he didn't argue and could not be drawn into an argument.

Having observed this to be true over many years I was completely astonished when I had a conversation with him one day in which he said that he had had an argument with Rosanna. Even more unexpected was his statement, "I was surprised to find that it had some benefits."

One of the foundational precepts that Swamiji shared was: Do what works. Even if we were personally able to resolve all our own karmas inwardly, as long as we are interacting with those who have not yet reached that level, life will be asking us to love and serve in a way that actually works. If we don't, the situation/relationship will break down. And sometimes no matter how hard we try, things don't always turn out the way that we would prefer. I gradually began to realize that Bhavani wanted me to be a person that wasn't me. She had a view of what she needed and every right to that view. It isn't that I couldn't see her perspective: I just couldn't yet see what to do about it.

Along with shifting sands at home I began to feel that working in the store was becoming too much of the same thing over and over again. I was losing interest and feeling hemmed in by the financial pressure. So I decided to sell the store. It took some months, but eventually two fellows and their families from the Bay Area who were retiring from corporate jobs, decided that Roseville would be a nice place to retire and running a music store would be fun.

Now that the store was sold I needed to come up with a new plan for income creation. Searching around inside of myself I came up with the idea that independent video production should be my next adventure. So I started shopping for video equipment to set up a video editing space in an outbuilding that was in our backyard. By this time online shopping had been going for a some years and you could get good prices. I checked locally and there was one professional video equipment shop not too far away. It then occurred to me that purchasing locally might be a good idea even if the prices were higher. Quick service would be important if I had any problems. So I decided to buy locally and make friends with the owner and service manager.

Figuring I would need a demo reel to get jobs and wanting to get familiar with the equipment, I walked over to Folsom Lake and took some nature shots. Then I went to the county fair and got a wide variety of shots. Soon I was editing, recording voiceover and adding music that I wrote and played myself.

I placed an ad in the newspaper and printed up flyers to hand out and post around town. Soon I was doing weddings, corporate training and promotional videos. All was going well until one day things went to a whole new level. My decision to purchase locally payed a huge dividend that I had never imagined. I got a call from the California Public Defenders Association (CPDA) which had its headquarters in Sacramento. They had just purchased a complete portable video production and presentation system from my friends at the local video equipment store to record continuing education seminars for Public Defenders. They were looking for someone to operate the system and the owner of the store had recommended me. For the next seventeen years, no matter where I lived or what else I was doing, I traveled to various cities in California to do about eighteen weekend programs a year for them. In all those years I never missed a program.

For the CPDA I operated a two camera live switching and recording system with public address system, wireless mics, lights, screen and projection for powerpoint presentations and sometimes live green screen. Along with working for the CPDA, I did a wide variety of independent video projects in Roseville: How to assemble newspapers, weighing your truck at a scale station, a Ropes Course, a Charter Airline, weddings, high school graduations, dance recitals, soccer, martial arts and motocross. Whenever possible I would also write the script and compose/play the music.

That year I was invited to take the test for 1st degree black belt. Along with the successful completion of the test I was offered a position as a part time instructor in exchange for monthly dues. Additionally I was invited to compete and be a referee for youth matches at a competition that our training center was putting on.

My three years of martial arts training had been good for me. I felt more calmly centered in my self both physically and emotionally. Certainly my spiritual life enhanced these changes, but I also found that in learning to not overreact to a physical attack I had also become less reactive to the energy of any confrontational situation.

I remember the training session in which I first put all of the techniques of blocking, punching and kicking together into a cohesive flow while sparring with one of the instructors. I was able to automatically react without physical or mental over reaction. My inner energies bonded with my increasing confidence and I began to hold my own in our match. I could feel a growing freedom from my childhood fear of being hit and it brought a smile to my face.

The inadequacies that I had felt when that fellow came into the piano store with a baseball bat and when I faced that fellow in Carpenteria who was beating on his partner were greatly diminished. I haven't been tested to see if they are completely gone, but so far so good!

At our training hall's tournament I competed in the over thirty-five age group in Form, achieving a first place, and in Sparring, getting second place. More interesting than my participation as a competitor was my role as referee. Just like the scouting Soap Box Derby, parents and coaches took the competition very seriously. The head student of our school gave all of the referees a stern talking to before things got started. He said, "This is our tournament and we make the final decisions. Make sure each punch or kick not only touches the opponent, but actually impacts with proper technique. Don't let anyone bully you into letting them make decisions!"

Well, I thought he actually meant what he said, so...

I was working with six to eight year old kids and after a couple of bouts I started to feel comfortable with the process of being a referee, both parents and coaches had behaved with acceptable decorum. In the third bout everything changed. About half way through the bout one of the competitors put a side kick up in the air about six inches from his opponent. Instead of stopping while the foot was just hanging in the air the opponent kept moving forward until he simply walked into the attackers foot. So the kick was not a proper kick and should not be scored.

Well, when I announced that there was no score for the attempted kick the boy's coach went wild. I tried to explain to him what had happened, but he had no ears to hear. He trotted off to complain to the powers that be. The next thing I knew the fellow who had told me to stand strong was replacing me without even asking my side of the story. No one wanted to hear the truth. So that was the end of my career as a Tae Kwon Do referee.

Had this happened to me before I arrived at Ananda I would have stormed out and never looked back. Now I found it disappointing but not completely unexpected. The head student later told me that he had done what he did to maintain harmony – certainly a noble thought – but he had at the same time caused the match to be falsely scored, thusly fixing the match... otherwise known as cheating.

Just a few months after starting with video production our landlord informed us that they wanted to sell the house. We ended up moving to Old Mill Circle, which was a newer suburb on the eastern side of Roseville. It worked well for us because I could turn the garage into a video studio and it was closer to the kids school where Bhavani now worked full time. Along with a grass backyard there was a nearby trail with open fields for walking the dogs. Even more importantly, the circular street was a neighborhood unto itself and the kids could go trick or treating on Halloween!

The fourth of July that year was also Ananda's 20th anniversary. We went up to the village to join the celebrations.

In spite of the problems that Bhavani had when we had lived at the village, she had many Ananda friends and loved the spiritual family living in the country lifestyle. The kids embraced the whole atmosphere of being in the community and we all had a great day.

Ananda's Anniversary was noted outside of Ananda as well. There was an article published in the L.A. Times giving a brief history and accomplishments of Swami Kriyananda and Ananda. In Nevada City an advertisement wishing Ananda Village a happy 20th anniversary was sponsored by thirty-five local businesses. The Nevada County Board of Supervisors even passed a resolution proclaiming "Ananda Village Week," praising the village as "one of the most respected, successful . . . New Age . . . communities in the world."

Certainly, the accolades of the "world" are not the signs of success that would be most meaningful to Swamiji. For him it would be the God Presence that he could see in the eyes of his spiritual family, which had not only embraced discipleship of Paramhansa Yogananda and the Self-Realization line of Masters, but had tread along with him the challenges of fulfilling Yogananda's vision of World-brotherhood Colonies. But after much negative energy in the past from Nevada County, it was certainly a pleasant change and a reflection of Ananda's positive influence on the surrounding community in spite of its years of resistance to our presence.

At the 1949 garden party in Beverly Hills, Swamiji had vowed to bring Yogananda's dream, "To aid in establishing, in many countries, self-sustaining world-brotherhood colonies for plain living and high thinking," into manifestation. Ananda was proof that it could be done and that it was worth doing. Efforts to reach out to the world at large had been happening side by side with our successes in America. Not a person to rest on his laurels, Swamiji inspired us all to go deeper in God and to serve with ever greater dedication.

Swamiji reminded us through the years that no matter how far out we go or are sent, we should return to our polestar spiritual energy source inwardly, and outwardly as often as possible. We had seen over the years that family members would go off to have adventures – some sanctioned and some not – and we never knew how long they would be gone or if they would return at all. My journey finding Master, Swamiji and Ananda had felt arduous, but I had also seen when I looked back at my journey that each step of the way I had been cared for and subtly guided – often less clearly than I would have preferred – but guided none the less.

We wait to see the doctor, we wait in line to pay for groceries, we wait before a baby is born. So we think we need to wait for God. It takes time to fully enter into the knowing that God was always with us while we thought we were waiting.

Swamiji taught us to include God in every life circumstance. When it came to physical health we tended to ignore the body's aches and pains. I have mentioned that my back continued to cause me pain at night after the construction I did on the music store. The disturbance of waking up multiple times per night in discomfort had pushed me to my limit and one day after years of ignoring it I decided that something had to be done. I inwardly put it out to the Universe that if the pain had not gone away on its own within three months I was going to look into surgical options. I made this inner declaration with full strength of will, giving the issue completely into God's hands. I didn't think much about it until about two and a half months later when I one day noticed that I was no longer waking up at night in pain. The pain was gone! And that particular pain never returned.

One of the advantages of being self-employed and working out of the house is that you have more time with the family. But according to Bhavani, me being around the house so much was also a disadvantage. Oh, I don't mean that she never enjoyed my company, she just would prefer that I had a job with regular hours and a steady income without financial pressure. I finally asked her one day, "Most of the people in America experience financial pressure, why do you think we should be immune from it?" No answer was forthcoming.

It came to me one night while Bhavani and I were lying in bed back to back, as distant as two people can get in the same bed. I realized that I would never be able to change in a way that would satisfy her. I didn't blame her for feeling the way she did. I didn't see her point of view as being against me, but more as a reflection of her own inner challenges. In the same way that I couldn't be different than I am, she couldn't be different than she was. I inwardly released all resistance to the situation and told God that I accepted that this is the way it was going to be.

Bhavani continued to pressure me about getting a job with regular income. So one day on impulse I drove up to Ananda in search of employment. As it happened, the Ananda Builders Guild needed a backhoe driver: I was hired. The fact that I had never driven a backhoe didn't seem to be an issue for them, so I didn't make it an issue for me. I was a little concerned about what Bhavani's response would be, she didn't know that I had gone job hunting at Ananda. When I told her, she was pleased that I had gotten a steady job!

The next thing I knew we were planning to move back up to Ananda! How did this happen? I didn't plan it in any way. It was a completely unexpected turn of events as far as I was aware. The fulfillment of my vow to return Bhavani to Ananda had come about in its own way and time. In fact, it was Bhavani's expressed discontent that had activated it happening. Another perfect example of why we shouldn't assume that all actions that may increase stress are wrong. I was deeply thankful.

Over the years I have heard many people say that the spiritual life is not practical. That seeking God is a waste of time, or at most should be left to the later years of life, when you are basically too old to do anything else. As individuals we might look at the Universe's spontaneous fulfillment of our life's needs/desires as coincidence, but when we see this happening in a whole group of people who are consciously attuning themselves to higher consciousness over a period of many years, it becomes clear that spiritual practice is the most practical of activities. Through attunement to Universal potential our individual efforts are supported by powers far beyond those who do not take advantage of these truths. The teachings of yoga completely concur with one of Jesus's best known precepts: Seek ye first the kingdom of God and His righteousness and all these things shall be added unto you.

20TH ANNIVERSARY CELEBRATION

Join Sri Kriyananda and the Ananda Family...

...in a Gala Celebration of Ananda's 20th Anniversary. As Sri Kriyananda is planning to return to Italy in mid July with his wife, Rosanna, his presence at this celebration will be especially honored.

This fall marks Kriyananda's 40th Anniversary as a disciple of Paramhansa Yogananda. A special tribute to this relationship, through which Ananda was founded, will be a part of the commemorative weekend.

HIGHLIGHTS INCLUDE:

Saturday, July 2
10:00 am Sri Kriyananda will give a talk: "What is Ananda? Where Have We Come From, Where Are We Going?"
2:00-5:30 Activities: Community tours, ball games, hot air balloon rides, bandstand performances, Ananda slide showings in firehouse
5:30-7:00 Picnic dinner, contra dance, family games
7:00 Processional
7:30 Choir performance
8:30 Speeches
9:00 Fireworks

Sunday, July 3
10:00 AM Discipleship Initiation
11:00 Sunday Service

Sunday, cont.
1:00 20th Anniversary Banquet
3:30 Community High Teas
5:00-6:30 Spiritual Practices (Energization, Chanting and Meditation)
6:30 Dinner
7:30 Special Attunement Service

Monday, July 4
7:00-8:30 am Spiritual Practices
8:30 Breakfast
10:00 Class: "The Mission of the Masters" with a panel of Ananda ministers, ending with a candle ceremony.
Lunch & Goodbyes

If you are planning to come and share this special time with us, please call ahead to make your reservation at the Expanding Light (800) 346-5350 or in California, call (916) 292-3494.

Chapter 14

Faith in God

"Fearlessness means faith in God: faith in His protection, His justice, His wisdom, His mercy, His love, and His Omnipresence... To be fit for Self-realization man must be fearless." –Paramahansa Yogananda

I had learned to live with the spirit of Ananda in my heart when Haridas and I developed the center in Sacramento. Even in Santa Barbara with Bhavani and the twins I lived for God, and served God as a photocopier salesman along with starting a meditation group. When we moved back to Roseville I flowed with the journey that God presented me and opened the music store followed by diving into video production. I was able to live with an inner equilibrium that had only come to me after years of discipleship to Paramhansa Yogananda and living under the positive life transforming influence of Swamiji and the Ananda spiritual family. So why did I feel the urge to return to the village?

While an awareness of soul-rooted joy grows through the years, inner struggle at times is still a common companion. Spiritual equilibrium is not a static state, it is ever-new. Compared to my pre-Ananda consciousness I was way ahead, much progress had been made, but I had no illusions about how far I still had to go. I also maintained an inner dedication to helping Swamiji bring Master's teachings to the world. Being closer to the group energy of those efforts would increase my opportunities to participate. Even more importantly, the goal of Self-realization was ever on my mind, I didn't want to just get by spiritually, I wanted to keep pushing forward dynamically.

Along with my own enthusiasm for life at Ananda, I knew that Bhavani, Kai and Sabari would be positively influenced by the environment as well. I didn't know for sure that Bhavani's experience at Ananda would now be more comfortable then previously, but I hoped for the best. As for Kai and Sabari, I couldn't imagine a better place for them to grow up.

Human interaction is the playing field for some of mankind's greatest joys and most horrific pains. Throughout history humanity has banded together for not only survival's sake but because of the simple fact that people working together, no matter what they are doing, can accomplish more than individuals alone. From a spiritual point of view, human interaction is the grindstone that wears down the rough edges of the ego until we are smooth and the soul can shine with its elemental divine radiance. So for Ananda Village to be a perfect place to grow our awareness of inner joy it also needs to be an environment that can challenge that happiness.

When I first came to Ananda I didn't realize that I did not know how to be happy. I knew that I knew how to be unhappy, that was a powerful part of my motivation to arrive at Ananda, but I didn't realize that I had never learned how to be happy from the inside out, to experience soul/Universally rooted peace, joy, love, instead of emotional ups and downs based on my ego reactions to life experiences. What I found at Ananda was a place where people were learning how to embrace inner happiness – each at their own stage, guided by a man who radiated a very high level of having achieved that state himself.

I had often wondered through the years why people living in caustic environments don't just move to more pleasant places. Certainly there can be many reasons, but one of the contenders for top spot on the list is the fear of change, fear of the unknown. Thus the common saying, "Better the devil you know than the devil you don't know."

This saying also points out that there are forces of light and dark, beyond the outward details, at work under the surface of all life circumstances. These most commonly unseen influences are much more powerful than most people realize. In *Autobiography of a Yogi,* Paramhansa Yogananda explains that there are great souls subtly and powerfully guiding the spiritual upliftment of mankind. The spiritual family that Yogananda represented is guided by a lineage of avatars including Mahavatar Babajji, Lahiri Mahasayya, Swami Sri Yukteswar and himself, as the last in this line. These great expressions of the Divine radiate into the Creation rays of blessing and if we consciously bathe in those radiations our lives, and those that we come into contact with, will be uplifted.

Ananda Village is a place where everyone, no matter their current level of success, is daily attempting to deepen their attunement to this Divine flow of consciousness. The spiritual family's group magnetism greatly enhances each individual's efforts and each person's effort helps build the group magnetism. This powerful group energy, inwardly guided by the great Masters, is an incalculable benefit to each soul's progress.

Recognizing that Ananda Village is not just a community, but an ashram (place of spiritual practice) community based on the teachings of Paramhansa Yogananda, is essential to understanding Ananda culture. This foundational basis was the cornerstone of Swami Kriyananda's leadership. Even though his commitment to Yogananda's vision of World-Brotherhood Colonies was an important part of his focus, his most central avenue of service was to inspire and nurture all who were interested to seek and experience God within and then to bring that inner experience into manifestation in all life activities. This environment of unrestrained commitment to discipleship was home to me, I loved and cherished it.

There is nothing like driving a backhoe down a hill with no brakes to raise the energy in your spine! When I started working at the Ananda Builders Guild I received two days of training and then I was driving the backhoe on my own. The thing about backhoes and new operators is that situations can get dangerous quickly and the automatic reactions or non-reactions of inexperience aren't always conducive to safety.

I had been warned that the brakes didn't work very well. The best way to control the speed going down hill was to keep it in a low gear. Unfortunately, if you accidentally stall the motor, gravity – according to the steepness of the incline – will send you hurtling in a forward or backward direction, depending on which way you are facing. This happened to me twice, once in each direction.

The first time I lost control I was headed forward with the front bucket just above the ground. When I stalled the motor I reflexively pushed down hard on the brakes, the quickly increasing speed of downhill descent reminded me that they didn't work. My mind went into slow motion...I took a moment to panic...I thought, "Panic isn't good!" What can I do? There was a momentary pause in thinking, I inwardly reached out to the Universe and then the answer presented itself. I lowered the front bucket and it began to dig into the earth, eventually bringing the backhoe to a halt. Whew!

The second time it happened I was driving up a hill when I stalled the motor. Racing backward down a hill out of control is much scarier than doing the same thing facing forward! This hill was steeper. I was going faster, faster! I twisted around to see what I might hit...there was a tree approaching quickly. It finally occurred to me... LOWER THE BUCKET! When the backhoe finally stopped I got out to gather my whits. Behind the backhoe was a large pine tree, just about twelve inches away. Om Guru!

For my final scary trick in the backhoe I was facing downhill with a heavy load of dirt in the front bucket. I had not properly thought out the physics of the situation. I started to raise the bucket and for awhile everything was fine, but when the load got about four feet off the ground, the next thing I knew the back of the backhoe was lifting up in the air. Soon the bucket had returned on its own to the ground and the backhoe was doing a bucket stand with its rear pointed towards the sky! Had I not been attached by the seat belt I would have gone flying over the front of the backhoe to the ground below.

After some moments of astonishment at the position of the backhoe and the joy of not yet being dead, I began to contemplate a solution. It was no surprise to me when my backhoe mantra once again presented itself to my mind with a small change: Lower the Bucket... slowly!

Most of my time on the backhoe was digging trenches and holes of various sizes. I also did a lot of brush clearing. At that time the Lotus cluster was mostly manzanita and Scotch broom, it became my job to clear it out for future development. The thing about brush clearing is that branches, like the tail of a dragon, love to reach back and whack you in the face as a parting comment on how *they* feel about brush clearing.

While I started driving the backhoe, Bhavani found us a rental house on Tyler Foote Road about two miles from the entrance to Ananda Village. Soon Kai and Sabari were enrolled in third grade at the Ananda School and Bhavani began to volunteer at the Expanding Light. Eventually she was hired to serve in the kitchen for two years, filling in occasionally to lead sadhana practice. The karmic flow of every soul's journey will naturally have ups and downs, one of the benefits of spiritual practice is the even-mindedness that helps us through life changes. Bhavani had recognized her need to step away from village life but had not let the difficulties of one period of time define her whole life. Her willingness to return to the village for its many benefits was additionally rewarded when she became the head instructor of the Yoga Teacher Training Program. Her experience of village life had definitely improved.

Along with driving the backhoe I continued doing video trips for the CPDA. I would drive to Sacramento, pick up the equipment at their office, and then drive to cities as far south as San Diego or as far north as Santa Rosa. The income from these trips made life at Ananda financially feasible.

While it was a job driving the backhoe that made our move back to the village possible, it was not long after our arrival that I also found myself at Swamiji's dome helping to videotape a series of twenty minute programs to be aired on cable television as part of his efforts to share the yoga teachings to an ever-expanding audience.

Swamiji was able to give spontaneous talks on an endless number of subjects. One day he started with the subject of *Finding Inspiration at Will* and followed his own advice in that talk by then speaking on: *Coping with Bereavement, How to Attract Money, Overcoming Harmful Emotions, and Who Are You, Really!* These talks were incise expressions of the application of the yoga teachings to some of the everyday life challenges that many people experience. He used his inner access to Truth, which he had developed through his own personal spiritual practice, to access a stream of insightful thoughts that not only communicated valuable information on the subject at hand but also radiated a vibration of calm inner knowing.

Along with practical teachings Swamiji wove in the use of humor that was soul/heart based. He never laughed *at* situations or people, he laughed *with* the countless creative and often humorous ways that the Divine could express in this world. While it was meditation that most powerfully awakened my ability to experience deeper inner perception it was attuning myself to Swami's way of laughing that helped me understand how to bring inner joy into outward manifestation.

Ego based laughing often promotes separateness, where as expressions of inner joy create an atmosphere of inclusion and oneness. It was an aura of childlike (unrestricted) joyful expression that Swamiji brought to every life experience that taught me how to not only experience greater levels of soul happiness, but to let it shape the way that I live.

Sometimes during Swamiji's talks we would have to stifle our laughter so as to not ruin the recording. This wasn't always easy. Through meditation the yogi experiences an inner stillness that the restless mind can't perceive. This deep level of calmness/peace becomes the foundation of shifting from ego, emotion based consciousness, to soul based Universal consciousness. What I observed in Swamiji is that he laughed from soul stillness rather than ego identified emotionalism.

Emotion based feelings create agitation in the mind, soul based feelings are rooted in stillness/calmness and do not disturb inner peace. This soul based way of laughing revealed a way to bring inner joy into outward manifestation without disturbing inner calmness.

I began to understand more about laughing with people and situations by taking on the practice of laughing with Swamiji. I don't mean that I just laughed when Swamiji laughed. I mean that I would inwardly reach out and try to feel what Swamiji was feeling while he was laughing. I would consciously attune myself to Swamiji laughing.

This attunement to Swamiji laughing caused me to shift from the subject of the laughter to the experience of joy that was flowing through Swamiji's consciousness. I began to feel its root in stillness and complete lack of ego motivation. In spite of Swamiji's aura of maturity and wisdom, his laughter was childlike, innocent and wholehearted, never with a barb, always with a warm embrace. It felt like it wasn't just a surface point of laughter, but that the whole Universe was expressing its joy.

I didn't actually know for sure what Swamiji was feeling, but through this process of attunement I was inwardly transformed. Over time, when laughing with Swamiji I began to perceive a kind of joyful soul satisfaction that I had never experienced before. The unrestricted flow of inner well-being was new and wonderful. We learned to not just seek God's joy, but to live in God's joy. It wasn't yet *all* of God's joy, but compared to the dissatisfaction of the lives that we had all come from before living at Ananda, it was heaven on earth.

The practical application of the spiritual precepts that Paramhansa Yogananda shared were being applied in all aspects of life at the village. The village included areas of life that any community might include. Master's Market was at the hub of community life. Along with groceries, baked goods, sandwiches, warm lunches and fresh produce from the garden, there was indoor and outdoor seating for not only eating but visiting with both members and guests.

On Friday nights there was pizza and most afternoons there was a variety of sports along with a play area for young children. On July 4th there were games, entertainment and a parade, followed by fireworks. Swamiji's above ground pool was installed and eventually the old barn that I had lived in after the fire was replaced with a large metal building with a hardwood floor for year round indoor basketball and volleyball.

The school developed a thrift store and taught the students how to run it. There was an auto shop for car repair, craft businesses and a mail room – because there were so many people living at the same address. There was a large garden maintained by full time gardeners and volunteers, a dairy with cows and goats, apple orchards and a horse club.

Dr. Peter opened a health clinic which served not only Ananda but residents of the surrounding North San Jaun ridge. The village planning and maintenance team had offices and up on the hill above the market the publications building housed Ananda Publications – which became Crystal Clarity Publishers. Eventually the publication building was transformed into a temple. New offices for businesses and ministry outreach were built further up the hill and dedicated to Yogananda's most advanced disciple Rajarsi Janakananda, who was also a successful businessman.

The Ananda "How to Live" school (later called *Living Wisdom schools*) went from kindergarten through high school at that time. Kai and Sabari spent the next six years receiving not only an excellent academic education but an experiential adventure that taught them how to live consciously and develop the skills of body, mind and spirit to accomplish whatever they decide to do. It was truly a holistic process.

Swamiji's book *Education for Life* was based on precepts that Yogananda put into practice as a young swami when he started a school in Ranchi, India. The thing about this educational system is that it addresses the whole being, not just the intellect. Yoga teachings give unique insights into the foundational principles that guide the way life works from the inside out. The understanding that energy, magnetism and consciousness flow are essential components of inner transformation gives educators tools to develop their own ability to creatively understand and guide their students in the best possible way. A good education will prepare the student not only for high test scores, but for all of life.

The *Education for Life* system also requires that the educators practice what they preach. Teachers are trained to develop their own inner sensitivities so that they can inwardly reach out and attune to every student as an individual in order to understand their upward flowing or downward pulling qualities. Through this subtle process the instructor can discover ways to guide each student in helpful directions.

In order to increase the effectiveness of this approach it is extremely helpful if the parents of the students understand and apply these principles at home. At Ananda not only were the parents practicing this inner approach to life, but the whole community was also living this way, thus supporting in the best possible way the truth that all of life is a school.

Here are a few examples of learning by doing experiences that Kai and Sabari had growing up at Ananda. It isn't that these are unique activities to Ananda, it is the attitudes and understandings that are added to common situations that makes the difference.

Go-kart

One day Kai heard about a go-cart for sale, so we went to look at it. The motor ran, but the connection between the motor and the driveshaft was missing. We decided to buy it and fix it. A friend of ours was an antique car restorer so we went to him for expert advice on how to proceeded. His list of steps to complete the job was so long and complicated that we went home dejected and the cart sat for months in limbo.

I felt bad that we had given up on the project and one day I woke up with a positive determination to get the go-kart working. Kai and I then applied ourselves to figuring it out, went to town and bought some parts; two days later we had it running.

We learned to not over complicate something that can be done simply and to believe in our ability to accomplish whatever we put our minds to. We also observed that things that appear to be obstacles in the beginning may dissolve as we are able to change our perspective.

Deer Necropsy

When Sabari was about nine years old her class was out on a hike when they came across a dead deer. As they stood looking at the deer they began to wonder why it had died. Their teacher then asked if they wanted to try and figure out what had happened. The kids that chose to participate then performed a necropsy in the field. They didn't determine an exact cause of death, but Sabari awakened a lifelong interest in animal medicine. Openness to new experiences can lead to previously unawakened potentials.

Monet Artwork

At school Kai and Sabari were guided to look at and understand how great works of art are created. They studied the art of a number of history's greatest painters. Then they focused on a painting by Monet and proceeded to try and duplicate it on their own. After that they went on to making their own original paintings. This learn by doing approach was surprisingly successful.

Snow Day

One day it snowed and all the kids at school went outside to have fun. Soon there was a huge snowball fight. After some time one of the teachers redirected the groups energy toward cooperation and they built a large snow village. When they all went inside the teacher asked the students to describe their feelings during the two different types of activities. It was determined in the end that they enjoyed working together more than working against each other. When we take the time to reflect on our life experiences we can learn previously unrealized understandings that can improve the way that we live.

Baseball

Sabari was on a girls baseball team. During her first year they lost every game. Their coach guided them in encouraging each other to do their best and be positive no matter the outcome. They began to not only cheer for each other, but they would applaud for the other team when they made a good play. Even though their team was known for losing, they began also to be known for their positive attitude. During the second year when Sabari's team finally won a game, the losing team applauded them.

Art and music are also central parts of Ananda culture in general. Swamiji's upbringing gave him an education in the classics both intellectually and artistically. In university he was considered a talented writer and as we already know; he could dance! Not only did he "cut a rug" on the dance floor in his youth, but he sang in a band and could play the piano. When he left school he joined a theater group thinking that he would become a playwright. The arts were part of his DNA.

When Swamiji arrived at Mt. Washington and became a disciple of Paramhansa Yogananda he thought that he was leaving all of that behind, only to discover that Yogananda himself was a prolific writer, poet and composer/musician. It was through the spiritual practice of chanting, which awakens devotion and leads to the Universal heart in stillness, that Swamiji discovered how to awaken, as Yogananda's guru Swami Sri Yukteswar described it, the natural love of the heart. By connecting to Spirit through deep meditation, devotion and attunement to his guru, Swamiji began to receive intuitively the thoughts and melodies that he was destined to share.

In the earliest years of Ananda we sang mostly Master's chants and commonly known Hindi and Sanskrit chants from India. Gradually over the years Swamiji would present a chant of his own creation along with the "philosophy in song" music that he composed with a guitar. Swamiji's musical inspirations motivated others to create musically as well, some of which have become Ananda classics. As mentioned, Haridas made his own arrangements of Master's chants on the piano, Mukti wrote the song *Oh Master*, and Maitri transformed Yogananda's poem *Keep Calling Him* with a soul stirring melody.

During the 1980's Swamiji's tours across America included a support team of singers and at the village there was a growing choir. In an effort to compose and record his music with realistic sounds he purchased a cutting edge Synclavier keyboard, but its complexity ended up being a distraction from his creative purpose. So one day he asked me to help him choose a new keyboard. We traveled to Sacramento in his car with him behind the wheel.

One of the subjects we talked about was why some former Ananda residents were so against Swamiji. Most of the people who passed through Ananda left with positive feelings, but there were a few people who had lived at Ananda for years that left not only with bad feelings toward Swamiji, but a determination to in some way act against him.

Sometimes when people leave a situation in which they feel uncomfortable they support their decision to leave with negative energy. In some cases their negative reaction may be understandable, even if not beneficial, if they were treated unjustly. In the case of one man, Swami shared with me his side of the story and the numerous efforts he had made to help and harmonize with his antagonist. Swamiji wondered if there was anything else he could have done to help the situation.

Swamiji's openness to understanding and improving his ability to help people was a foundational element of his nature. He was completely willing to be wrong if he could understand how he was in fact wrong. Or, if he wasn't wrong, how could he be more effectively right.

When it was my turn to speak on the subject I expressed, "People put you up on a pedestal that looks like their expectation of who you should be in their mind, and not who you actually are. When you do something that doesn't fit their expectation it upsets them."

I continued, "Some people think you are all knowing and never make a mistake." To which Swamiji responded, "That isn't true and I have never claimed it."

I followed up with, "Swamiji I have never needed you to be perfect. Whatever problems you have are yours, between you and God"

I later regretted using the word problems, instead of challenges or shortcomings and I wished that I had made it more clear that I was interested in helping in any way that I could.

We also discussed the use of drums in music. I pointed out that drums are a part of virtually every culture's music. We use drums when chanting, but not for music in general. Swamiji was not against the use of symphonic style percussion but he felt that the western style drum kit was not generally used in a way that was vibrationally conducive to inwardness.

Some time later I was told that Swamiji said he had valued our conversation and was "proud" of me.

Our search for a keyboard was eventually successful in that we purchased one, but later Swamiji exchanged it for a different keyboard. I felt a little bad that we hadn't gotten the right keyboard the first time, but I didn't regret the time spent with Swamiji.

There were additional points of interest on this trip. After keyboard shopping we discussed stopping for lunch. We decided to get pizza and made our way to a place in the general direction of home. The traffic was quite heavy and in the parking lot of the restaurant we came to a stop sign where the cross traffic had no stop sign. The cars passing in front of us were lined up as far as we could see. We waited for quite some time because no driver was willing to pause and let us proceed even though they could see that we had been waiting our fair share. It seemed that we would be stuck there for a very long time when Swami did something that completely surprised me.

Having never been driven by Swamiji before I was naturally curious about his driving style. Thus far his piloting skills were consistent with what I knew of him, comfortably capable. The cars crossing in front of us were hugging each other's bumpers in order to keep anyone from cutting in. It appeared to be a gridlock situation for us. When our car lurched forward unexpectedly I looked over at Swamiji. He had a big grin on his face. I then turned to look at a large truck that was moving toward us with imposing presence. Swamiji announced with absolute faith and unexpected relish, "He won't hit us!"

As proclaimed, the truck stopped and we safely moved forward. The thing that was so surprising to me was that I had never seen Swamiji assert his will in a way that was self-serving. We had certainly waited longer than *all drivers being courteous* would have allowed, so it wasn't in any way inappropriate for

Swamiji to take the bull by the horns, still, it was completely unexpected.

It wasn't so out of the blue when Swamiji asserted himself again after lunch. When the bill for our meal arrived at the table Swamiji grabbed it before I could. I expressed that I expected to pay, it was a tradition that we paid for Swamiji's meals, but he responded by saying in a sweetly insistent voice, "No one ever lets me pay. You have come to help me and I want to show my appreciation."

I could completely understand his point of view and acquiesced with a thank you. Suddenly I was doing Swamiji a favor by letting him pay when I would gladly have paid a substantial amount to spend the day with him. As if this wasn't enough, I had one more moment of observation on the way home.

While traveling from the city of Auburn toward Nevada City there was a comfortable silence. We had been trained to keep silence unless there was a reason to speak in order to develop and maintain inner calmness. When I saw Swamiji reach for the car radio and turn it on my brain stopped. I had never been in a car with other Anandites and the radio on, use of the radio was generally considered a restless activity. It was difficult to imagine Swamiji being in any way restless.

The radio was already tuned to the classical station... Swamiji had cultured tastes. In some ways it was Swamiji's refined nature that made it difficult to see him as other than a Divine being. When I was with him I had to constantly monitor my consciousness to make sure I was paying attention properly. There was distance between my deepest inner experiences and my everyday personality. With most people I could get a sense of what I perceived as the distance between their soul and personality. With Swamiji it was an endless process of perceiving more soul which secondarily led to understanding personality more clearly.

Nevada City Baseball
Little League 1992

Jewel in the Lotus
ANANDA SCHOOL
THRIFT SHOP
COUGARS
AMERICAN RIVER TRAVEL
EUREKA YOUTH
SOCCER
COUGARS
1988

Chapter 15

Karmic Storms

"Truth burns up all karma and frees you from all births."
–Paramahansa Yogananda

Our return to life at Ananda Village was very meaningful to me. At my first private meeting with Swamiji in the summer of 1972 I had told him that I was at Ananda for God, not community. Over the years my understanding of the word community was deepened from a social/economic perspective to a recognition that it was life in a spiritual community that had given power to my personal transformation. Yes, Swamiji was the point of inspiration and guidance, and each individual's daily effort powered progress, but it was the group dedication to living the precepts and ideals that Paramhansa Yogananda represented that made Ananda a place that was not just a community, but a spiritual family.

Having grown up in an earthly family in which I never felt at home, the Ananda spiritual family had become my true family, my true home. I had given my heart to Yogananda, Kriyananda and all of my brother and sister disciples. This inner feeling of communion and belonging became central to the evolution of Larry from Beverly Hills to Vijay a life member of the Ananda spiritual family.

Just as each individual has personal karma, so do families, communities, countries, worlds and the whole Creation. The dual nature of life itself dictates that there will be ups and downs, twists and turns, comforts and discomforts, according to the incredibly intricate web of Truth underneath the surface of life's polarities. Paramhansa Yogananda addressed this subject in *Inner Culture* magazine, April 1941, answering the question: **Why is life so full of challenges?**

> "Through life's challenges you learn life's lessons. Challenges are not meant to crush you but to help you develop your powers. They come through the natural law of progress, so that you might advance from lower to higher levels of spiritual attainment.
>
> In order to pass life's tests, you will need to develop elasticity of the mind. Never allow your mind to entertain thoughts of illness or limitation, and you will see your life change for the better. Do not grieve or worry about anything.
>
> When you are asleep you are not conscious of the body, but when you awaken you remember

whether you slept well or not. This shows that your consciousness continues even when you are not conscious of the body. No matter what happens, you must become free in your mind. When your mind can remain completely apart from the body at will, you will be free.

The key to all happiness, power and health lies within your mind. But what often happens is that if you are ill for six months after enjoying good health for many years, you think you will never get well again. Your mind must not be affected by the conditions of the body. Your mind should convince your body.

Sometimes you think it is easy to believe that this universe is a dream, but as soon as you encounter the challenges of daily experiences, you often have difficulty seeing life as a dream. You have had many experiences through many incarnations and you will have others in future incarnations. You must learn to play all parts in the motion picture of life, inwardly saying, "I am Spirit."

Let nothing sit on the throne of your heart but God. Break this dream delusion by waking in God and you will be safe forever."

Through the practice of meditation the yogi becomes more aware of inner realities and gains increasing skills of body, mind and spirit to face life challenges with an equanimity based in calmness and peace. Eventually we can connect to inner joy even in the most dire of circumstances.

Up to this point in Ananda's history numerous karmic storms had been weathered. The creation of a community of light will inevitably draw forces of darkness to test that light. Karmic fires that had sparked in the past were about to flare up again and create personal and community wide changes that were even more dramatic and transformative than the fire of 1976.

By the time we had moved back to the village, the Ananda ministry had matured and Swamiji's outreach was supported by an ever growing number of committed and experienced ministers. I was added to the list of available ministers and scheduled to do occasional Sunday Services at the Expanding Light Retreat and at the chapel at the Crystal Hermitage.

The rapid growth of any organization is a challenge, with an influx of new representatives it is difficult to maintain the quality of representation. The development of qualified ministers isn't just an issue of information – although this is certainly important, the real challenge has to do with vibration; which shouldn't be confused with personality charisma. The qualities of consciousness that flow through a person are the truest representation of what they are presenting. A minister's most basic responsibility is to represent/radiate the vibration of their inner connection to Spirit.

It is a practical truth that not all minister's would be equally able to instruct and vibrationally touch people. Swamiji's thoughts took him not only to solutions for the short term but also to understandings for the extended evolution of the ministry. While in Assisi, Italy, supporting the rapidly growing work there, he was divinely inspired to write what became a ceremony called *The Festival of Light*. This ceremony includes a poetic prose description of our most central spiritual origins and teachings, original music that represents those teachings and uplifts the soul, along with an opportunity for every participant to step forward to the altar and receive from the minister(s) a blessing at the spiritual eye. It is not just a beautiful blending of the Indian arati ceremony with a Western communion service, but a vibrationally uplifting experience that represents the universal non-sectarian nature of the future.

In spite of Swamiji's enthusiasm, the *Festival of Light* was not equally appreciated by all. In fact, some people were so upset by it that they left Ananda. The first ten years of Ananda's existence was very East Indian. Our guru, Paramhansa Yogananda, was Indian. Swami was a Swami and he commonly wore Indian clothes. Many of us took Indian spiritual names and we all ate Indian food as often as possible. We sang many Indian chants and loved the Indian epics Mahabarata and Ramayana. We started Sunday Service with a sanskrit chant to the guru and we ended the Service by singing Yogananda's translation of Guru Nanak's chant *Oh God Beautiful*. This is the flavor of what we had grown up with at Ananda.

Swamiji's music had some Indian style which thrilled our souls, but we also loved the bulk of his songs which were wonderful western melodies that were gradually filled out with beautiful harmonies. Over the years Swamiji's music evolved with additional influences from Italy, Egypt, Eastern Europe,

Ireland and the Holy Land. The *Festival of Light* was the first major change to our style of worship. It wasn't in any way a change of teachings, but it was a style change.

The service was now started with something that Yogananda often did. He would ask the congregation with volume and enthusiasm, "How feels everyone!" And they would respond, "Awake and ready!" Yogananda would then ask,"How is everyone!" And they would again respond with more energy, "Awake and ready!"

I believe that most people enjoyed that Master did this, I certainly did, but I wasn't convinced that we should do it every week.

After the traditional chanting, meditation, reading, sermon, moment of silence and donation with a song, the *Festival of Light* with individual blessings, which lasted about 30 minutes, would end with everyone singing Swamiji's song *Sing Out With Joy,* followed by a prayer and then the minister pronouncing, "Go out with Joy!"

Each component of these changes was by itself something that most members could appreciate, but when connected to the changes in Swamiji's life over the past eight years it was a shift that unbalanced some people. Since 1978 and the *Joy Tours* which reached across America, Swamiji had been westernizing his public presentations. He cut his long hair, shaved his beard and wore a suit instead of the ochre robes of a Swami. He got married and spent a lot of time in Italy, eventually writing the *Oratorio* – a musical expression of the life of Jesus Christ – and the *Festival of Light*. The Sunday Service took on a more formal *churchlike* and less spontaneous feel.

I had my own list of preferences in regards to these changes, some pro and some con; which I kept mostly to myself. In spite of the things I didn't feel drawn to, over the years I had a number very deep experiences during the *Festival of Light*. More than once I felt so uplifted that I had trouble standing up when called to do so during the ceremony, I had to hold onto the chair in front of me to stay steady. It wasn't from lightheadedness, I was deeply indrawn to the flow of soul joy moving up my deep spine.

My overarching thought was: Wow! Swamiji is an incredible human being. He has broken free from the pressures of the preconceived ideas – both his own and those of others – of what his life and service should look like and has charted a course into the unknown with incredible energy, integrity, courage and capability. He is truly a noble captain of his ship. In my mind Swamiji would say, "Master is the captain of the ship." And I would respond, "Well then, you are his worthy representative."

It will be helpful at this point to explain Ananda's traditional process of internal communication. Keep in mind that there were no cell phones or internet during Ananda's first 30 years. When I arrived at Ananda there were about 50 resident members plus children, potential members and guests spread out on 700 acres of land. Swamiji did multiple classes, satsangs and services every week. Attendance at these gatherings was the number one way to know what was going on for most members. There was also an inner circle of members who interacted with Swamiji on a regular basis as part of operating the ministry, community and publications.

Over time there developed a close-knit group of dedicated disciples that met with Swamiji in various combinations of members as the flow of life presented opportunities. During these satsangs – even business meetings were satsangs if Swamiji was present – there would be an atmosphere of complete relaxation and active inner attentiveness. Whatever the subject at hand Swamiji would share his thoughts with complete openness to questions and comments. He would offer not only his current view of an issue – which included a willingness to evolve that view – but how he had arrived at that view.

These satsangs were both educational and soul satisfying. There was always lots of heartfelt laughter rooted in joyful Spirit. The discussion of the subject at hand *increased understanding* and *dissolved uncertainties*. Even the most difficult subjects were resolved, or tabled for future discussion, with a feeling of respectful caring. The group shared a oneness of mind and heart that was bonding in a way that I had never before experienced.

If a decision or resolution was come to at the meeting, communication to the affected person or group was arranged via person to person contact or community wide announcement via written notice in the village newsletter or printed notice in every mailbox. This system worked well when the community was relatively small, but as we will see, when the number of members grew and the issues more intense, there developed gaps between the inner and outer circles.

As I have mentioned, Ananda as a group was very sensitive to energy that was perceived as *negative*. Difficult questions could be presented if the vibration of the presenter was harmonious, but if there was any agitation (or againstness) in the question or comment you could feel people withdrawing from complete openness. It was not opposing points of view that was at issue, but the spirit with which these views were perceived to be presented. Adding to the complexity of the dynamics was that not everyone was equally able to gauge the true intent of the speaker or express their ideas confidently (with humility), clearly and diplomatically, so many people kept their thoughts to themselves.

Ninety-nine point nine percent of the time life at Ananda was devoid of negativity, I don't remember ever hearing a raised voice argument. But life wouldn't be life if situations didn't boil over once in a while.

Over time there emerged a group of people who at various times felt comfortable speaking up in challenging circumstances and I was one of them. Initially I spoke up because I restlessly wanted to participate, gradually I learned that feeling inwardly guided to speak was a better motivation. Along with speaking up came the challenge of what to say and how to say it.

Speaking truth had been important to me from my earliest days of discipleship. Meditating deeply took time to develop but speaking honestly I could do, so it became part of my foundation. It took me some time to realize that it isn't enough to speak the facts, the tone of the communication is also important, especially in a group of vibrationally sensitive souls. In the late 1970's I evaluated a piano for Jack, an Ananda member who offered to let Swamiji use his Steinway piano, and he passed my recommendations on to Swamiji. Swamiji wrote back to him saying:

> Jack:
>
> I agree that we should get other opinions on what the piano needs. Vijay is speaking from experience in the piano business, but not from exhaustive experience. I'm sure he wants the best for the piano. He does manage to express his views in a manner that grates.
>
> Kr

This tendency to unintentionally offend others was a karma that would haunt my life at Ananda in spite of my efforts to minimize it. Strangely, growing up in a home in which I had been frequently yelled at had inured me to feeling bad just because someone was upset with me. When trouble found me I always, as Swamiji taught us, looked at it with detachment to learn its truth and grow accordingly. I also found that getting into trouble was often – but not always! – a precursor to an unanticipated blessing.

In the same way that I experienced blessings from hardship, all of Ananda was about to do the same, only for Ananda it was to last for the next twelve years. In the beginning of 1990 Ananda changed its legal name from the *Yoga Fellowship* to *Church of Self-Realization*. SRF immediately threatened to sue us if we didn't change the name because of its similarity to their own. They had threatened us in various ways in the past and it was uncertain if they would follow through now. Shortly after the threats arrival, Swamiji held a meeting in the dome at the Crystal Hermitage. Not only was it disturbing that SRF would sue us, but Swamiji began to talk about a counter suit. The idea that we would sue SRF brought the situation to a whole new level in my mind.

Swamiji led the discussion and we looked at the situation from many different angles. In the past Swamiji had often separated his reasoned opinions from intuitive perceptions. In order to clarify my understanding of Swamiji's perspective I asked him, "Swamiji, how much of your view is reason and how much is intuition?"

My internal upset must have come through my voice in some way because my question was interpreted as an accusation and not a sincere question for greater understanding. Swamiji answered by saying, "Vijay, why do you have to be so negative?"

History tells us that it was completely right and proper for Ananda to stand up to SRF's bullying. But at that time we didn't know what the future would hold. For me, this moment was not only disappointment that SRF could be so adharmic (against right action) but it was also the beginning of my acceptance that being misunderstood would not be a temporary circumstance in my life. I don't make this statement against anyone who has misunderstood me, especially not against Swamiji, it is a karma that I carry from a time and place that I do not remember. While it has caused me suffering, it has also led me to opportunities and blessings that might not have come another way. While I accept it, I do not embrace it, I continue to improve myself so that one day that karma will be dissolved.

In spite of the momentary setback at that meeting Bhavani and I were added to the list of Lightbearers who are authorized to lead the *Festival of Light* and bless others as channels for the Masters. There were now so many ministers and lightbearers in the village that there weren't as many opportunities to share on Sunday as I would have preferred. I began to think about other ways to share the teachings. Swamiji had encouraged me to develop my writing skills, and he often talked about his writings as being seminal and that we should "Make the teachings your own" indicating that we should live them and then apply them creatively to all life activities. He eventual went so far as to say, "It is the responsibility of the disciple to activate and expand the guru's work."

The idea of writing in Swamiji's shadow was a daunting thought. I had composed numerous chants and songs thus far, feeling deep inspiration, but getting no interest or support beyond a few close friends. I considered the thought that I should wait until after Swamiji had passed from this world to begin writing, but that just didn't feel right – for all I knew he would outlive me! I wrestled with how and when to start writing for a couple of years, often praying for guidance but not feeling anything definitive.

SRF's threat to sue became tangible when we were notified that it had been filed in court. Needless to say this was disturbing in a wide variety of ways. SRF was a financial Goliath and we were David, our monetary slingshot did not radiate confidence that we could survive. The Ananda way of life was at risk and the enemy at the door was our own fellow disciples who we loved and respected.

Court proceedings of this kind are slow and a classic wealthy corporation strategy is to stretch them out because time is money and they have plenty while their prey generally does not. An added element to our situation is that we gradually came to know that SRF had spies in the Village. Our internal discussions and communications were arriving at SRF's door faster than we could disseminate information within our own community. The pressures and uncertainty of the situation began to heat up and the lid of the community's equilibrium began to rattle.

While the wheels of justice slowly turned, other more personal storms were kicking up dust. Swamiji's marriage to Rosanna was in flux. Rosanna began to spend more time in Italy. While the original reason was her father's health, it became clear over time that there was more to the story, but that story is not mine to tell. I will say that while Swamiji's and Rosanna's life paths diverged, the radiant beauty of her soul's blessing to Swamiji and the whole Ananda family is written in the hearts of those she touched and that endures.

During this same period of time Bhavani and I were experiencing our own divergence. On the surface things looked fine, but beneath the calm exterior Bhavani was once again feeling a deep dissatisfaction of which I was only distantly aware. The turning point of our relationship presented itself in a dramatic series of events.

After wrestling with the issue of when to start writing I had finally decided that it was time. I didn't want to write anything that would be seen as competing with Swamiji's books, so I chose a subject that was interesting to me but not one that he was likely to write about: *Doorway to a New Lifetime: Childbirth from a Spiritual View,* which years later I changed to *Positive Flow Childbirth*. I rented a small home at the village and planned a four week writing seclusion. I was scheduled to start the seclusion on a Monday, arriving at the rental house on Sunday night. My state of mind upon arrival was the result of two unexpected occurrences.

On the Thursday before my writing seclusion I traveled to Roseville and spent the night at Yolanda's house because I was going on a video job for CPDA. On Friday I would get up early, pick up the equipment at the Sacramento office, drive to the program site, do the Saturday program and return Sunday. While sleeping at Yolanda's I had a unique experience.

In 1977 while in Bangkok, Thailand, with Swamiji I purchased a 2+ carat emerald which I had mounted on a silver chain. I began wearing it just before meeting Bhavani for the first time and never took it off. In the middle of the night I woke up suddenly from a sound sleep with what felt like a whole body twitch. As I woke up, my attention was immediately drawn to the thumb and forefinger of my right hand in which I was tightly gripping the emerald. While asleep I had somehow found the gem, perfectly pinched it and then held it firmly enough to jerk the whole chain off my neck. It had not been a conscious action, but one that had spontaneously happened on its own. It occurred to me that forces beyond my knowledge were at work.

The import of the emerald's message was made clear when I arrived home late Sunday afternoon. Shortly after beginning to relax from the long drive Bhavani informed me that she thought we should separate. An hour later I was on my way to four weeks of seclusion.

My mind, not in the calmest state due to various life pressures, a long drive and the state of my ending marriage, was a swirl. We all had been taught to "Give your problems to God." To the atheist this is a ridiculous idea. For the average churchgoer it is a good idea with hopeful but doubtful results. To the yogi, with specific techniques of inner concentration, it is known to be possible but for many not yet experienced. I had certainly attempted to do so many times in various ways over the years with what I would describe as fair to middling results. I had experienced deep inner stillness, peace and a feeling of upliftment/blessing that was wonderful, but I had not experienced clearly crossing the line into what I would describe as dramatic Divine intervention versus a good or even very good meditation.

The thing about intense feelings is that if we can redirect them toward the direction of our goal, the energy of that intensity can be brought to positive purpose. In meditation that night I focused myself and practiced Kriya Yoga. When I got to a calm inward state of consciousness I wholeheartedly gathered all of my frustration, disappointment, uncertainty and anything else I could think of and offered it to God at the spiritual eye. The strength and completeness of my inner offering was greater than ever before, and so was the response.

My first inkling that something unusual was happening was that even though my offering was only heart and mind, it was somehow heavy and as I mentally pushed it up and out in offering it was as if the burden was going over a cliff edge, it dissolved away from me and I felt inwardly light as air. The Universe was accepting my offering. This feeling of complete release from the weight of my challenges was followed by an infusion of soul satisfying well-being that was a heady blend of love, joy, appreciation, reverence and the embrace of all that is good. I couldn't help smiling and thinking, "Lord, what else can I offer you?" I would willingly receive problems in order to experience the blessing of offering them to God. Little did I know that God would take me up on that offer, but first I had to write a book in seclusion!

My plan was to keep silence (no speaking), meditate four to six hours a day, eat little and write, write, write. In the middle of my second day of seclusion there was a knock at the door. It was Bhavani, she was worried about me and wanted to make sure I was okay. I didn't speak, but I wrote with paper and pen responses to her concern. I was still filled with an enhanced inner intuitive connection to Spirit and my thoughts flowed easily without any level of agitation. She didn't stay long, later telling me that she could see that I was feeling inwardly connected and she was surprised at how deep I had gone in such a short time. I didn't share with her at that time what had taken place.

I had no plan for what I would communicate about childbirth, no outline, no research, no chapter titles, nothing but the title. I sat down at the computer and looked at a blank screen. It occurred to me that I should explain why I was writing about this subject so I titled the page *Preface* and set the stage for the book. At the beginning of each chapter I looked at the empty page and inwardly asked what the title should be.

Each time I did this an answer presented itself. Because I was in such a calm state the amazing nature of ideas flowing from the ether into my mind seemed natural, there was no doubt present to block my access. I wrote 154 pages in three weeks and spent the last week editing and enjoying seclusion.

It is possible that I would have had a successful writing seclusion without the unexpected news that we were separating, but there is no question that when I turned the difficult energy of that circumstance toward greater connection to Spirit it became useful instead of destructive, it led to greater joy rather than greater suffering. I see this experience not as an accomplishment, though in a way it was, but as a gift that I was blessed to receive.

It was during the following year that Swamiji edited and published Paramhansa Yogananda's interpretation of *The Rubaiyat of Omar Khayyam*. This deeply mystical work was so inspiring that it was decided to use it as the subject matter for Sunday Services. As it happened, I was scheduled to lead the Service at the Crystal Hermitage Chapel on the inaugural Sunday. Unbeknownst to me, it had been decided that in an effort to monitor the quality of ministerial performance, this Sunday my presentation would be evaluated.

By this time I had been serving on Sundays on and off for almost twenty years. From the beginning of my public speaking efforts I had been determined to follow Master's basic instructions to ministers, which was that they should gather a couple of stories and jokes to share but mainly let Spirit speak through you. Jesus taught his disciples to let Spirit guide their words. Swamiji practiced this approach and so over the years I had followed in his footsteps, at first stumbling but eventually finding my stride.

The *Rubaiyat of Omar Khayyam* and its history was unfamiliar to me so I did much more preparation than I would do when addressing subjects with which I was familiar. The fact that it had existed for 950 years before being translated by Edward Fitzgerald and becoming famous in the West as bawdy literature, only to find its way as a gift to Paramhansa Yogananda who saw the large blank pages under the stanzas and was inspired to reveal the deep mystical truths which had been invisible to most readers, is an epic "behind the scenes" view of God's long game.

I later learned that my representation of the *Rubaiyat's* journey was well received and I continued to be scheduled to give Sunday Services. One Sunday at the Chapel while looking at the congregation I discovered that Swamiji was sitting in a back row, eyes closed, head slightly bowed in humble self-offering. I internally observed that I was a little surprised that his presence didn't rattle me. I then had a short moment of concern that my observation that I didn't feel disturbed would cause me to feel disturbed. Fortunately this quickly passed and just in the way I had realized the value of letting Swamiji pay for my meal on our trip to Sacramento, I completely accepted that he was present not as the leader of Ananda but as a devotee on the spiritual path.

While speaking my thoughts flowed comfortably and I even told the story of an interaction with Swamiji as an example of the subject at hand. We moved on to the *Festival of Light* and I was absorbed in doing my best to channel Spirit while blessing each person individually at the spiritual eye. It didn't occur to me that I would be blessing Swamiji until he appeared in front of me. In order to place the forefinger of my right hand on the correct spot I had to look at Swamiji, suddenly time stretched and in half a second I took in the totality of the moment. His eyes were closed, his palms touching in humble openness, it was a holy face that I loved, a doubt tried to enter my mind *Who was I to bless this great soul?*, but I pushed past that thought without pause and gave myself fully to the sacred mutual blessing and touched his spiritual eye.

After the service I greeted people as they left. When it was Swamiji's turn his smile radiated joyful loving support and he said, "That was sweet."

I later learned that Swamiji felt I had read the *Festival of Light* too quickly because I was nervous. I never told him that the real reason I read it so quickly was because I thought it was too long. Interestingly, Shivani, who was currently stationed in Assisi, was visiting and had also attended the Service. Her comment to me was, "With Swamiji present, I can't believe it, you didn't appear to be nervous at all."

Diverse reactions to my words and actions became everyday fare for me. No matter what I did there were those who understood me and those who clearly in that moment didn't. There seemed to be an aura of controversy around me. Often people would support my view in private, but not in public. While I appreciated that some people agreed with me, I didn't take that as proof of rightness. Nor did I assume that those who disagreed with me were always wrong. As I had experienced Swamiji doing, I would review past problems and try to glean new understandings that I might have previously missed. I practiced following my inner compass as best I could, saw where I had been clearly correct and when I had led myself astray. The good news is that over time I saw that no matter what happened, things always worked out beneficially, eventually.

Upon my separation from Bhavani I moved into a yurt up on the hill above St. Francis pond at the village. We arranged a schedule where the kids would stay with me on a regular basis and life went on. I continued my CPDA jobs and did various paid and unpaid video jobs for Swamiji, the ministry, the Builders guild, dance recitals, high school graduations and anything else I could come up with. I even did odd jobs for Ananda Electric doing basic new home wiring and construction for the Ananda Builders Guild. After some months I moved to a cabin below the school and next to frog pond.

One night I was awakened in the middle of the night to what sounded like a blood curdling scream. By the time I was fully awake it had stopped. I wasn't exactly sure of what I had heard, I sat upright listening intently. After a few minutes it happened again. It was definitely a high intensity full bodied scream, the kind that in the movies it would be associated with a big knife that was being plunged into a place where it definitely didn't belong.

I wrestled in my mind about what to do. There was no way to call for help. It was the middle of the night and I didn't have a flashlight. There was potentially a crazy person with a knife out there...who knows where? There was also a chance that someone needed help. I couldn't in good conscience ignore that possibility. So I put on my sandals and wondered off into the unknown.

The sound had come from the far side of the pond and there was no trail, so I shuffled through the grass in the dim starlight to circle around the water. The frogs were quiet, so they knew something weird was going on. The stillness of the night was once again pierced by a full-throated large-lunged bellow that made me stop and question what I was doing wandering about in the dark. For reasons unknown to me I felt compelled to continue.

Ahead of me there was a full sized homemade brick igloo-shaped sweat lodge that had been built as a school project. Sabari had been involved in the construction that was led by Michael Gornik. As I neared the entrance another chilling scream burst from the interior. When it stopped I hesitantly called out, "Hello? Are you okay in there?"

"Is that you Vijay? It is me Lakshman (The brother of King Rama. This Lakshman is not the Lakshman who was Swamiji's secretary for many years.) We are okay, we are just having a sweat. Sorry if we disturbed you."

What a relief! I kept the, "What in the hell were you guys thinking!", to myself and didn't stay around to chat about my opinion of the value of primal screaming, I just said goodnight and shuffled right back the way I had come as fast as I could. I didn't hear any more shrieking and soon the frogs were once again singing; life was back to not being so frightening.

Doorway
to a New
Lifetime
Childbirth from a
Spiritual
View
by Lawrence Vijay Girard

Positive
Flow
Childbirth
Lawrence Vijay Girard

Chapter 16

The Pot Boils Over

"Greater love hath no man than this, that he lay down his life for his friends." –John 15:13

This will be the most difficult chapter of this book for me to write because some people may be tempted to think that I am being critical of Swami Kriyananda: which couldn't be farther from the Truth. It contains a most personal and potentially controversial experience that I will share at the risk of it losing some of its luster, which has benefited me since it happened. As of this writing it took place thirty years ago and only after twenty years did I tell less than a handful of close friends.

I share this and some of my other spiritual experiences not with pride because they happened to me, but to reassure you that because they could come about even to me, something similar could occur in your own life.

By January 1995 the SRF court case was just starting its 5th year. Additionally, in 1994 a second lawsuit, believed to be instigated and supported by SRF, was initiated. The hordes weren't on the plains heading our way, they were at the gate with battering rams and the sounds of their attack were devastating. The tensions and uncertainty of the situation was reaching fever pitch, a ministers meeting in the dome at Crystal Hermitage was announced.

Let me set the stage. Swamiji was just recovering from heart surgery. The court case team was struggling to keep up. The financial burden was staggering. The Ananda leadership was under severe pressure from both internal community turmoil and external havoc, including everything from bad press, keeping the ministry alive, publishing Swamiji's books, running the retreat, staying connected to all of the Ananda communities and meditation groups around the world, normal personal life challenges, the lawsuits, SRF spies and harassment, the list goes on and on.

The inner circle, which had naturally tightened because of SRF spying caused more people than normal to be pushed toward the outer circle in terms of communication, meaning that they were in the dark as to what was happening. Additionally, during a court case there are some things that can not be legally discussed outside of the legal team, and other items that should not be discussed publicly whether it would be legal or not. There was simply no one thing that could be done in the short term to solve all of these challenges.

The issue of communication was partially the lack of available information, but even more importantly it was an issue of processing what we did not know, and dealing with the anxiety that came with that lack of knowledge.

One of the reasons I had strong feelings on this subject is that I had been in both the inner circle and the outer circle. I could see both sides of the fence and had appreciation for both views. I understood that people in the inner circle knew what was happening, had heard Swamiji's analysis, shared their thoughts and concerns with him and digested his responses. As I said in *Chapter 15* when referring to discussions with Swamiji: The discussion of the subject at hand *increased understanding* and *dissolved uncertainties*.

This observation is not a criticism. It is just a description of what I perceived was happening. The people in the outer circle did not have access to the same level of Swamiji's stabilizing influence. Additionally, the great souls that were in the inner circle were capable of handling more challenge than the average member and even they were being stretched to the limit.

When I entered that meeting I had no thoughts of being against anyone. I was convinced to my core that it was essential someone advocate for the outer circle. Because of my history of standing up to address challenging issues it occurred to me that speaking up could cause me to be ousted from the community. Whether that was actually true, I don't really know, but I believed it could be true. I felt deeply concerned for the survival of the community and was knowingly, and willingly, prepared to sacrifice myself in order to help my spiritual family survive.

I don't remember why I was late to the meeting. My best guess is because I was driving from a distance that didn't allow me to be there on time. My history was that I would come early and stay late to any opportunity connected with being around Swamiji. I made my way as quietly as I could to the lower left side of the steps that connect the upper and lower sections of floor. I looked at Swamiji and he was smiling and energetic, I saw no concerning signs of illness.

The meeting proceeded with two main messages. The first was, and I am paraphrasing a bit crudely: Get with the program or leave. The energy behind that kind of statement was clearly a circling of the wagons while being under attack. Ananda's way of life was no secret. If people made mistakes than they should be dealt with, honestly and with compassion. But a scorched earth attack from outside of Ananda was not going to be accepted without a fight. This statement was saying with the necessary strength to fend off our detractors, "If you don't believe in this way of life, why are you here? Why not leave?

The second message was a reflection of our dedication to the spiritual teachings that Paramhansa Yogananda gave us which described meditation as our most powerful tool for inner transformation. We were told by one of leaders that meditation is the solution to our current situation. I know that it wasn't intentional, I but I found that statement demeaning. Telling a group of dedicated meditators that they should meditate, as if they didn't already know its value, was not respectful or effective.

When the fire of 1976 threatened the community we all didn't sit down on the ground to meditate it away, we put on our firefighting clothes, grabbed our tools and fought the fire as best we could. We also welcomed help from people who were not good at meditating but trained to fight fires. Every life challenge needs to be faced with the tools appropriate for that situation and the capabilities of the people using the tools: solutions that you can actually successfully use.

From the early years of Ananda some people had tried to add a psychological approach and we resisted that influence as a dilution of our path. It isn't that anyone was against others using that approach, it just wasn't our way. I believe that pressures from this direction were part of why that response was presented the way it was.

The meeting began to wrap up, we had not achieved a satisfying *increased understanding* and we certainly had not *dissolved uncertainties*. I began to inwardly edge up to the cliff in preparation for diving off, at the same time desperately hoping someone else would speak up. It shouldn't have been so difficult, but it was, no one was willing to take the chance.

Swamiji asked a couple of times if there were any questions. I continued hoping that someone would step forward. There was an atmosphere of incompletion, Swamiji asked once more in a tone that said final chance. I resisted until the last possible moment and then spoke his name "Swamiji" and stood up.

I am telling this story after many years of reflection and I am convinced that there were unseen powers of light and dark that made what happened happen the way it was supposed to happen. The line between Universally powered karmic control and free will is very narrow, I see the actions of everyone present at that meeting as the fulfillment of their allotted part and not in any way a failure. As I have previously said: Sometimes what we might perceive as a *wrong* has to happen so a greater *right* can be manifest.

I made a serious mistake in judgment when I stood up without having clearly thought out what I would say. I knew there was a problem with communication and had a general sense of the distance between the inner and outer circles but I could not articulate it the way I have here after thirty years of refection. In fact, not only did my access to intuitive thought flow fail me, but because of the intensity of the situation I could hardly speak.

It was an untenable situation. I couldn't blame Swamiji. I didn't want to blame anyone. What I should have said is that there is a gap in communication and we need to talk about how to bridge that gap. But nothing of real value was coming out of my mouth. Swamiji asked me to give an example of the problem. But, again, I didn't want speak against anyone, these were my dear friends, their service to Swamiji and the community was unparalleled, I was stuck between the proverbial rock and a hard place.

Swamiji urged me again to explain and I hesitated. Instead of using anyone's name I referred to "the leadership". I don't remember exactly what I said but it was clearly taken as an attack. The next thing I knew Dr. Peter stood up and said, "As Swamiji's physician I insist that we end the meeting, this is detrimental to his health."

Why the subject of communication should be so controversial as to risk Swamiji's health is indicative of how out of kilter the energy in the room had become. The next thing I knew Swamiji was once again berating me publicly for my many faults, but I couldn't keep track of the details because something out of a science fiction story or an epic Himalayan yogi account began to happen.

Perfectly synchronized with the beginning of Swamiji's words a force field of protection projected outward from my spine, extending beyond my physical body about one foot in all directions. The intensity of the moment caused time to stretch and I was able to observe in detail the incredible nature of what was taking place. With the expansion of the force field I was infused with peace, calmness and bliss. Needless to say, my attention was completely captured by this unbelievable – except that I believed it because I was experiencing it – experience of spiritual blessing. I could hear Swamiji's words but I felt no discomfort from them. In fact, paradoxically, I realized that the longer he went on the more time I would have to enjoy this amazing turn of events.

Just as Swamiji stopped speaking the protecting aura dissipated, leaving me with an intense afterglow of joyful Divine Presence. I spontaneously sat without speaking, absorbed inwardly while the meeting ended. As soon as the group stood to leave I tried to exit without interacting with others. A couple of people asked me if I was okay and another thanked me for speaking up, but I didn't want to lose my awareness of this inner blessing in conversation so I escaped as quickly as I could to sit in meditation and savor my good fortune.

Such is the reversal of the yogi's view of life than the worldly person's, instead of being upset with Swamiji for misinterpreting my motives, I was thankful to the depths of my soul for one of the greatest experiences of my life. It isn't often that we get such dramatic confirmation that our motives are pure and that the Universe has seen and approves.

I don't believe this experience swelled my head – according to Swamiji it was already swollen!, but it did give me reassurance that God is always present and that I should trust that Truth even when I make mistakes. Additionally, it gave me strength to reach past misunderstandings and to accept the life journey that I was given even if it wasn't always comfortable.

Not long after the meeting I received this letter written January 31, 1995 from Swamiji.

> Dear Vijay:
>
> As you know, I have often been not only your supporter at Ananda, but, on many occasions, your sole supporter. I was reflecting on the time, some twenty three years ago, when you came up for acceptance at Ananda. At that time, though I saw much good in you, I didn't feel you belonged here and was about to give my reasons for not accepting you. Just then, seeing a pleading look in Mukti's eyes, I got the picture and for her sake remained silent.
>
> Since we'd accepted you, I decided to do my best to help the goodness in you to come out. And, in fact, I think Ananda has always been an important, even a wonderful, experience for you. Not always easy. Sometimes not wholly pleasant!

Still, I can't imagine you having spent these more-than-twenty years in some other setting. I believe, also, that my friendship for you has been reciprocated.

In this time you have shown yourself not a team player, but what of it? To live in a community *requires* teamwork, of course, but to be a team player is not in any way, in itself, a criterion of spiritual fitness. Being a member of Ananda hasn't been natural for you, but you've been sincere in your spiritual search and service. To me, this is what matters most.

You've been rebellious, egotistical, often angry, unwilling to cooperate with others or even to see their points of view. I've tried again and again to find a niche for you, only to have *you* veto my efforts – most recently with Dave and the video work. What can I do? I can't think what, except to let you decide when and in what way you want to cooperate.

But I have seen you grow more negative, more insensitive, more certain of your rightness over other people's. Vijay, I don't want to see you go the way of so many who have sacrificed attunement for self-will. You are dear to me, and I have invested many years in trying to draw out the potential I see in you.

I must tell you, though, that last Saturday I felt you had betrayed our friendship, I think you

> left with the same chip on your shoulder as that with which you'd entered. For my part, I felt betrayed. You do not seem to realize what you have received here at Ananda. If you do not change, Divine Mother will take you away. And what will become of you then? My heart grieves to think of it.
>
> In Master's Love, Swami

I will share three of my many observations about this letter. The first is that for some reason Swamiji's perception of me was incomplete, his observations contained items that are clearly true but also a number of conclusions that are easily proven factually not correct. Secondarily, the tone of his letter is not so much accusatory, but of hurt based on deeply caring. Lastly, most importantly, he knows that *I am his friend,* and he said, *"You are dear to me."* While I am sorry to be a cause of distress, I don't mind getting into a little trouble to hear those words.

It took about a month to arrange a private meeting between me and Swamiji. This was facilitated by Gurudas (Servant of the Guru) who was at the time in charge of Crystal Clarity Publishers and in regular contact with Swamiji. Through our mutual interest in the martial arts we began to talk and he saw the value that could come from a private meeting. I am extremely thankful that he lobbied on my behalf and was successful.

We met in Swamiji's office at the Crystal Hermitage. On my arrival he was just finishing up something on his computer so I sat down and had a little time to gather myself. In spite of the potential tension of the situation, I felt completely calm. I loved being near Swamiji and rested in that feeling until he was ready to talk.

Swamiji initiated the conversation by taking up where he left off at the Ministers meeting. His list of my shortcomings was quite extensive. There was no protecting force field, but I didn't feel reactive, I just listened without comment until he was done. Part of my challenge in that moment was that in the past Swamiji had encouraged me to not be defensive. So I really didn't want to defend myself. Also, we had been trained not to share our spiritual experiences. Had I told him about my experience it might have changed my whole future at Ananda, but I didn't, I kept it to myself.

I have often wondered if it was a failure on my part, as a friend, that I didn't tell him. Even worse was the thought that I might hurt his feelings in some way by sharing. It was a quandary that I eventually had to put on a metaphorical shelf as unsolvable.

When it was my turn to talk I explained that I had been unavoidably late and had not heard Dr. Peter's concerns about his health. Upon arrival I saw him rosy-cheeked and energetic so there was no sign that I should be concerned. With my explanation Swamiji's demeanor shifted immediately to acceptance and relief. His feeling of betrayal instantly dissolved. Swamiji then did the completely unexpected, which was classic Swamiji, he apologized to me with clear remorse and humility for his misunderstanding.

We then moved on, but without any tension, to his belief that I didn't get along with others in the video department. It was a complete mystery to me as to where this idea had come from, I informed him that it simply wasn't true. His face lit up with a smile and he said, "I am so glad to hear that!" He asked me to double check with the Dave and Linda (Later named Maitri – not the Maitri that wrote *Keep Calling Him*) to confirm they had no hard feelings. (Days later after doing so I reported to Swamiji that there were no conflicts. He smiled, happy that it was confirmed true.)

Once we had cleared the air our conversation moved on to heartfelt communication between old friends. I explained a little more clearly my concerns about communication. Swamiji brought me up to date on his latest activities. We moved from his office to his private apartment. Time alone with Swamiji was not a common occurrence, once again something special was happening because something unpleasant had taken place. We sat together on the couch and conversed, I was very happy.

Just before leaving it occurred to me that there was uncertainty in the community about how things stood between us, so I brought up the subject. He immediately responded by saying, "Don't worry, I will take care of it."

The very next day the following letter appeared in every mailbox at the village.

February 28, 1995

Dear Ones:

For those of you who have been concerned over the controversy between me and Vijay at the minsters meeting last January, I want to say that it has ended in harmony. I had a nice talk with him yesterday. He had come to that January meeting late, and hadn't heard all the discussion about my health. He therefore didn't realize that I'd already extended myself well beyond my strength in giving a long discourse to the group. My distress with him lay in the thought that he, as a friend, would be so determined to air his ideas as to be indifferent to my health. That was something I wouldn't have expected anyone to do. Anyway, he explained that he hadn't realized, and was surprised to learn, that I wasn't well since I *looked* so well. (In fact, now that all my blood is pumping in the right direction instead of a third of it pumping backward, I do look rather like the applecheeked housekeeper in P.G. Wodehouse's "Honeysuckle Cottage.")

I apologized to Vijay for my misunderstanding. He has always been very dear to me. I'm relieved therefore, that this problem has been resolved – as problems of this sort ought to be – by simply evaporating.

As for the problem of communication in the community, which he raised at the meeting, I agree with him. Jyotish and I have been discussing how that communication might be improved.

In Master's Love,
Swami

When I read Swamiji's letter for the first time I was appreciative of the public apology, not many leaders would be willing to do so, but what I cherish is the *He has always been very dear to me*. Yes, Swamiji definitely took care of it!

The issue of communication did not get solved right away, in fact, it erupted instead. One day there was a new letter in every mailbox, it wasn't from Swamiji, it was from an anonymous author who wrote against Swamiji, urging Ananda members to revolt. This invasion was followed by a number of signed letters by members in support of Swamiji and the Ananda way of life. It ended up having the reverse effect that the original author intended. Instead of weakening the community it strengthened our resolve. It also served as a spontaneous release valve that helped outer circle members to let off steam.

Eventually, small satsangs and teas were held around the community in which members could participate in dialogue. This led to *increased understanding* and helped to *dissolve uncertainties*.

Even though I didn't yet have my first book in print, I decided to start my second book and have another writing seclusion, which I would do at my Frog Pond cabin. While working on the new book, in which I made good progress but did not complete during seclusion, I had another special spiritual experience.

During seclusion I was in the practice of eating less and meditating more. This time, along with keeping silence I would try to meditate six hours a day along with writing whatever came through me.

About three weeks into the seclusion during my evening meditation I was swept up into what I can only describe as an elevated state. I felt the energy in my spine flowing up to the spiritual eye with strong, but not overwhelming, waves of peace/bliss. In the past, special experiences would last a few minutes and then withdraw, this time it persisted. In fact, it lasted so long that I decided to finish my meditation, even though I expected the experience to end when I stood up. To my surprise the uplifting energy flow didn't stop. I prepared for bed and lay down. Previously I sometimes had trouble getting to sleep during seclusion because of a generally increased energy flow. I fell asleep with no problem, once again thinking that the experience would end, and woke up rested and still elevated, it was wonderful.

I sat again to meditate and everything was blissful. After some time I heard a noise under the sink on the other side of the cabin. Apparently a rat had gotten in and was rummaging around. I tried to ignore it. I was convinced that if I got up to chase the rat I would lose my elevated state. I continued trying to ignore the rat but it was like being told not to think about monkeys, you immediately can think of nothing else.

In spite of my concern about losing the elevated state of consciousness I felt compelled to remove the rat, so eventually I got up and tried but failed to find the rat. When I returned to my meditation seat I was thrilled to realize that I was still elevated, so I continued to enjoy the upward flow of energy. For a while all was quiet, but eventually the rat couldn't stop banging around and I once again felt compelled to get up. Again I failed, returned to meditation, and smiled...I was still elevated! It was by far the longest lasting continuous experience of my meditation career thus far.

The third time the rat disturbed me I thought twice about getting up. I knew I had been pushing my luck. The fact that the experience had not stopped even with two rat hunts was just as amazing as the experience itself. But once again I felt compelled to get up. This time I didn't chase the rat, I just opened the cabin door even though it was cold outside and hoped that it would exit on its own. By the time I returned to my seat the state of elevation had withdrawn. An interesting feature of blessing experiences is that they leave an afterglow of well-being and thankfulness. So I didn't feel bad, I just wasn't floating in the same way.

My small home at Frog Pond was nearing the end of its life. It was on the list of old non-code dwellings to be demolished. One day I came to know that a small three room cabin on five acres next to Ananda was for sale by a man who had lived at Ananda in the past. I went to see the property and discovered that he was willing to sell it with a low down payment and owner financing. I couldn't have qualified for a bank loan, but I was able to borrow the down payment from earthly family and with his no credit check financing I was able move in with minimal out of pocket expense. So suddenly I was a land baron!

The *new to me* property gave my *do it yourself* tendency ample scope. I fixed leaky windows, tiled the rough concrete entrance, installed a large tub in the bathroom and upgraded the kitchen. Sabari and Kai visited regularly and life proceeded on down the road. Along with video work I was occasionally teaching Tae Kwon Do classes that had been started by other students of Master Lee in Auburn and Nevada City. I had passed my test for second degree black belt in 1992 and often visited martial arts training centers when I traveled to various cities for CPDA jobs.

During these years, along with baseball, soccer and Sabari's continued dancing, we took up skiing and then snowboarding. We started at Donner Ski Ranch and eventually visited most of the ski resorts in the Lake Tahoe area including Squaw Valley (since renamed Palisades Tahoe).

It was on the day that I rented a snowboard to try it out for the first time that I practiced something I learned from Swamiji. Kai and Sabari were on ski's and I was riding the snowboard rental. We were having a great day, the snow was good and my surfing skills were translating to snowboarding at a good rate, my interest in snowboarding was rapidly increasing.

In the afternoon we decided to take a break and during our time in the lodge my rental snowboard was stolen. It ended up that the staff at the lodge knew there was a thief on site and they decided to stake out the likely area. They actually saw the thief take my snowboard but failed to catch him. They would take no responsibility for my loss.

It would have been easy to let the day turn into a downer, being upset I could have threatened to sue the resort. But I had seen over the years how Swamiji met unexpected problems with a positive attitude, he would say, "If anything or anyone distresses you, think how you'll feel a week – a month – a year later. If you can imagine yourself being happy and peaceful then, why waste all that time? Be happy and peaceful now."

I couldn't really afford to pay for the lost rental board, but I was now so enthusiastic about snowboarding that I not only paid for the stolen board, but I bought a new one to use in the future. Seeing me deal with the situation with a good attitude was the kind of example that Kai and Sabari grew up with, not only at home, but in the school and throughout the community. Okay, I didn't *always* react so well, but I did improve every year!

One of the things that I was learning is that we don't need to be perfect to experience Divine blessings. We need to be persistent, sincere and occasionally moderately fanatical in seclusion. The tools of energization and meditation that Yogananda taught are not complicated, they just need to be practiced correctly and with the right attitude. Swamiji said, "I never expect anything when I sit down to meditate." This is nishkam karma, action without the desire for the fruits of your actions. But he also said that we should expect the best, we don't want to be so detached that we meditate without joyful expectation. His advice to *meet luck half way* is valid for both inward and outward goals.

The pressure of the lawsuits and the evolution of Ananda's ministry were strangely intertwined. To SRF's dismay, the harder they attacked us the stronger we became. As a part of the growing commitment to a householder community four couples were assigned to giving services at the Expanding Light and single Ministers were only scheduled for the chapel at the Crystal Hermitage. This caused there to be a large gap between sharing opportunities. Over time I became frustrated by this lack and prayed a number of times as to whether I should give up being a lightbearer/minister.

The good news about prayer is that God *can't not hear* our prayers. The less good news is that God doesn't always respond in the time and way that we would prefer. During this period where I prayed about the ministry, each time I prayed I got a call within a day or two about filling in for a minister on Sunday. This happened three times over a period of about six months. So I was fairly convinced that I should stick with it, but I also felt the urge to be more active.

When I traveled to different locations for the CPDA I began to give satsangs when that city had an Ananda meditation group. A number of the devotees that I met during those satsangs became life members of Ananda. I am not saying that I was the deciding factor in those cases, just that I felt blessed to support that possibility.

In the fall of 1995 I self-published my first book *Doorway to a New Lifetime: Childbirth from a Spiritual View*. I gave a copy to Swamiji and shared it with a couple of Ananda members. One said, "It was surprisingly good." I wasn't sure if that meant it was good or they were surprised that it was good: maybe both? The other person questioned my qualifications to write on the subject. Mixed reviews!

This is also the year that Sabari had an acute case of appendicitis. The surgery lasted longer than originally predicted. We spent some hours in the hospital uncertain about the outcome. When she first became sick we took her to the doctor and I suggested that she might have a flu bug that was making its rounds at school. But when it persisted, blood was drawn and showed a very elevated white blood cell count, indicating an infection. We rushed her to the hospital, it was quite serious, her appendix had burst. I had unintentionally delayed her treatment with my suggestion of the flu. Fortunately she came through it with flying colors and healed fully in good time.

It was also around this time that I wrote a song with Sabari. I jokingly challenged Sabari to help me write a song, but it turned into something very sweet. It was a bedtime lullaby.

In the Night by Sabari and Vijay Girard

(Chorus)
In the night
Inner light
It surrounds you and lifts you
To Her arms of infinite peace.
All your dreams
All your hopes
They are with you in heaven
You are free in the ocean of love.

(Verse)
There are Angels
All around you
Throwing petals of blessings
They protect you from all worldly harm.
Now your soul

It can soar
And expand into Spirit
To explore your true inner home.

(Chorus)

May your sleep
Be as sweet
As the flowers of springtime
May you soar on currents of joy
And I pray
When you wake
You will smile from sweet dreams
Which will carry you into your day.

(Chorus)

As the years went by, it became clear that living at the village had been wonderful for Kai and Sabari. They matured into caring and capable young adults. They didn't take on the rituals or daily practices of our spiritual style, but they did respect them, absorbing the values that we not only preached but lived, they were able to reach past our imperfections and embrace our sincerity. We never felt that we should impose our beliefs on them, but encouraged them to experience as much of it as they comfortably could and let them make their own decisions about what to do with those experiences. Since the day they were born one of my greatest joys in this life has been to spend time with them, just the way they are, the selves they choose to be.

While I wasn't kicked out of the community after that dramatic minister's meeting, Swamiji's prediction that Divine Mother might remove me from life at the village began to manifest in a way that took me some time to recognize as Her hand. As you will come to know, the twists and turns continued in unexpected ways.

Chapter 17

Where You Lead I Will Follow

"He is your Polestar on the dark seas of mortal existence. Seek His guidance." –Paramhansa Yogananda

In nature, the changing of the seasons happens every year, and even though every year those changes are unique to that year, we recognize those changes and flow comfortably from season to season. Every life has seasons, the seasons of individual lives are driven by personal karma synchronized with larger karmic flows which are not always easy to recognize.

During 1996 I experienced another gradual changing of the seasons in my own life that I was very slow to fully grasp. In May, a junior high graduation ceremony was held in the Expanding Light Temple. Kai and Sabari were completing their education in the Ananda school system. They decided to travel different educational paths; Sabari going to public high school in Nevada City and Kai to a private high school in Colorado Springs, Colorado. When school started in the fall I saw much less of Sabari, and Kai only on school vacations. I experienced a kind of empty nest syndrome, except I wasn't unhappy, I just began to realize that I was no longer needed in the same way, I could consider new options.

My ministry in the village continued to shrink and also my economy. I began to survive financially only from my trips for CPDA and gradually my credit card debt blossomed. I decided to start looking for a job in other fields than video production. In the past when I had tried to get a job the first place I went hired me, but now I was turned down by everyone; all the doors were closed. I finally got the message when I was one day turned down for a job delivering pizza! When the manager turned me down, I asked him, "You are turning me down for a pizza delivery job?" He responded with a confident, "Yes!" In that moment it all came to me, Divine Mother was having fun. I didn't mean to be rude, but I couldn't help laughing out loud on my way out.

I now knew that I would be moving away from the village to have a new adventure, I just didn't know where I would go. I was not rejecting life at Ananda, I wasn't upset with anyone, disappointed that I wasn't included in a more dynamic way, yes, but in my mind and heart it would not be an act of separation, it would be an extension of my vow to live for God and serve Master's work.

Once again I was experiencing how something uncomfortable was leading to new potentials that I wouldn't explore without that discomfort. I had served away from the village in the past so I had no fear of moving forward. Kai and Sabari had grown up in the village, for that I was immensely thankful. People make a mistake when they turn away from the good of relationships that evolve in unpreferred directions. I would not make that mistake.

Along with this new clarity of change came unpleasant calls from bill collectors. I explained to them that I would send money when I could, but if they harassed me I would be forced to seek bankruptcy protection. Strangely, they encouraged me to file for bankruptcy, so I did. I had misgivings about the rightness of doing so, but gradually accepted that I was following the laws of man which accounted for the possibility of this happening to people and provided a solution.

When considering where I might go I sought inner guidance. Not receiving any clear sign from the heavens I came up with Boulder, Colorado, as a good possibility. It didn't seem like a good idea to arrive at the onset of winter so I spent the Christmas season at the village, attending the eight hour meditation and all of the other Christmas activities.

After Master's birthday on January 5th it occurred to me that I should try once again to get a job to carry me over until spring, at which time I would move to Colorado. I went to the nearby Mother Truckers store to get a copy of the local newspaper so I could look through the classified ads at job opportunities, only to find that they were sold out of copies. I then traveled farther to North San Juan, arriving at the gas station/mini mart only to discover they too were out of newspapers. I thought it was strange that my attempt to seek employment was once again being blocked. That night I was to discover why.

When my land line telephone rang that evening I was surprised by the voice on the other end of the line; it was my father. He was calling to offer me a job helping him sell undeveloped land in Arizona to people in Las Vegas. My first response was to break out laughing. When I stopped laughing, which took some time, I said to him, Dad, the last time I worked for you, you fired me twice the first day!"

I hadn't been in touch with my father for months. He knew nothing of my financial challenges or my decision to make changes in my life. We had never gotten along well and the whole idea was absurd. As our conversation developed my father turned on his salesman charm, which had made him very successful over the years. As he talked I began to wonder if this was a sign to move forward even if it was temporary.

Swamiji had explained to us that sometimes when the energy of a situation gets stuck you just need to do something, anything – under the guidance of common sense – to get the energy moving. Once the energy starts to flow you can make adjustments as new understanding presents itself. My forward momentum had definitely been stuck, the timing of my father's call was serendipitous. I had decided to look for a job in the morning and a job offer called me that night. That doesn't happen every day.

I told him that if I were to consider it he would have to sign a minimum six months contract. I could not afford to move and be concerned everyday about being fired. He said, "Send me whatever you want, I will sign it." Taking a few days to consider the possibilities I sought confirmation in meditation. It came to mind that when I had previously been in Las Vegas I felt that it had potential for outreach. People came there from all over the world. Not all of them were there to attend wild parties, get drunk and gamble. If it didn't work out I could always move on. So I sent the contract to my father with an addition: You can not yell at me!

At first I assumed that I would need to stop working for the CPDA, but then it occurred to me that I could continue with them if I was able to keep the equipment with me in Las Vegas, so I wouldn't have to pick it up at their office in Sacramento. They agreed, so now my monthly income would be sufficient for my needs, it was a big relief.

Suddenly the energy was flowing and everything fell into place. I easily rented out my cabin home, loaded my piano trailer with all my worldly goods, picked up the video equipment at CPDA and hit the road, driving over Donner Pass in the Sierras and heading south down most of the length of Nevada.

Before leaving the village I wrote the following letter to the community:

To my Spiritual Family, 1/21/97

> I am writing to you all because I am making changes in my life and would prefer that you heard about them directly from me rather than the rumor mill. Ordinarily I wouldn't publish the going on's in my life, I am by nature a private person, but in this instance I feel that it would be

better, and possibly helpful to others, if I share my thoughts and new directions.

The "What's going on?" is that I am moving. On Feb. 1st I will be moving to Henderson, Nevada, which is just south of Las Vegas. The why are you moving — and even more incredible, why there? — is what I want to share with you.

In recent years I have felt that I was supposed to be more involved with the ministry. It has been a frustrating time because I haven't been able to find a niche in which to apply myself. As the result of finding doors closed to me I have often doubted that I am supposed to serve in this way. Yet, whenever I have prayed for a sign concerning the correctness of my serving as a minister, definite positive responses have been the result.

One time after a particularly difficult period I told Master that I would give up any thought of serving as a minister unless I got a definite sign to the contrary. During the following month I found myself — through a series of unexpected events that I in no way controlled — giving Sunday Service 3 times! And each time I felt a wonderful blessing as a result. So... what to do?

The truth is that for a long time I have felt that I was supposed to go out and serve somewhere, but there are two things that have held me back. The first and easiest to understand is my children. I have wanted to be here for them. I have been savoring my time with them because I know that it is limited. They grow up so quickly!

The second thing that I have had more difficulty digesting is my desire to be a part of the "mainstream" Ananda Ministry. The problem is that apparently, I am not a "mainstream" type of person. It isn't that I consciously try to be different, but my inner sense of truth doesn't allow me to follow the crowd, unless I feel that the crowd is right. So how can I be loyal to my "mainstream" family — which I really want to be a part of — and also be loyal to the truth of who I am?

Just before Christmas I was able to take a 3 week seclusion. Along with writing about half of a new book called, *The Way of the Positive Flow,* I was seeking a resolution to these conflicting energies. I was praying that Divine Mother would give me a sign and a feeling of peace about my future. And in Her own sweet way, She did.

It was like trying to solve a mystery and seeing all of the pieces, but not quite being able to see how they fit together. Then, when I got far enough inside during my seclusion, suddenly it all came into focus. It made sense. And even though it isn't the way I would have necessarily preferred it, it was beautiful. It became very clear to me that it is time to move forward with my life. I can no longer cling to the past — whether it be my children, or my golden days of Ananda past.

So suddenly I found myself free to go anywhere and do anything! Wow! After opening myself up to going anywhere, my initial pull was towards moving to the northeastern part of Colorado. It was my intention to get a part time job until spring or summer, and then move. A few days after Christmas I went to buy *The Union* newspaper to start looking for a job. When I found both Mother Truckers and Tom's in N. San Juan out of copies, I thought that was a little strange, but decided I would get one the next day. That night my father called and asked if I would come help him with his land sales business in Nevada.

I had to laugh when my Dad asked me to come work for him. The last time I tried to work for him he fired me twice the first day! But I tried to open myself to what was right, and as my father spoke to me I felt a very different energy coming from the situation than I had in the past. I also felt that it was time for me to push forward, and that even if the short term directions weren't optimal, getting the energy going forward would give me momentum towards an ultimate destination. Besides, there are devotees everywhere, why not serve those in Nevada?

Of course, since my father's office is in Las Vegas my first thought was that I was asking for nothing but trouble. But it ends up that I will be able to live about 12 or 15 miles south of Las Vegas, in Henderson, which feels much different than Las Vegas. And along with that, the job that I will be doing will give me the time and financial flexibility to give a realistic amount of energy towards developing a ministry.

Most importantly, I feel that God is guiding me in this direction and that no matter whether I succeed or fail outwardly, as long as I feel that inner connection strong and vital, that will be the indication of my success.

Some people may wonder if this represents a breaking off of my relationship with Ananda. I certainly hope not. In fact, I don't think that it is possible for me to be disconnected from Ananda. The very fiber of my life has been transformed through my association with Swamiji and the rest of you.

Besides, family is a state of mind, not a place. But just as a child grows up and leaves the home of it's parents, so I feel that it is time for me to reach out in whatever way my inner inspiration takes me.

It is true that I have not asked anyone's permission nor discussed this new direction with anyone until I felt guided to make these changes.

It is also true that I feel the need to express our Ananda Traditions in ways that feel comfortable to me: that may be different than that which feels comfortable to others. I hope that my experiments in serving Master will provide a harmonious addition to what is already available and not be seen as a "putting down" or "disconnecting from" the preferences of others. I consider myself an Ananda Minister and will, as I have been inspired through Swamiji for these many years, do my best to represent Master.

If you find yourself wandering aimlessly through southern Nevada, feel free to contact me! The village office will know my phone number and address.

I wish the best for all of you and trust that the future will bring us more opportunities to share the blessings of God and Gurus.

In Friendship Divine, Vijay

I experienced a surge of optimism as I drove towards the unknown. I had always been comfortable with going to new places and starting fresh. Numerous times in my life one door had closed and another opened. This might seem like a cliche, but it is not to people who have experienced and observed its truth.

I rented an apartment in Green Valley, just east and a little south of the airport. Before the end of the month I was settled in and on the job. As an officer of the corporation I could legally sell real estate without a real estate license. The property was about a two hours drive from Henderson, across the Hoover Dam, over the border into the northwest corner of Arizona....lots of driving!

There were two areas of property, one with sloping hillsides and a distant but beautiful view of Lake Mead, and the other with very flat square parcels, all pristine undeveloped desert spaciousness. The customers were from the general Las Vegas area. The thing that really sold the land was the financing, 5 acres for $75 per month for 10 years. No money down, just make your first payment and you can start using the land. My father had sold hundreds of parcels with an about 80% closing rate. The challenge was to get customers into the car to drive them out there. If a person appreciated desert landscape the property sold itself.

I don't remember a single time in my life that my father ever praised me. Until one day he almost did. We were taking a customer to the land and I was driving. It was decided that we should take a shortcut down a small dirt road that I had never driven before. It was clearly a road that had not been used for a long time and was basically a continuous series of potholes. In the early years of Ananda the roads were just like this "short cut". So I felt completely comfortable.

I had always enjoyed the challenge of driving intuitively on dirt roads, it is much more interesting than pavement. Dodging the holes, braking and accelerating in a flow, moving as quickly as possible without anyone hitting their head on the roof of the car. It was fun! After our drive that day my father said as a flat statement with no emphasis of tone, "You drove that road as if you knew it by heart." In my mind I thought, "Was that a compliment?" I took it as such.

Unfortunately his appreciation of my driving skills didn't carry over to any other part of life. After five months on the job I was in his office one day and something I said or did set him off. He just couldn't stand my style, my approach to life, he called me up on the carpet, got in my face, and yelled at me with vigor.

As he berated me I observed my reaction. I was pleased that I was calm. Growing up I had been afraid of him. Now I could see him as a soul caught in the current limitations of his life's journey. It was disappointing that we couldn't be more compatible, but I accepted that it was what it was. The next day he informed me that I was fired and he sent me a check for my final month of the six month contract. We had made it for five months, amazing!

During those first five months I began to go through a process of midlife evaluation. I was now forty-six years old. I had been a disciple of Paramhansa Yogananda for twenty-eight years and had been associated with Ananda for twenty-five of those years. Without the preconceptions or pressures of the opinions of others, or the responsibilities of parenthood, who was I and what did I want to do with the rest of my life?

I told myself to be completely honest with myself, I consciously released my own preconceptions of self to allow whatever was true to be true. I decided to get fit, so I joined a fitness club and attended aerobics classes. I also joined a Tae Kwon Do training center and went regularly. Within three months my body was brought into good order and I felt stronger than I had in years. I also participated in a coed recreational volleyball league.

I heard about the volleyball league from the leader of the aerobics class that I attended. When she told me about it I hesitated, not sure how I felt about making a commitment to the team. Swamiji had said I was not a team player, I didn't think he was referring to volleyball. But it was true, I didn't fit in. I was not adept at making meaningless small talk, I didn't swear, and I didn't really care if we won, I just wanted to try my best, get exercise and have fun. During one game my serve was having a much better than average day. I even served a few aces. But when I missed a serve the team acted like I had shot them in the back. I couldn't help thinking that these adults could learn some useful lessons from Sabari's baseball team.

My aerobics instructor started offering Kardio Kickboxing classes. I attended because kicking and punching appeals to me. She noticed that I had some skills in this department and invited me to co-lead a session. It went well and she asked me if I would be interested in co-leading on a regular basis, I gave it some thought but decided that it wasn't a direction that appealed to me.

There is an SRF meditation group in Las Vegas and I occasionally attended their programs. I couldn't go regularly because, while I always felt touched by Spirit when I went, it also broke my heart. I knew too much of what was going on behind the scenes in SRF. I could feel the restrictions of officialdom in the chanting and the readings. It was not bad, it was good, but there was no compelling transmission of Spirit in that place and moment. It was an institutional diminution of Master's offering. Had I never experienced Swamiji's incredibly dynamic living expression of Spirit I wouldn't know what I was missing, but I had and I did.

I started searching for a new job, the first place I went hired me: the doors were once again open. My new boss, Dave H. was operating a small production support company on his own, he needed help. He provided whatever you might need for putting on a show, event or trade show booth. He was a brilliant theatrical lighting designer and all around theatrical production expert. While attending high school in Las Vegas he had become involved in the Local Stagehands Union and even though he was younger than me he was already a twenty plus year member. He had extensive connections all over town and I was soon introduced to some of the network of people who worked behind the scenes of the shows and events in Las Vegas.

As his employee I was able to work on both union and non-union jobs. Dave would make connections and give me the details, I would then write up proposals and contracts. Once we got a job I would go with Dave to the site and do whatever needed to be done. I was being paid to learn skills far beyond those that I already possessed. The diversity of Dave's areas of interest allowed me to quickly pick up a wide variety of stagehand skills.

After about six months Dave decided that he wasn't cut out for having an office so he closed up and helped me get signed up in the stagehands union. Once that happened I was then authorized to go out on jobs in the following categories: Camera Operator (fixed and hand-held), AV Tech, and Tape

Operator. The union is basically a temporary employment agency. They get requests for workers with specific capabilities. The dispatcher then calls down their list of members who have those skills until the job is filled with available people. Once you finish a job you call back in to say you are available again. This rotation can be circumvented if you are specifically requested by the people putting on the show/event, which they would do because you have proven that you can do the job well.

My first handheld camera job came through a friend of Dave's who managed one of the ballrooms at the Flamingo Hotel. They were putting on a summer series of *Oldies but Goodies* concerts. The first artist in the series was Brenda Lee. I was stationed in the downstage right corner of the stage, completely unfamiliar with the broadcast quality equipment I was using, but of course acting like I knew what I was doing.

There were also two fixed camera operators on the floor in front of the stage. We were doing what is call *Image Magnification* (I-Mag), along with being recorded to tape, our camera shots would be live switched to large screens on the sides of the stage. I was informed through the headset that Brenda Lee would be coming out through a curtain from backstage and that my camera would open the show. Before I could set up my shot all of the lights went out. I wasn't exactly sure where the curtain opening was and was definitely unsure about my focus. Somehow, when the spotlight appeared and she stepped forward through the parting curtains, I had the shot and the show went on without a hitch.

I knew I had done okay because I was requested for the rest of that concert series. It didn't quite hit me that I was now a cameraman in Las Vegas until I found myself onstage with Kenny Rodgers. Although his career was declining at that time, he was still popular and one of the all time greats of country music. It made me laugh inside, God through my karma was guiding my life to unexpected places.

My trips to California for CPDA continued and my jobs through the stagehand union were increasing, plus the rental money from my house next to Ananda continued, so my personal economy had recovered from the previous hard times. My year of willingness to honestly evaluate myself had led me right back to who I was before moving to Las Vegas, I was a disciple dedicated to Master and Ananda. So I began to think about how I might begin outreach locally.

In December of 1997 my father unexpectedly passed. He was sitting at home watching TV and he had a heart attack, gone in just a few minutes. Consistent with his limited social skills, except as a salesman, he specifically requested in his will that we not hold any kind of service on his behalf. So there was never any opportunity for group grief or celebration...according to the preference of those who knew him. I found out a few years later that he had helped Rosie, the owner of a shop/restaurant just over the border in Arizona, and her son financially. I also had seen him get down on the floor and play with his Chihuahua dogs, so I new he had heart, he just couldn't sync that with his kids or people in general.

Some months after his passing I had a dream. In the dream my father came to me and apologized, which I accepted. After waking up I reflected on the dream and observed that it was clearly my father, but the body I saw was of a small dark skinned boy. Since my father had often exhibited prejudice against people of color I thought it was karmicly correct.

Through my stepmother, Mary, my siblings and I received a substantial inheritance. It included some cash and also the land in Arizona. One of the financial wisdoms that I had learned by that time in my life is: if you find yourself with a windfall, don't piddle it away, do something big with it. So in the spring of 1998 I purchased a house. The story of how that purchase came about is one of quintessential Universal response.

With the idea of spiritual outreach in mind I looked at a map of Las Vegas and drew a large circle where the two main traffic arteries meet. My criteria was that the dwelling be in the circle, suitable for guests with sufficient parking, I should be able to afford it, and: Oh please, if possible, let there be a pool!

One day I was driving and I saw a stand alone storefront that looked like it would make a perfect center. I was pretty sure it would be too expensive, but I couldn't resist calling the number on the for sale sign just to find out the details; market research. The woman who answered the phone gave me the details – yes it was out of my price range – and I tried to get off the phone, but as the woman spoke I began to appreciate her saleswoman technique. She was really good. In fact she was so good that I decided that she had earned my story. So I told her about the circle I had drawn on the map.

Within a week she took me to see a four bedroom, two car garage, home of over 2200 sq. ft. on ¾ of an acre – in the circle – and it had a pool! It hadn't even been put on the multiple listings yet. It was a fixer upper, so it was in my price range. I bought it with deep gratitude!

Before moving in I ripped out all of the carpet, applied new texture to the walls, and painted the walls and ceilings. The new carpet was thick for comfortable yoga postures. After moving in I remodeled the garage like we did in Sacramento, except I added a soundproof control room for recording and a separate entrance so visitors could go directly into the temple through a book room without going through the house.

During my first year in the newly renovated house/center I had another unique experience. This time it wasn't in seclusion, it was something that gradually built up over time and I didn't realize it was happening until one day I realized it was happening. What I hadn't realized was happening is that I was experiencing an increase of inner well-being that was not connected to a specific meditation but to a shift in the average level of my consciousness. I can't explain the reason that it happened when it did, but it was remarkable.

I discovered that I was aware of life around me in a new way. Previously I viewed life in the city as unnatural and separate from nature, while seeing life outside urban environments as being more natural, and wilderness being fully natural. I now saw all of life as nature of different vibrations, but still all the same nature. The freeways were arteries of life force flowing through the body of the city, the way a river would flow through a plain or valley. The pollution in the air was like the dust that is kicked up by a large herd of bison, car exhaust is less pleasant than field dust, but still nature. Car horns and other sounds of man were as much a part of nature as the noises of birds in the trees. I was feeling a greater level of the unity with all life underneath its surface of diversity. The intensity of this greater awareness did lessen over time, but it didn't leave me completely.

Along with increased well-being and greater harmony with all life, I experienced a kind of permanent spiritual healing. Almost as far back as I can remember to this point in my life, I had lived with an internal feeling of angst; a feeling of inner unease that I could never quite put my finger on. It was like an old wound that you don't remember how it happened but it aches now and again, never quite healing fully. This anchor from my unremembered past had quietly fallen away and I was aware that an internal weight was gone, never to return. I felt lighter and freer.

While these changes in my consciousness didn't remove my personal preference for country living and life in spiritual community, they completely removed any resistance I might have had to city life. When I met people through the center and they heard that I had moved from Ananda to Las Vegas they were incredulous. They asked, "Why would you do that?" I didn't tell them that I no longer saw the differences that they saw in the same way. I was experiencing on deeper levels the reality that my life is driven by unseen forces and my responsibility is to harmonize with that flow and serve the light along the way.

Another aspect of my inner changes had to do with expectations, both my own for myself and the pressure I felt from fitting in at Ananda. The pressure that I lived with growing up was my reaction to the Judeo Christian values of the culture my parents grew up in and shared with my generation. I lived in a world that I never measured up to. I was always falling short of the expectations that others had for me. And I unknowingly took on that same attitude toward myself: I saw myself as not measuring up.

I was around eight or nine years old when I started inwardly fighting against the opinions of others in this regard, but I didn't fight against having this opinion of myself. My public defense of self which was often described by others as stubbornness gave the impression that I had a too high opinion of myself, but that wasn't what was going on inside of me. It wasn't that I thought I was the greatest thing since Swiss cheese, it was that I was trying to keep my head above water under the onslaught of parental and societal pressure to be other than just the way I was.

In the early years of Ananda there were fewer people and so there was room for greater diversity, Swamiji was open to helping almost anyone, everyone was a potential diamond in the rough. Over the years Ananda evolved, and even though it courageously resisted organizational restraints, they became necessary so that a greater good could be accomplished. Unfortunately for me – in terms of my personal preferences – I have never fit comfortably in restraints. For me *the truth of the moment has always stood first,* I believe this is certainly part of what Swamiji was referring to when he wrote that life at Ananda wasn't always comfortable for me.

In addition to organizational challenges are the pressures that many raja yogis put on themselves to achieve self-realization in this lifetime. As glorious as this goal is, over pressurizing ourselves with preconceived ideas about what a graduation lifetime should look like is not helpful to the goal itself. Positive motivation is excellent, but endless feelings of failure when unrealistic or simply preconceived goals are not achieved can be detrimental to a disciple's purpose.

As a part of my inner transformation I was able to shed many of the discomforts of the past, allowing me to make friends with myself. I had been touched in my heart with the awareness that God loves me – and all – just the way we are today. I don't mean that positive progress isn't needed for greater self-awareness, but that God's love isn't dependent on that progress. Our spiritual progress gives us more access to Divine awareness, not the other way around.

The experience of the awareness that Universal Love is real and that the substance of that love is who and what we truly are completely changes the perspective with which we see the world. As we grow spiritually this Truth becomes more and more the reality in which we live. I wasn't experiencing all of that Cosmic love, but the amount that I did experience was life transforming.

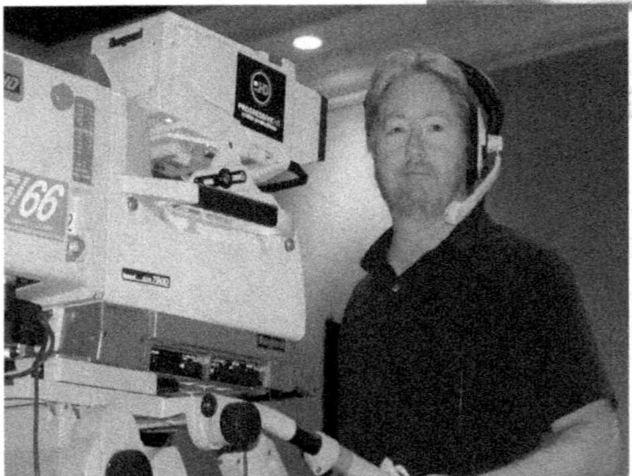

Chapter 18

Inspiration and Entertainment

"You have come to earth to entertain and to be entertained."
–Paramhansa Yogananda

I won't deny that my life in Las Vegas was entertaining – which only seems right since it is considered by many to be the entertainment capital of the world, but it was also – in spite of the preconceptions of many – filled with much inspiration, which reminds us that God is everywhere.

I never heard Swamiji express a lower opinion of a city than he did of Las Vegas, but I didn't really feel that I had chosen Las Vegas, just that the Universe had swung me that way. I figured: "If Mother Teresa can do Kolkata, I can do Las Vegas!"

For seven years I navigated the hallways of resort industrialism surrounded by the desert sands of the northeastern part of the Mohave desert. Away from the big hotels Las Vegas is a city like any other, people going about their lives in search of they don't know what. I took on a practice that I had observed in Swamiji. It is easy to think of ministry as official church programs, but what I had seen from Swamiji was that he was always on the job, paying attention in all circumstances for opportunities to see Truth underneath the surface of life and act in harmony with it.

Being a channel for the light is not just for special programs, but an everyday 24/7 way of living. When we recognize that our path through life is guided by Universal forces, we can anticipate that the opportunities to serve that are ours will present themselves and that we need to pay attention so that we don't miss them.

Serving the light through the stagehands union wasn't always easy. Unions were created because of adversarial attitudes between management and workers. Without those negative circumstances unions wouldn't be needed, so while they talk harmony, they don't really want it. There is also on many jobs an attitude of mediocrity – don't shine too bright because you will make others look bad. Most difficult for me was the *stay in your own lane* rule. At Ananda we all pitched in automatically, and happily, when we saw that we could help others.

In the union it was against the rules to help with jobs that were not specifically your responsibility. One day I was called out on a large job, there were so many workers that there was a union steward who's only job was to keep track of everyone and make sure the rules were being followed. When I arrived on site the steward took me aside and said, "Here is what I want you to do. Walk around acting like you are busy, but don't do anything."

On another job, I was there as a cameraman and warned beforehand that the hotel might try to get away with putting up a second camera without an operator, which was against the rules. So when they did just that I called the union office. After the call we discovered that the fellow who was hired to run the videotape recorder didn't know how to set it up properly. I jumped in to fix his mistake, but the program was delayed by a few minutes. I was blamed for the delay and banned from that hotel. The union failed completely to seek the truth and stand up for a member who had followed union policy. Another karmic debt paid!

One of the things I liked about union jobs was the variety of things we did in many different locations. Jobs were a minimum of four hours and the longest one I had was ten days. The people who crewed each job were constantly rotating so you would work with many different people. Over time you would meet up with people you had worked with before. Initially I was in spiritual stealth mode. I was Larry with almost no backstory.

Gradually I began to do what I call spiritual fishing. In conversation I would throw out the bait of a spiritual idea and see if I got any nibbles. Occasionally this would lead to meaningful conversations. This always took place when I was with one or two people during a break or at lunch. Except one time I relaxed my guard on headsets.

I was one of three camera operators, a director, switcher operator, tape operator, lighting director and sound director. There was an extended pause during a rehearsal and so people were making light conversation over the headsets. One of the camera guys said that he heard I had written a book and wanted to know what it was about.

Well, anyone who knows Ananda sharers knows that we can launch into a long explanation at a moments notice. My words were flying over the wires when I suddenly realized what was happening. I stopped midword and then said, "Too much information, sorry." There was some laughter and the moment passed.

One day I was on a long break in a big hotel and came upon a beautiful grand piano in a large empty hallway, so I sat down and played it for about twenty minutes. Just before I finished one of the union crew in the building walked by and dropped a twenty dollar bill on the piano and thanked me for playing. My first and last paid piano gig!

Kai spent two summers plus other shorter visits with me in Las Vegas. We – meaning I did most of the work – bought a classic fixer-upper 1965 Mustang and did a mechanical update, including removing the engine and having it rebuilt at a machine shop, new leaf springs – which meant I had to use a torch to burn out the bushings with lots of stinky smoke, and new shocks and tires all around. Once fixed, Kai drove it to his job as a lifeguard at *Wet and Wild* water park. We also drained the pool, acid washed it and gave it a fresh pool paint job. The pool was a lifesaver during the summer.

Sabari also spent time in Las Vegas. During one visit the three of us went indoor skydiving. It was amazing! During the winter we went snowboarding. On one visit Kai and Sabari helped me cut down a tree that was old and leaning towards the neighbors property. We did some preliminary cutting until we reached one large branch that was the most difficult and dangerous part of the process. Sabari came up with a plan to use a couple of ropes to guide the branch as it came down. It looked pretty iffy, but her plan worked perfectly, and it all came down safely.

One time we went to the Luxor hotel which is shaped like a pyramid. Some of the elevators move at an angle, which is weird. We went up to a higher floor to look out on the open interior and I got vertigo for the first time, that was also weird.

The big story at the Luxor was a ride that we decided to go on called *In Search of the Obelisk.* It was an IMAX 3D motion simulator. We stood in line for about 25 minutes. Several times the line moved forward and at each new stopping point there were fresh signs that warned riders about the dangers for pregnant women and people susceptible to motion sickness or heart attack. We laughed at how serious the warnings were.

When it was our turn we stepped into a huge room in which there was a massive metal platform on hydraulic cylinders with about 250 seats facing a screen that was 84 feet wide and 68 feet tall. As impressive as the seats and screen were we still weren't overly concerned. Even the seat belts didn't bother us. It was when the ride operator took the time to inform us all that if we felt the need, all we had to do was raise our arms above our heads and he would stop the ride so we could get off. At that point we began to doubt!

At the beginning of the ride the whole platform rose straight up into the air, the screen was so large you could see nothing else, and then we began to fly and do *loop de loops.* The whole platform rocked front to back and side to side. It was overwhelming. I had to close my eyes for about half the ride because it was just too much. The whole time I fought with maximum determination to not raise my hands.

When the ride was over we walked out without talking. I had literally broken out into a cold sweat, which I had never before experienced, and was a little wobbly on my feet. When we were away from the crowd we stopped to laugh for a long time. Then we all admitted that we had struggled to keep our arms from going up. We decided that they were serious about the warning signs!

Our outdoor adventures went to a whole new level when I bought a boat. It was an 18 foot 1976 Seaswirl tri-hull with an inboard/outboard motor. It had been stored in a garage for many years and looked almost new. I bought it at a great price and had it professionally checked out and tuned up. It had very low hours and ran perfectly. The house was less than 30 minutes from Lake Mead and soon we were on the water wakeboarding.

Sabari had a natural talent for driving the boat. Kai was the best at wakeboarding. I was fifty years old and doing my best. We had a lot of fun on the boat, but one day it almost sank.

On that fateful morning I backed the trailer into the water and we got the boat off with no problems. After parking I made my way to the dock, stepping into the boat I discovered a pool of water: The boat was sinking! I ran back to the car, backed up the trailer in a rush, and just barely got it under the boat before it was too low in the water. We discovered that I had forgotten to put in the plug for the drainage hole. Once we had drained the boat I put the plug in and we headed out on the lake; no damage done. Whew...disaster averted!

While people trickled through the center, just enough to keep me optimistic that it could improve at any time, I was much more productive in the writing department. During this time in Las Vegas I published five new books and wrote a sixth. The industry for printing books-on-demand was just taking off and it made book publishing affordable for authors. Advances in computers and software for cover design along with typesetting were also making it easier for do-it-yourself publishers. I was able to design all of the covers for my new books, do the typesetting and prepare files for e-book versions.

The books that I published during this time were:

Way of the Positive Flow

Positive Flow Parenting

Flowing in the Workplace: A Guide to Personal and Professional Success

The Adventures of Harry Fruitgarden

Book #1 ***What's it All About?***

Book #2 ***Who Would Have Guessed?***

All of these books are about how to apply yoga principles to everyday life. **The Adventures of Harry Fruitgarden** is a young adults series that follows the life of Harry Fruitgarden, a young philosopher, life explorer, who is living consciously and trying to improve his life. My publishing company is named after him: Fruitgarden Publishing.

Along with the advances in software for book publishing and video production, computers themselves were also making great progress. In order to update my system affordably I decided to build my own computer. I researched the subject online, purchased the parts at wholesale and when it was all plugged in and working, I smiled like a Cheshire cat. Once this was done I informed CPDA that I had new capabilities and could add graphics to their videos for a reasonable fee. So not only did I save money on the cost of the computer, but it also increased my income.

Over the years members of the Ananda spiritual family have experienced countless examples of God's hand in our everyday lives, sometimes in unusual ways. For many years I drove the same model truck, but one day I got it into my head that I would buy a different brand truck. So I went to a dealer's lot, traded in my old truck, drove a new truck off the lot, and before I was half way home I completely regretted buying the new truck. It just didn't drive with the feel that I liked in the other brand truck.

My case of b*uyers remorse* didn't stop the next day, my mind churned all day between regret and determination to accept my mistake. It never occurred to me to seek Divine intervention. In the afternoon I received an apologetic call from the dealer, "The bank changed its mind and your loan has been rejected, please return the truck." I drove there straight away, got my old truck back and smiled all the way home!

Some people will be tempted to chalk my new truck return up to coincidence, but there is no way to say that about this next occurrence. I had placed a number of potted plants in my living room as decorations. Unfortunately they would occasionally attract gnats and one day a gnat flew straight into my open mouth. Before I realized what was happening I reflexively swallowed and the gnat went, as they say, down the hatch. It was such an odd thing to happen that it took me some time to process what had taken place. My response to the situation was to ask the Universe semi jokingly: Am I still a vegetarian?

One of the powers that is attributed to advanced yogi's is that if they swallow something that they regret eating they can consciously regurgitate only that one item from their stomach. I had heard of this but it never occurred to me to try it – possibly because you were supposed to be advanced! About twenty minutes after swallowing the gnat I was in the shower and something began to happen in my stomach that was unfamiliar and strange. I want to make it clear that I was in no way controlling or attempting to control what happened. I began to feel a kind of tickle in my stomach and the tickle began to move slowly upward through my esophagus to the top of my throat where it caused me to cough and spit into my hand the dead gnat, and only the dead gnat. It was a completely unanticipated answer to my question: Yes, I was still a vegetarian!

It was during my time in Las Vegas that I decided to get Lasik surgery done on my eyes so I wouldn't need to wear glasses. The price had dropped dramatically through a clinic in Vancouver, British Colombia. When researching the costs I discovered that it would be less expensive if I flew to Seattle, Washington, rented a car, and drove to Vancouver rather than flying there directly. So I made arrangements and started on my way.

Everything went smoothly until I found myself on Interstate 5 driving north from the airport toward Seattle at one o'clock in the morning. I had taken a Saturday night flight with the plan of driving to the Ananda Center in Seattle, parking there and sleeping in the car so I could attend Sunday Service. It was a good plan except I had neglected to get their address. Don't forget, this trip was before cellphones, internet and GPS.

While I am in the habit of sharing my thoughts with God I don't often ask specifically for help. This was another approach that I had learned from Swamiji. On this occasion I thought it would be appropriate to hold a *What are we going to do?* conversation with the *Universal powers that be*. I had no idea how far south I was from Seattle or where in Seattle the center might be. I drove for some time thinking about my options and decided that I should look for a gas station where I could find a telephone book and a map.

I drove for a long time without seeing any gas stations. I just kept driving on and on being concerned that I might have already passed the area in which the center might be located. Eventually I saw a station on a parallel street to the freeway, but there was no off-ramp so I kept going to the next off-ramp, turned right and then right again onto the parallel street heading back toward the gas station. It was the middle of the night with no traffic and I found myself slowly going through a commercial area with a variety of shops on both sides of the street. I peered out the windshield catching some of the shop names. One of the signs caused me to stop the car, it said: Ananda. I had somehow driven directly to the center.

Once I had published *Way of the Positive Flow* I began to carry a copy with me most of the time. In this book I describe the basic process that yogi's use to live in harmony with life under all circumstances without the coloration of religion or personal style preferences. The first step is living consciously, observe what is going on within you and around you. The second step is to inwardly reach out and attune yourself to Universal potential in that moment. The third step is to experiment with the inspirations that present themselves under the general guidance of redirecting negative energies rather than going against them. This simple non-sectarian process can open up potentials that some call miraculous but Anandites call the miracle of every day life.

I discovered that I wasn't very good at selling my books but greatly enjoyed giving them away. Some of the people I gave books to were well known, including Jay Leno – who made me sign it for him, Mary Tyler Moore and Magic Johnson. I also had meaningful conversations with Ben Stein and James Taylor. From this time onward I took on the practice of carrying a copy with me when taking airline flights. I would throw out the bait of meaningful conversation to my neighboring passenger and if we communicated successfully I would offer them a free copy.

Giving books away was also something I learned from Swamiji. It was during the lawsuit years and money was very tight. In spite of this, or actually because of this, in an effort to help us break free from limitation consciousness he printed 5,000 copies of his book *Do It Now* and invited us to help him give them away. This attitude of meeting challenges in life with expansion instead of contraction was a hallmark of Swamiji's approach to life.

One of the ways this concept manifested in my own life had to do with helping to pay for Kai and Sabari's student loans for college. While they did get substantial scholarships, they would still owe a total of $25,000 between them when they graduated. I determined that I would pay this amount but had no idea how that could come about. With two years to go before the money would be due I had somehow saved $10,000. At that time a good friend of mine was having serious life challenges and so I decided to buy a modest rental house, using this saved amount as the down payment and rent the house to my friend at a discounted rate. Well, my friend only lasted two months in the house and left without notice, leaving a big mess.

At the time it seemed like a disaster, but I rented the house out at full rate and sold it just before the money was due for the kid's loans. During the time I owned the property, values rose with enthusiasm and when the dust was settled at the end of closing, I had almost exactly $25,000. If I hadn't been helping a friend I wouldn't have bought that house, and if I hadn't bought that house, well, I can't say for sure the money wouldn't have come another way, but it did come that way.

There were two historical dates that affected my work through the union. The first was Y2K. During 1999 there was so much concern about what computers would do when they turned from 1999 to 2000 that the last six months of conferences in Las Vegas were filled with Y2K compliance sessions. I suppose it was a boost to the economy, but as a camera operator it was really boring. In the end I guess they did help because there were very few problems when the date turned, but I have to admit I was a little disappointed that it wasn't more dramatic.

9/11 was a different story. I was working at the MGM Grand Hotel on the morning of September 11, 2001. We had set up for a conference the day before and were onsite, ready to start when the news began to spread. Soon we had a live broadcast on the big screen and audio through the sound system. Everyone milled around not knowing what to do. We watched in horror as the towers came down. After some time the conference was canceled and we packed everything up and went home. It was one of those days that is not just another day.

There was one celebrity that I didn't dare approach, that was because his security staff specifically warned us to stay away. It was on a camera operator call to the Colosseum at Ceasar's Palace. I had been there before on a couple of occasions, but this time it was for a series of Elton John concerts. Unfortunately, or fortunately as it turned out, I was told that they had decided not to use the camera that I was there to operate.

Just as I was about to leave they approached me with an alternative position. They needed some stagehands to help with the inflation of three 25 foot tall balloon figures during the finale of Elton John's Red Piano show. It didn't take me long to realized there was huge entertainment potential here so I said, "Yes!" What I hadn't accounted for was the costume that we had to wear. We were dressed in all white farmer coveralls and beanie hats. We looked like Oompa-Loompas from the original *Charlie and the Chocolate Factory* movie.

On the night of the first concert everyone was pretty hyped up. Right before the start of the show, Elton John arrived and stood just off stage to perform his warm up, which consisted of him letting out one big yell at the top of his lungs. After that we just hung around waiting for the finale.

When the time came we sat in three teams of three in the stage left wing. One team for each balloon. The balloons were already on the stage, we just had to go out, unfold them and connect them to the blower that would quickly fill them up with air. As they rose up we had to stabilize them and generally keep them from getting out of control. We would stay on stage during the whole finale.

On opening night I got into a little trouble. A stage manager was there to give us our cue to go out. Each team was sent out one at a time to blow up their balloon. The first team went out with no problem. Even though I was in the third team, for some unknown reason to everyone, including me, I ran out with the second team. I didn't realized I had jumped the gun until I was half way to the second balloon, it was too late to go back, so I just kept going. When I got to the balloon I acted like I was helping while trying to stay out of the way of the guys who knew what they were doing. Once the third team came out I switched to my proper team and everything was fine after that. I didn't get fired so I guess it wasn't that big of a deal.

One day I received an invitation to dine out with a fellow who had visited my home/center. When I arrived he introduced me to two others that he had invited. One of them was a young man named Jemal. Our little group had a friendly spiritual conversation during the meal and the evening ended with an aura of satsang.

Not long after that dinner I was contacted by Jemal and he began visiting me. He asked me what he could do to speed up his spiritual progress. Along with developing his skills in meditation I suggested he spend as much time as he could at the center. Often when newcomers arrive their sincerity is tested. I didn't do this with testing him in mind, but when he asked me one day what he could do to help I suggested he weed the small garden I had developed mainly for growing tomatoes.

Weeding the garden was a brutal job. It was overgrown with Bermuda and crab grass that took serious effort to remove. It was a job I had neglected because it was so difficult. When I saw Jemal approach it with a smile and finish each round with a bigger smile I knew that something good was happening. It didn't take long for us to begin discussing the idea of him moving in with me and after two weeks he was in residence.

Jemal grew up in Las Vegas and went on to attend university at Princeton – where he graduated with an engineering degree. He also become a competitive diver at Princeton. Upon returning to Las Vegas he was hired to supervise a large industrial construction project but he found no joy in his job so he quit. He was now a struggling diving instructor with college debt.

Determined to pay off his financial responsibilities Jemal applied for a job at the Treasure Island Resort which had two large sailing ships and a pirate show on the famous Las Vegas strip. He struggled with the worldliness of the job but decided that it was worth a year of diving off pirate ships for money to pay off his student loans. We discussed the subject at length but I never told him what I thought his decision should be, it was completely up to him. I can tell you now that I thought he made the right decision.

Having Jemal around was good for me as well. His youthful spiritual eagerness was invigorating for me. I had opportunities to pass on what I valued most to a worthy student become friend. I was thankful and honored to serve in this way. When he finished his yearlong contract and paid off his student loan he turned in his pirate slops (A 17th-18th century term for inexpensive, ready-made clothing issued to sailors, including baggy trousers, shirts, and vests.) and moved to Ananda Village. When I look back at what his time with me led too, his discipleship and service through Ananda, I would have happily signed up to live in Las Vegas for seven years just for him.

When I had four books in print I decided to attend a large wholesale book expo in downtown Los Angeles. I rented a small booth and invited Jemal to come with me. We had company shirts printed, large mounted prints of the book covers and a company banner to hang in the booth.

At that time the Harry Potter books were already hugely popular, there were signs promoting them all over the place. Since one of my books was about a boy named Harry Fruitgarden, when I met people I would ask them, "Have you heard about the other Harry?"

They have book signings at these events, authors can choose to give away free books to attendees who are all professionals in the book industry. As I have mentioned, I am much better at giving books away than selling them so it seemed like a good idea to me. What I hadn't realized is that if you aren't famous, people don't get in your line to receive books. It is quite humbling when you just sit there and can't even give your books away for free.

Fortunately I had unknowingly brought my solution to this unexpected problem: Jemal. Once I realized what the situation was I asked Jemal to see what he could do to help the situation. It didn't take him long, he just put on his big smile and started ushering people down my line. He was amazing. Before you could say *there's a crowd, there was a crowd!*

I did make some sales at the Expo, but the only profits that I know about were that we had a lot of fun.

Fruitgarden Publishing
"Information and Inspiration for Living in Harmony with Life"
You can find us on the web at
WWW.FruitgardenPublishing.Com
Positive Flow Parenting

Chapter 19

I Know This Man

"There is a magnet in your heart that will attract true friends."
–Paramhansa Yogananda

The SRF and Bertolucci lawsuits were in their 11th year and because their cases were so weak their lawyers spent most of their time slinging mud at Swamiji in an attempt to tarnish his reputation and credibility. It was very frustrating for many at Ananda because we couldn't stand at Swamiji's side and defend him. In the fall of 2001 in order to speak the truth about the lawsuits a website was created, called AnandaAnswers.org (This website is no longer online.)

One of the features of *Ananda Answers* was that Anandites were invited to contribute by writing in support of Swami Kriyananda; sharing their own experiences with him. When I heard about this I was very enthusiastic about standing up for

Swamiji. There were two unexpected results of my efforts. The first one was that when I sent my first draft to Asha she wrote back that she liked it, but requested that I say more. This made me laugh because I wasn't used to anyone requesting that I *say more*! When I sent the expanded version, Asha's reaction was "Wow!" A wow from Asha is good news indeed.

The second thing that I didn't expect was that people in the office would take the time to write notes of appreciation to me. In my life to this point I wasn't used to receiving appreciation very often. Rather than puffing me up, it made me a little uncomfortable, because I didn't always know how to process it.

When giving Sunday Satsangs and greeting people afterwards I was very aware that people were thanking me as a representative of Ananda and so I felt less personally connected to the praise. I have also felt that way when writing. If I am in an inwardly connected flow the thoughts feel like they are being presented to me. So while I am actively participating, I don't feel that it would be proper for me to take full credit. Over the years I have recognized more and more that God is doing everything, even when we think we are doing something.

Here is what I wrote:

I Know This Man

(written October 2001)

Dear Truth Seekers,

The spiritual life, according to the saints of all religions, is a challenge to experience God within our own selves. As a teenager I read *Autobiography of a Yogi* and recognized that

Yogananda was my Guru and that his teachings and the Kriya technique were my path. I started to follow this path in 1969 by taking the SRF lessons. I found it difficult to meditate in the beginning but I kept at it. In July of 1971 I took Kriya initiation at the end of the SRF Convocation at the Biltmore Hotel in Los Angeles. I was just 19 years old at that time and felt very alone in my attempts to improve my life. On the Monday after convocation I had a private interview with Brother Anandamoy at Mount Washington. I told him that I wanted to be a monk and live with other devotees. He told me there was a two year waiting list.

During the next year I went to college (as Brother Anandamoy suggested I should.), practiced kriya as best I could and tried to wait out the two years. During that year I felt desperate to find more spiritual support and friendship than weekly lessons from SRF could provide. My inward pleas were answered in June of 1972 when a series of "coincidental circumstances" brought me to Ananda. Since that time it has been my good fortune to be associated with Swami Kriyananda and many other devotees at Ananda who have dedicated their lives to knowing God through the teachings and inspiration of Paramhansa Yogananda.

Shortly after arriving at Ananda it became my job to tape record all of Swami Kriyananda's talks. This allowed me to be in his presence on a regular basis. I found that just being around him was incredibly beneficial to my connection to God and Yogananda. I was so thirsty for growing my inner life that I found as many excuses as possible to be with him in both public and private settings. In retrospect, the fact that Kriyananda put up with me during those years is proof enough that he wasn't simply seeking his own pleasure.

I have traveled around the world with Kriyananda. I have been with him in intimate settings where he shared many of his personal views of life, of the spiritual life and of Yogananda's teachings. I have seen him relate to princes and paupers from many different countries and cultures. Over these years I have seen thousands of people who have been positively influenced by his life and efforts to share Yogananda's message. I have also personally known many of the people who now are his detractors.

I tell you these things because I believe they point out that I am in a position to comment on him as a man and as a spiritual leader. My knowledge of him comes through personal experience over a period of three decades. It is true that my thoughts on these subjects are only my view. But if there is any truth to my words: this is a man worth knowing, not persecuting.

I am going to cover just a few of the main areas of attack that have come from SRF and their supporters. If there is an area of concern that I have not covered that you would like to discuss, please contact me through Ananda.

Accusation: Kriyananda is a control freak and he unfairly uses his position to force people to do what he wants.

My Experience: I can't help laughing at this. I spent many, many years trying to get him to tell me what to do and he wouldn't tell me! So this accusation goes directly against my personal experience.

I am not saying that Kriyananda never makes suggestions to people about what they should do. You have to realize that people are constantly asking him what they should do. If you met someone who you felt was truly wise wouldn't you want to hear their guidance? Should he never respond? Is that the only way he could avoid being accused of controlling others? The fact that so many people have come to him for help time and time again should speak that he is in some way being helpful. Many people write to SRF for help. Do you think everyone likes the response they receive? Not likely. The most consistent guidance that I have heard Kriyananda share over the years is that people should learn to stand on their own two feet. This has never sounded to me like the advice of a person who wants to control others.

Isn't it true that one of the signs of a person of wisdom is that they do not impose their view on others? If that should be true for Kriyananda it should be true for SRF as well. The fact is that SRF and some of their followers (not all) are acting in a way that is consistent with the very accusation they make towards Kriyananda. They are trying to impose their view on others. If the people connected with Kriyananda and Ananda are happy why would they want to destroy that happiness? If they were just trying to get people to question their lives and the influences of Kriyananda that would be one thing, but they are trying to impose their view on others by actively trying to destroy Ananda.

SRF has been living in the past for so long they simply can't see that people today don't want to be controlled by their spiritual leaders they want to be inspired by them. Kriyananda has been inspiring people to improve their lives for a long time. Why is SRF having such a difficult time in their efforts to destroy Kriyananda and Ananda? Because Kriyananda's efforts to help people have been incredibly successful.

SRF claims that they are suing Ananda to "Keep the teachings pure." This is so patently false that it shows the height of their arrogance that they would even say such a thing. SRF has edited Yogananda's writings extensively since his passing. What is one of the most consistent messages of those changes? The insertion of their name and the claim that they are the only authorized place to receive the teachings of Yogananda.

Hasn't 2000 years of Christianity taught us anything? Do the Catholics and the Protestants need to go to war again? These are just the kind of squabbles that support those who turn away from the spiritual life. No group or individual can or will ever—including a Master—be able to fully express for all time the multifaceted truth of Spirit. When groups try to claim sole proprietorship of Universal realities, intelligent people have to simultaneously laugh at their immature childishness and weep for the pain that their ignorance will inevitably cause.

While Yogananda was alive there were other great saints doing good works all over the world. Did Yogananda claim that he was the only source for truth? No. So how can SRF make such a ridiculous claim. They claim that they are the only reliable place to get the teachings and blessings of the Self-Realization line of Gurus. Can a group of people that consciously set out to destroy the lives of hundreds of people who are doing their best to live in harmony with the inspiration of Yogananda's teachings be a place where the teachings are being kept "pure"? Common sense tells us no.

If you take the time to meet some of the people who have benefited by the inspiration and positive way of life that has been made possible by Kriyananda's efforts I believe you will find an experience very different than those described by a few detractors. Also take the time to find out how the relentless and dishonest attack from SRF and their "unofficial" representatives has caused untold anguish and financial hardship to hundreds of disciples of Yogananda.

Most importantly, you should base your own evaluation on personal experience and not the opinions of others. (Including mine!) The accusations against Kriyananda and Ananda are purely and simply yellow journalism. When people with a negative cause have no truth on their side they fling lies in the hopes that the sparks of sensationalism will distract people from what is really going on.

Accusation: Kriyananda is a sexual predator.

My Experience: When I first came to Ananda I was 20 years old. As a young man I was certainly interested in sex. I had just spent a year in college where the sexual revolution was in full force. In college, sex and partying are often more important to students then studies. That was certainly the case with me. The only difference for myself was that I desperately wanted to be a devotee of God and Guru; not wine, women and song. I just needed to find an environment that would support me in those positive directions.

One of the interesting things that I noted when I arrived at Ananda was that sex was not really an issue. It isn't that people weren't doing it. It is just that it was very secondary to the place that most people were putting their attention. Meditation, service and satsang (spiritual fellowship), these are the staples of motivated devotees. What I found at Ananda was a group of devotees who were putting all of their energy into growing their spiritual lives. Those who were having sex were doing so in private with the same mix of reasons that people all over the world have.

Since non-sensuality is one of the tenants of our teaching we were all aware that the goal is to draw our awareness in and up the spine rather than out towards the world through the senses. Each of us wrestled with these energies on our own. Yogananda taught that it is often better to put out lots of positive energy into the good things that we can do rather than fighting constantly with our shortcomings. This doesn't mean that we don't get bad karma when we do wrong, it just means that if we wallow in our imperfections we will never raise ourselves up out of them.

In all of my years around Kriyananda I have never heard him impose the teaching of celibacy on anyone. He never claimed that he was celibate. It is true that his vow as a Swami gave the impression that he was celibate. But that was our definition not his stated one. Swami never claimed to be perfect in any way at any time that I was present. He never told others they had to be celibate. He spoke of the principles involved and encouraged people to face these challenges with patience and humility.

Are we so naive as to think that every priest and nun that takes a vow of celibacy and living only for God is successful in that vow? The rarity of saints among the thousands of vowed renunciates in the world should tell us that there is a distance between trying to live up to a vow and actually succeeding. Are the millions of aspirants through the generations that have failed to be perfect in their vows all evil? Of course not.

Swami never encouraged us to hold him up on a pedestal. He has always turned people towards God and Yogananda, never towards himself. This is something that he has done consistently through all of the years that I have known him. I struggled for many years to put my relationship with him into a perspective that honored all that I appreciate and love about him with the fact that he is not perfect and never claimed to be. This process was made difficult not by Swami, but by the lack of context that our society has on people who inspire us. We don't know how to relate to them. We are also trying to translate teachings from India—a very different culture—into our American perspective. These challenges are not Kriyananda's fault. They have made his life more difficult, as well as our own, but he did not create these issues.

When we elevate someone to a status above us we are the ones putting demands and expectations on them much of the time, not the reverse. Why should we expect our spiritual leaders to be perfect in every way? It might be nice if they were. But personally, given all of the failings that I have, it gives me hope that someone as great as Kriyananda could still have challenges like the ones that I face. That tells me that I can focus on the good and be hopeful about the areas that aren't yet perfected.

Do we really believe that a person who isn't perfect shouldn't try to help others? I don't think so. If that were true then very little helping would get done in this world. The reality is that we are all improved as we try to help others. This is the way that life works. Imperfect people must help others in order to perfect themselves. In so doing goodness and light is brought into the world and all are benefited.

I have noticed over the years that Kriyananda is not really gender oriented. He treats everyone the same. His interactions with people are based on a loving, compassionate interest in helping others. He is incredibly patient. While he is very discriminating, he is not judgmental about the opinions or actions of others. He takes a humorous approach to the foibles of human life—including sexuality—not to raise himself above others, but to keep a humble, honest and healthy view of the world we live in. This openness manifests in spontaneous acts of matter-of-factness about life.

One day I came to his house unannounced with a woman friend and walked in on him while he was not fully dressed. He was lying on a couch in an Indian style loin cloth reading a book. Rather than being offended by our intrusion or embarrassed by his lack of attire he simply got up and moved to his bedroom where he quickly dressed and returned as if nothing at all had happened. He did this in the most natural and unassuming way. All of the immature ideas of modesty and propriety that I had been brought up with were dissolved by his calm presence of mind. He was totally unaffected by the unexpected turn of events.

We all have to face our sexuality. If we can accept it and work with it without shame or self-deception we will find that these issues can often be put into a larger perspective that removes them from the negative view that our Judeo-Christian upbringing has imposed upon us.

I don't believe that every choice that Kriyananda made in dealing with his sexuality was perfect. I believe that he struggled in the same realm that we all struggle in: trying to reconcile our humanity with an ideal view of our divinity. I am reminded of Jesus's admonition: "Let him who has not sinned cast the first stone."

It is my belief that Kriyananda did not force himself on anyone. That is so inconsistent with the totality of his life as I have known him that I am simply not able to see it. I have seen him interact with literally thousands of women in public and certainly many hundreds in more private settings. I have never known anyone so consistently respectful of the wishes of others. I personally know most of the women that he was accused of treating inappropriately. These were not young innocents who were sexually ignorant. Nor would I consider them timid people who would give in to a sexual involvement that they didn't want. These were consenting adults.

The idea that Kriyananda would rape a woman would be laughable except that it is such a serious charge. The American judicial system is not always about truth and justice, it is often about deception and innuendo. The fact that falsely accused people are found guilty in courts of law is well documented. The ultimate truth is that only those personally involved actually know for sure what took place. All I can say is that if you were able to inspect the totality of the lives of the people involved I believe you would find Kriyananda to be a much more credible speaker of truth than his accusers.

The bottom line is that having sex doesn't make Kriyananda evil. It also doesn't negate the incredible good that he has done for thousands of people.

The current day facts are that this is a dead issue. Kriyananda is in his mid-seventies. Did he make some mistakes? Yes! Is he perfect? No! Did he ever claim to be perfect? No. Is he likely to sexually influence anyone in the future? No. The only reason this is still being discussed is that it is flashy and it distracts people from the real issues that need to be looked at today. SRF and their supporters in the effort to destroy Ananda are no longer really concerned with Kriyananda. They are actually worried about the scores of ministers that Kriyananda has trained to carry on Yogananda's work without SRF control.

The incredible irony of all this is that in their very attempts to destroy Ananda, SRF has made Ananda stronger. History now repeats itself. Like the early Christians, the disciples fought amongst themselves while they were being persecuted by the people in power that could see their powers slipping away. What was the end result? The teachings spread all around the world and no one group could control it. That has happened in pretty much the same way with every world religion. That is what will happen again.

Accusation: Kriyananda allows no dissension or self-direction.

My Experience: As it happens, I am what some would call a free thinker and others might describe at times as a loud mouth. I was a teenager in the 1960's. I cut my teeth on going against the establishment. So when I came to Ananda I was up front with my thoughts and questions. There were some at Ananda that thought I didn't belong, even Swami. He once said that he only accepted me because I was friends with one of the solid members of the group.

It is important to understand that people who are seeking harmony in their lives do not like to be around people who cause disharmony. While it is true that we can become strong inwardly by learning to deal with the restless or negative energies of others, why go looking for trouble? We certainly are not likely to want to live in close proximity to troublemakers while we are trying to develop our peaceful nature.

What I found over the years at Ananda is that I often voiced the thoughts of others who were too timid to speak up themselves. I also found that my style of communication was so caustic that it distracted people from seeing the issues that I was trying to discuss. In spite of my brash outspokenness the group did put up with me. I was accepted into the group of people that spent the most time with Kriyananda. Kriyananda invested his efforts in helping me to improve myself. And apparently those efforts held some success because he took me around the world with him for 7 1/2 months. That was not the act of a person who can't stand to be around people who think for themselves.

The truth is that I have never met a person more able and willing to hear truth no matter where it comes from. I have heard newcomers lecture Kriyananda on what he should or shouldn't do and watch him listen attentively like an earnest student. He is amazingly willing to receive new information and change his views.

Some years ago I had what appeared to be a disagreement with him at a large gathering. At the time, he thought that I was speaking against him and he was very disappointed. He scolded me in public. Later we had a talk and he realized that he had misunderstood what I was trying to say. At the time I was a little concerned that people in the community would get the wrong impression of the situation. He told me not to worry but didn't tell me why. The next day there was a letter from him in the mailbox of every community resident. He started the letter by apologizing to me and then went on to say that he agreed fully with what I was trying to say. That was not the act of an egomaniac or a person that can not abide the views of others. It was the act of a person that is self-integrated enough to admit a mistake publicly.

I was deeply touched by Kriyananda's letter. Not only for myself, but for the incredible example that he showed about how to get beyond misunderstandings without holding grudges or hard feelings. This seems particularly appropriate for the current situation with SRF and Ananda. The real issue is: Can we all rise up to the table and find harmony in our commonalities rather than animosities in our differences?

Once I was at a conference in Vancouver, BC with Kriyananda. He was one of the main speakers at the conference. He also led a morning meditation that was open to the public. The room we had on the first morning was too small so he asked me to see if a larger room could be made available. Knowing that I would probably insist on a larger room when talking to the program coordinators Kriyananda looked me right in the eyes with a smile and said, "Don't insist, offer." This advice that he gave me was true advice, not only because it helped me to interact with others more respectfully and successfully, but because I have seen him live it for all of the years that I have known him.

There is a very real difference between nagging negativity and sincere critical thinking. What always amazes me about Kriyananda is that he treats both the same way. He respects the right for others to seek and express their own truth. The only times I have ever seen him go against negative people is when their energies are causing undo damage to others. He never seeks to save himself the aggravation, but he does try to protect others when he thinks it is appropriate. To people who are grappling with thoughts that they don't yet fully understand he is ever patient and respectful. I know, because that is the way he has treated me.

In 1980 I was the first of Ananda's "inner circle" to be married not by Kriyananda, but by other Ananda Ministers. This was unheard of at the time. I made this bold move because I believed that it was the right thing to do. I didn't ask anyone for permission, I just posted a general invitation to all in the Ananda Newsletter making no special invitation to Kriyananda. I was deeply touched when he arrived at the wedding to sit humbly with the rest of the group. He took no offense at my actions. Had I known that he would attend I certainly would have prepared a special seat for him. Truthfully, I didn't think he would come. I found that I was the one that ended up being small-minded in not trusting our friendship fully, not him. We also had dancing at the wedding. That too had never been done.

But he nor any other Ananda member took any kind of offense to my self generated choices. In fact, I remember that Kriyananda danced a waltz and we were all amazed at his stylish footsteps.

Those who say that Kriyananda is against individuals thinking for themselves and speaking the truth as they understand it are simply wrong. They either have never met him or they have some other agenda that keeps them from seeing the truth.

Issue: Who are the people speaking against Kriyananda and Ananda?

My Experience: As I mentioned, I personally know most of the people who are speaking against Kriyananda and Ananda. These are not bad people. But they are doing a bad thing. One of the saddest parts of this is that these people are still loved by many at Ananda. We wish them well. We not only want to be their friends, we are their friends. But we can no longer stand by and let them destroy a way of life that we cherish.

On one occasion I was driving in a car with Kriyananda and he was talking to me about a man who had expressed deep anger towards him. Kriyananda was shaking his head back and forth with sincere regret. He was telling me how he had tried everything that he could think of to accommodate this man and create harmony, but the man just didn't want to give up his anger. I could easily see in Kriyananda's face that he was not angry with this man, but genuinely concerned about the man's well-being. This has been Kriyananda's consistent attitude towards those that speak against him. I have never seen Kriyananda feel sorry for himself at the cost of respect for others.

I can't say the same thing about those who once lived at Ananda and are now trying to destroy it. They are on what they have deluded themselves into believing is a holy crusade. They are not interested in the welfare of others, they are simply using this crusade as an excuse to avoid facing their own life challenges. I am not saying that life at Ananda is perfect. I have often pointed out things that I disagree with. But to destroy a way of life because it isn't perfect is not a holy cause but a foolish one.

These people claim that they are standing up for themselves and truth because they experienced pain and suffering. How do they righteously accomplish that "noble" goal? They cause pain and suffering to others without any regard to a positive potential. They have no plan to build something good out of all this. They only seek to destroy.

As we all know, it often happens when people get emotionally wound up that they will begin to exaggerate the injustices they feel were unfairly heaped upon them. They rationalize these expansions on the truth as being true because they support what they want to believe. Fact and fiction soon lose meaning and truth is replaced by anything that will support their point of view. Are these people intentionally lying? I don't know. All I know is that their claims are false. And even if they were true, this isn't the way to make things better.

I have seen thousands of people come and go from Ananda over the years. Most of the people that come leave at some point. Some leave with a positive attitude and some leave with a negative attitude. Considering the volume of people that have been to Ananda it is amazing that very few people have been asked to leave. Most people leave on their own when they recognize that it is time. The interesting thing is that no matter why people leave, if they ever return they are invariably met with smiles and welcomes.

I myself have come and gone many times over a period of thirty years. I have lived in almost every area of Ananda Village. I helped start the Sacramento Center which is now a community. I led a meditation group in Santa Barbara for a year. I lived on my own in Roseville, California for some years. I was a monk and I was married. Most recently I have been living in Las Vegas, Nevada for almost four years now. I write books and have started a group with a different name. Anandagiri instead of Ananda. It is the same as Ananda, but I am experimenting with ideas that have been rolling around in my head for a long time. Have I asked Kriyananda or anyone at Ananda for permission to do these things? No. Do my friends or Kriyananda think I am out of my mind and fallen off the path? I don't think so. They have fully supported me in following the inspiration that leads my life. Do they agree with everything that I do? No. Actually, they don't know most of what I do. I am a private person and I don't advertise what I am up to. But I believe that they respect that I am doing what I believe is right for my life. I visit Ananda as often as possible. I stay in touch with those that I am personally close with. Even with all of the changes that I have gone through and my independent approach to life, I have always found the door to Ananda open. I know that I could show up any day of the week and find people happy to see me and ready to make room for me in their lives.

Summation.

Throughout recorded history feuds of all kinds have have burned through the hearts and lives of many souls. This current circumstance is not about Kriyananda and his mistakes. It is not about Ananda trying to infringe on SRF's territory. It is about taking the next step in expressing the timeless truths of Spirit in a way that reflect the expanding consciousness that is a part of the times in which we live. Each of us must take the time to reflect on how we can express the insights that Paramhansa Yogananda has brought into the world at this time and place. Yogananda emphasized the need for each person to have a direct experience of God. The science of Kriya Yoga is not about a church or an organization. It is about the transforming power of Spirit. It is about the blessings that God has sent into this world through our line of Gurus. It is about each individual soul growing into the direct perception of oneness with God.

As a group—led by Kriyananda's example—Ananda has an incredible capacity to forgive the past and embrace a positive future. Even after over ten years of lawsuits and millions of dollars spent, Ananda and Kriyananda seek harmony and would instantly turn away from the past with no recriminations should the opportunity present itself.

While I love all the good that is at the roots of SRF I know that Yogananda has come to me most through Swami Kriyananda and my Ananda spiritual family. No court or dissenting group of people can take that from me. This is not an outward place, but an inward haven that fills my heart daily. If you can get this kind of support through SRF then I bless them in their efforts to help you and you in your efforts to receive that help. I can only hope that your growth in the love of Spirit will allow you to know that those who find inspiration through Swami Kriyananda and Ananda are also lovers of God and sincere disciples of Paramhansa Yogananda.

I invite you to investigate Ananda for yourself by visiting any of our meditation groups, centers, communities or the Expanding Light our public retreat. It is through your own personal experience that you can find out what place Ananda or any other group should hold in your life.

In Divine Friendship,

Vijay Girard

Here are two notes I received from friends in the office at the village. I offer them not as praise for me, but as examples of the feelings of those who worked on the Ananda legal team in defense of Swamiji and Ananda for twelve years.

Dear Vijay,

Asha has asked Sheila to help put together/edit/review material for the "Ananda Answers" web site, and Sheila shared your letter with a few of us today. I was deeply inspired. And felt the kind of deep satisfaction of seeing, in one seamless flow, beautifully written, the defense of Swamiji I've always longed for. Your letter was feeling and love, but not emotion. It's written for a real person, too, versus the letters many of us have written that are mainly an exercise in "venting." Every point you undertook to address you illustrated with your own experiences with Swamiji that were very alive and to the point...

So, I just wanted to say thank you, Vijay. Divine Mother was surely flowing through you. Your letter is our most on-point and powerful defense of the accusations against Swamiji that I've ever read – after all these years of many of us making sincere efforts to do so.

May God and Guru continue to flow through you,

In divine love and friendship, Catherine

Here is another:

> Dear Vijay,
>
> Your letter has been making the rounds of the office and I was privileged to get to read it today and look forward to sharing it with Sudarshan when he returns from a backpacking trip on Sunday. I was especially intrigued with Swami's response to your letter in which he says he had been waiting six years for a letter like yours and also that he was "chagrined" that so few people thought to write such a letter (sigh).
>
> Well, anyway, I just wanted to say thank you for all the time and thought you put into it. It truly hits so many nails on their heads in such a perfect way. Swami has amazing patience; he simply waits on us to do what we should know to do, but are too ignorant, lazy or whatever to do it. I'm glad you were the one who was able to do it (finally)!
>
> Considering how many letters, depositions, testimonies, etc., have been written in Swamiji's defense (mountains of them – I've written a few myself, and read most of the rest of them) you have pulled off quite an accomplishment here, to say the least. I sincerely hope that thousands of people can read it.
>
> Now, in retrospect, I wish we had thought of calling on you to go on as a witness, to stand up

against Flynn during the Bertolucci trial, instead of somebody like me and some others, who Flynn made mincemeat of, in about 5 minutes flat. I don't know if you could have saved the day, but through it all I felt Swami yearning for a champion to stand up for him in just the right way, but somehow no one of that caliber was forthcoming at that time. It was heartbreaking.

I know that many of us would gladly have offered our very lives in defense of Swami if that had been an option, and I know he knows that. Still, it is very revealing now to get a little peek into how Swami feels about our actions or lack thereof, and hopefully this will help us to get stronger/wiser and do what whatever it is that needs to happen just now.

I hope you are well and happy. Thank you again on behalf of your whole Ananda family.

Love, Savitri

This one is from Swamiji. The book he refers to is *Way of the Positive Flow*.

Dear Vijay:

Thank you for your insightful and well-written letter. I haven't taken the time yet to read your book, but look forward to doing so. Lila read it and pronounced it very good. Your reasoning in your letter is clear and convincing. Your grammar and spelling need a good copy editor, but apart from that you write well. Congratulations.

All's well here. I've just finished a new book, *Hope for a Better World! (The Cooperative Communities Way)*. It's the only book of mine that just might become a best seller.

I'd appreciate hearing from you from time to time, to know how you're doing. I'm sorry I missed you in Seattle some months ago. God bless you, Vijay.

Love, swami

I responded to Swamiji's letter with the following:

Dear Swamiji,

Thank you for writing. It means a lot to me.

I hope that my silence the past few years hasn't given the impression that I am separating myself in any way from you and Ananda. In many ways I have never felt more connected. For the past five or six years I have been experiencing a kind of maturing process that has been a wonderful next step in my life. It is like Divine Mother nudged me out of the nest so that I can explore more fully the life that She feels would be helpful to me. It reminds me of when Mr. Moses kicked me out of his house. I ended up doing things that I wouldn't have done without that impetus. I believe my experiences here have helped me to become a better person.

I am under the impression that some people think I have separated myself from Ananda because I am using the name

Anandagiri for the group. (Which is so small that I question the honesty of calling it a group). I remember when you came out with the idea of the nature channel groups. The use of different names for groups doesn't make them separate in a negative way. It just gives them a unique identity that they can use to focus their energies. That is what I am experimenting with. In the near future I will be launching an Anandagiri web site. I'll let you know when it is up. I think visitors to the site will find that my presentation is very much Ananda. I see this as a small branch of the same tree, not a different tree that is similar.

I am now working hard on my next book *Positive Flow Parenting*. It is already written, I just need to clean it up. And yes, I desperately need to find a good editor. I just don't know where. Any suggestions?

There is so much that I could tell you about what I have been up to…but I won't right now. Kai and Sabari are doing well in their second year of college. Kai will be going in January to a study abroad program at a university in Pueblo, Mexico. Sabari is working at a Zoo where she gets to feed the polar bears and work with many different animals. Bhavani is doing well in Roseville. She has 300 yoga students through her classes at Sierra College and American River College.

Most importantly, I want you to know that my love for you and my Ananda family has never been stronger. I can't tell you how many times I have wanted to hop a plane just to visit with you. I think of you daily and offer my love and appreciation for your presence in my life.

Love, Vijay

Chapter 20

Living the Path of Self-Realization

"Only by mental attunement with the consciousness of an already-liberated guru can we make that leap across the yawning abyss which separates the ego from infinity".

–Paramhansa Yogananda

I had known for many years that I would write about Swamiji and Ananda, but I hadn't yet felt motivated to start. It surprised me when one day upon waking I realized that I had a very clear idea about how to start the book. It felt like I had been injected with a *time to start and here is how* message. I immediately began writing the first book of *The Journey of Discipleship Series – Traveling with Swamiji.*

By the fall of 2004 I had written almost 600 pages. I knew it still needed lots of editing, but I felt that it was time to let Swamiji have a look. He had moved to India in November of 2003 at the age of seventy-seven, determined to establish Ananda India and bring Paramhansa Yogananda's name and teachings to contemporary India. He had established the work in an ancient city, transformed in modern times, just south of New Delhi called Gurgaon (now reverted to its original name Gurugram).

I was actually a little hesitant to go to India, especially to be with Swamiji. Not for any negative reason but that I had a strong intuitive feeling that once I got there I wouldn't want to leave. The idea of what it would mean to move to India was a little too big for me to want to contemplate it. I could have just mailed the manuscript to him, but of course at the same time, the idea of being in India again with Swamiji was just too much to resist, I had to go.

I was in touch with Jemal at Ananda Village and told him of my plan to visit Swamiji and present him with *Traveling with Swamiji*. He got very excited about the idea of going to India to be around Swamiji and asked if he could come along. I thought that was a great idea and we arranged to spend most of the month of December at Ananda India.

We traveled to New Delhi on December 4, 2004 with a several hour layover in Paris. While we were waiting for our connecting flight Jemal entered into conversation with some other travelers and the next thing I knew he had his harmonium out and he was leading them in a chant. It touched my heart. This is how the light flows spontaneously through society from person to person and generation to generation. I had a glimpse of Jemal's future in that moment, it made me smile.

Flights from America to India often arrive in the middle of the night. One advantage of this is that the traffic is much less, which makes it easier to take in the unique blend of sights, sounds, smells and vibrations of Mother India. Like meeting a good friend, no matter how long the outward separation, the inner connection is just the same, as if no time has passed.

I was reminded of arriving in India the first time with Swamiji in 1977. I sat next him in the car with the window open, warm air blowing in our faces and the magic of being in India with Swamji bubbling through my consciousness. No thoughts of what would come, just the sacred joy of the moment. Now I was once again entering into the arms of the unknown and there was again a warm thankfulness in my heart.

We had booked rooms in a small hotel just a few blocks from the main ashram house at B 10/8 in DLF Phase 1 and after getting some rest we walked to the ashram. Swamiji was living in another house just around the corner of the next street and around 10 am we were informed that we could go over there. The houses in DLF Phase 1 were all large with three stories and full basements. Gurgaon was considered to be among the most forward thinking cities in India and this was possibly the most prestigious neighborhood. It was clear that Swamiji wasn't thinking small, he was positioning himself to come into contact with movers and shakers who could help him serve all of India.

Swamiji was nowhere to be seen when we arrived so we sat in a small sitting area outside of one of the bedrooms which was his office. There were two sofas facing each other with a coffee table between them. It had been some time since I had seen Swamiji and I was a little wound up with jet lag and excitement so I tried to center myself. When he walked in to greet us he was disheveled from recent sleep and sweetly engaging in a very relaxed way. He sat down on the couch across from us and as we talked I began to feel what I feel when I am with Swamiji, inwardly drawn, openhearted, happy and thankful.

Swamiji began to tell us about his latest book, *Space, Light, and Harmony: The Story of the Crystal Hermitage*. He had a prepublication copy on the coffee table and he invited me to move over and look at it. I took the book on my lap, sitting next to him on the couch. As I looked at it he described its contents, but I became disconnected from what he was saying because upon entering his personal space I became like a rabbit caught in the headlights of a car, frozen by the intensity of the vibrations of his presence.

The next thing I knew Swamiji was lightly chastening me for not sharing the book with Jemal. That brought me back to earth because moving to the other couch released me from the overwhelming nature of what I was feeling. It also reminded me of when Master returned to India and met with Sri Yukteswar in chapter 40 of the original *Autobiography of a Yogi*:

> "Master, please permit me to get a new carpet for the sitting room." I had noticed that Sri Yukteswar's tiger skin was placed over a torn rug.
>
> "Do so if it pleases you." My guru's voice was not enthusiastic. "Behold, my tiger mat is nice and clean; I am monarch in my own little kingdom. Beyond it is the vast world, interested only in externals."

> As he uttered these words I felt the years roll back; once again I am a young disciple, purified in the daily fires of chastisement!

In the West we are taught that it is bad to be corrected by the teacher, but to the devotee, to be corrected by the guide is to be blessed.

Later that day we attended a video recording session in the living room of Swamiji's house. Swamiji had just the day before our arrival finished a grueling month of recording. He shared his thoughts in a letter to everyone.

> Dear Everybody:
>
> This is an emotional moment for me. I have just finished recording the last of 365 TV programs, twenty minutes each (not counting the introduction and announcements, but including the song at the end of every program). I feel I have done a major work for Master, and I am conscious of his happiness in my heart.
>
> There were quite a few days when I didn't think I could carry on. This last day was especially difficult for me – maybe the relief over being at the end. But people couldn't see what it cost me; it looked easy. Last July (or thereabouts), when I first decided to do the remaining 235 programs in November, I just didn't dare contemplate the challenge of it: ten programs a day, five days a week, back to back for a whole month and a day.

Last week, to make up for the five extra shows on the last day, I did 13 one day, and 12 the next.

I had many people urging me all month to go slower, but I felt that if I let up I wouldn't be able to come back and finish the whole job. As Jyotish said, I'll reach more people through these programs than the sum of all the people I've ever spoken to and written for in my whole life.

I felt like weeping at the end, for sheer gratitude at having finished this job for Master. I didn't weep, but, as I said, I feel deeply moved. Quite possibly 200 million people, and even more, will view this program not only all over India, but also in over 100 other countries.

Jai Guru!

Love, swami

Tarun, the owner of Quest Studio in New Delhi, was hired to record and edit all of the programs. Our arrival coincided with the videotaping of the singers singing Swamiji's songs, which would be added in rotation after each talk. Once all of the songs were completed it was time to create an Intro and an Outro that could be added to each talk. The next thing that I knew I was traveling most days to their studio so I could help with the post production process.

I thought my purpose in visiting India was to present Swamiji with the manuscript of *Traveling with Swamiji,* but that didn't happen until the last day before I returned to America. I had given zero thought to what else I might do on the trip. It ended up that the Universe had preplanned everything. That I was able to help with such a momentous project was not only an honor, but a great blessing. This kind of synchronicity, unseen until observed, is always present in the Creation.

During my visit I was so preoccupied with working on the TV programs that I didn't think of much else. I went to all of Swamiji's satsangs, and the Christmas activities, including the eight hour meditation. The only sightseeing that I did was to visit the "mile of malls" on the main street in Gurgaon with Jemal, where we took a picture together with the Santa Claus, and had tea with Swamiji and a group from the ashram.

Swamiji felt it was important to do something that would signal to the Indians that we were here in India to stay. So he determined to buy a house. The money was raised and a suitable home was found just another block or so from his current rental residence. One day he invited a small group of us to roll up some carpets from his current rental to carry over to the new house to see how they would look.

I should mention that Swamiji's health was very unstable at this point in his life. He was quite unsteady on his feet. Not having been around him for some time I wasn't as tuned into this fact as I should have been. After we had rolled up the carpets Swamiji decided to show me something in his current bedroom. As we turned toward the bedroom I noticed that the carpet I had rolled up was sticking out into the door frame of his bedroom.

I saw the carpet and I saw Swamiji heading toward it, it registered in my mind that there might be a problem, but I couldn't put my finger on exactly what the problem might be. Before I could reason the situation out, Swamiji had stepped into the carpet roll without lifting up his foot and was literally doing a superman over the carpet roll into his bedroom. His arms reached straight out from his body which was now parallel to the marble floor. I could tell that he had tightened the muscles of his arms, and forgive me for saying so, his form was quite good.

I could see him do his best to absorb the impact with his arms, but he did hit his forehead on the floor. I raced over on his right side and one of the ladies, Nirmala and Miriam were there but I don't remember which one lifted him, took his left side and we walked him over to a chair and sat him down. He was wearing a bathrobe over his clothes and it was pulled apart slightly, his shoulders were slumped over and he was panting slightly. I looked at his face and in his eyes, for a moment I thought he looked like an ordinary old man, but as I watched I saw – as if a dimmer switch was being turned up – the light in his eyes turned on and Swamiji was once again fully present, not in the least bit ordinary.

His first words were, "Vijay, why do these things always happen when you are around?" I am pretty sure he was joking, but I didn't think it was very funny.

A few minutes later he was up and we were carrying the rugs to the new house for the full tour. He had a growing lump on his forehead, but a smile on his lips. He commented that he should know how to pick up his feet by this time in his life. I later learned that he had fallen a number of times in recent years.

Another thing that I had given no thought to was what I would say to Swamiji when we met privately. He knew I wanted to talk to him, but he didn't know what I wanted to talk about, and neither did I. I wanted to personally hand him the manuscript, as an offering of appreciation for having something so special to me that I could write about. Beyond that thought I would once again be winging it. When we finally met, I was as surprised as he was at the words that came unbidden out of my mouth.

We met in the afternoon, as I said, the day before I was to leave. I gave him the manuscript and then we started talking. At one point there was a pause in our thoughts, and then out of nowhere, I heard myself blurt out, "Swamiji, what would you think about me coming back to help here permanently?" This idea had not visited my mind one time since my arrival in India. It was completely out of the blue.

Swamiji responded by asking me, "Can you pay your own way?"

I said, "Yes."

We discussed the financial challenges of the situation and he asked again, "Can you pay your own way?"

I replied, "Yes."

We talked some more and then he asked a third time, "Can you pay your own way?"

I smiled offering a third, "Yes!"

He smiled back and said, "Okay, when can you come?"

There was a big program scheduled for Master's Mahasamadhi Anniversary on March seventh, so I said, I will be back by the beginning of March.

As if this wasn't enough, we somehow found ourselves talking about renunciation and the Swami order. The next thing that came out of my mouth without forethought was, "Swamiji, say the word and I will get down on my knees right now to take the vow."

Swamiji's response was that, separate from the subject of appropriateness for my life, he simply wasn't ready to face that subject.

The next morning, just before leaving for the airport, I strategically walked by the open door to Swamiji's office, as Swamiji would say, "Meeting luck half way." As I had hoped, Swamiji called out, "Vijay." He was reading the manuscript. I could see that he was starting to skim. He mentioned that there was too much surfing. I said, "Sir, it gets better." We said a quick good bye and I headed to the airport. I was glad to have seen him reading it. If it went no farther, I would know that he had read it. It was now in God's hands.

As it happened, Jemal decided to stay in India. He had nothing tying him down in the States. He was a young man, footloose and fancy free. He was choosing to help Swamiji serve in India. I would see him again soon.

The trip home was filled with thoughts of moving to India. I had given myself two months to extricate myself from seven years in Las Vegas. I would sell the house/center and almost everything in it, quit my job with CPDA, suspend my membership in the union, and arrive back in India.

I smiled to myself, I had known this might happen, I was happy to have been right. When I arrived home I found the following email waiting for me:

Dear Vijay:

It was wonderful having you here in India. The timeliness of your visit, moreover, considering my work in recording all those TV programs, was miraculous. I look forward to your return here.

I've taken the time to read your whole book. Congratulations - or, as they say in Hindi (that means the same thing). The book is heartfelt, sincere, and insightful. I was deeply touched.

There were a number of facts that might be corrected, and some spelling mistakes. What I had in my hips was arthritis, not tumors. (The surgeon who eventually operated on them told me, "They were the worst case I've ever seen. I don't know how you could even walk!") A number of statements you make should be brought in line with the facts: for instance, the Portiuncola was the first, small hut where Saint Francis and his little group lived; the church he rebuilt was at San Damiano. Quite a few little things like that.

One spelling mistake you make repeatedly is to say "affect" when you mean "effect." Do look up the difference.

I felt that the first part – which, as you said to me, gets better after that; in fact, it gets *much* better – would be improved by editing and shortening. Few of your readers will be surfers or even ex-surfers. And though it is very painful to see how your father treated you, you make the point so strongly even the first time that I think less, later on, would be enough.

I agree with you: The reader needs to know you before your initiation of the spiritual path. And I don't mean to cut out the surfing, which was such an important part of your life. But I think that whole section would be stronger if it were shortened.

You write well. Moreover, considering all the negative energy that SRF has broadcast to the world against me, I think it's time someone wrote something to balance it. Asha has been working on my biography for years. Devi is writing a shorter one, and may have it finished by the time she comes to India in February. But what you've done is unique and very personal; it may become the most widely read of the three. So I think it merits the careful extra work I've suggested. I also hope that Crystal Clarity Publishers will be able to publish it; they'd do a good job promoting and distributing it.

Many blessings to you, Vijay. Your book was deeply moving.

In Master's love,
swami

Needless to say I was thrilled by his response. I wrote back:

Dear Swamiji,

I just got back.....I can't believe how sore my rear end is...way too much sitting!

I had been hoping you would write about your reaction to the book, yes I was a bit nervous, but still I believed that you would like it. So when I got home and found your email I was thrilled. I feel so honored to stand up for you in this way. I agree completely with your assessment of the surfing and my father issues...Bhavani had the same reaction and I knew it might be the correct one...but wanted to test the waters before making a final decision. I have also wondered if I should cut the trip to Europe that I took to visit my mother. There are some fun stories, but they aren't directly on point and could be removed fairly easily.

I am also open to including, expanding or clarifying any other areas in the book that you think might be improved. There are a few more stories that I have considered adding. I wonder if my description of life at Ananda during those years paints enough of a picture to be sufficient for that aspect of the book. And does the last chapter which covers the trip after India hold up? Or does it lose momentum? And does the whole thing get wrapped up sufficiently at the end?

I actually made up a list of questions (which Lakshman has) that I hoped readers at this stage would give me feedback on. The items you caught were on the list, as well as others.

What I think I need as well, is an editor to help with the technical side, which while I have improved, still needs more improvement. I just don't know exactly how to proceed with that issue.

I have felt for years that my books belonged with Clarity...possibly now is the right time to start in that direction. If this book were to be successful maybe Shaun would consider trying the others. In any case, I am open to handling things in any way that you feel is appropriate.

I am so pleased that you feel good about the book. Along with hoping that it is helpful to others...I really hoped you would like it.

My goal is to be back in India before Master's Mahasamadhi celebration. It will be a big task to make that happen but I am going to try. I felt very blessed while being in India with you and the others, and am very enthusiastic about helping with the work there.

With love in God and Gurus,

Vijay

A couple of weeks later I received the following email from Seva. She was on the trip around the world that I had taken with Swamiji and a key figure in Ananda's evolution. When I arrived in Gurgaon to see Swamiji she was there and had access to the manuscript when Swamiji was finished reading.

> Dear Vijay,
>
> I've been missing you. By reading your book you are always in my thoughts, and since you're not actually here, I'm missing you. So come soon.
>
> I enjoyed the journey of your life, especially the parts with Swami. That was very sweet and special. It's always fun to hear how another sees him and makes me realize that my perceptions were not necessarily the same. I wonder how it would have been for me if I had, but to me he was the best of friends, my older, wiser, wonderful brother always there. I knew there was more, but then I wasn't yet of a state to see that. Now, it's as though my being glows when I do see him with great joy. Hopefully this is more advanced.
>
> Swami said that he enjoyed your book and wants to have it published. That's great, Vijay. Of course, you realize that those at the village who make these things happen are wondering where the $$'s are coming from! It's very tight there, just so you know, if you didn't already. But if Swami wants it, Sean will certainly make it happen. And many will enjoy what you have written.
>
> I didn't realize you went surfing in Bali. Boy, what we forget. Did you not remember,

Anandamoyi Ma was very ill before we came? And that we saw Chidananda when he left from seeing her? Wasn't that a special visit. I often think of her. Her special greeting to Swami was so sweet and said it all. Sorry it's taken me so long to read the manuscript. I've been busy.

Catherine & Peter visited, along with Anandi & Bharat, Lisa & Brian. Swami wouldn't invite me to be with all of them when he had them visit. My personal karma with him is over, but that doesn't matter any more. I'm here just to serve Swami and Master in whatever way they want. We had a wonderful Birthday celebration, but it took the last out of many here. I & many got colds; a group went to Rishikesh; and of course, Swami and group went to Goa. So it's quiet now and wonderful, except we need to keep working on getting the new house together. Dharana is doing most of it with air conditioners, generators, etc. Phew!

Keep in touch. Have great joy, love, Seva

I wrote back to Seva the following:

Dear Seva,

Thanks for writing. I'm glad you enjoyed the book. And I appreciate you missing me. It has been one of the quirks of all our karma at Ananda that we are both close and distant at the same time. I hope you know that I feel great love and respect for you. Your path in this life might not be flashy, but you have faced your challenges with dignity and perseverance...it hasn't gone unnoticed.

I believe that our feelings toward Swamiji are more the same than different...we love him and God through him... and though I think our time of daily closeness with him is past...I believe this time in India is a gift that honors our journey with him. I felt so at home while I was there that it feels like I am visiting here.

I already have my ticket to return, I'll be arriving on March 1st. The house sold in a week, so as long as the escrow goes along with no problems, all I need to do is get my visa set up.

You expressed regret in your letter that your view of Swamiji wasn't more advanced...I think maybe you are experiencing what I might call the Sister Gyanamata Syndrome. She asked Master for samadhi, but she didn't need it in the way that she thought. Sister had an attunement that transcended the need for flashy experiences. I don't believe your life could have been linked so closely to Swamiji and Ananda unless Master had you close to his heart...from everything that I have observed, Swamiji won't ever leave you behind.

I can see your smile in my mind's eye and it warms my heart. See you soon.

With love in God and Gurus, Vijay

The thing about discipleship is that it looks different for every disciple. Master taught that every atom of the Creation is endowed with individuality. Every disciple has a unique and special relationship with our own higher Self: Life/God/the Universe. The yoga teachings take into account this truth and provide a framework that harmonizes with the essential way that life is made.

Even though we had been taught that spiritual experiences were not the guideline of spiritual advancement, we couldn't help thinking that flashy inner experiences were a necessary sign of advancement. I have heard a number of "old timers" at Ananda lightly bemoan a disappointment at not experiencing more dramatic meditations. The thing that we don't take into account when evaluating our spiritual progress is that we can't remember all of the incarnations that brought us to this point in our spiritual journey.

When the soul is drawn into a new incarnation, as it takes on the new physical form with its filter of DNA, it also takes on a karmic filter that limits what can and can not be spiritually perceived. This karmic filter is most importantly affected by the Satguru, our guide through many incarnations.

Swamiji wrote in Chapter 31 of *The New Path*:

> 'Sir,' I asked him one day, 'how long have I been your disciple?'
>
> 'Well, it has been a long time, that's all I will say.'
>
> 'But does it always take so long?'

> 'Oh, yes,' Master replied. 'Desires for name and fame, etc., take them away many times, until they have learned all their material lessons in this school of life.'

The practical truth is that it is not for us to know exactly how things stand in terms of ultimate graduation from the wheel of life, death and rebirth. It is possible that you have experienced samadhi in a past life and not now remember its wonder. The signs that will most accurately tell us how we are doing are directional, are we calmer and more peaceful, are we living to give or living to take, are we connecting more to inward soul joy rather than emotional ups and downs, do we live more with a sense of God's participation in our lives, do we talk to God and listen for the Divine response. These are some of the ways that disciples can know that they are progressing.

One of the best signs of spiritual progress is when we shift from the initially essential "I want moksha (Liberation) in this lifetime!" to the trusting awareness that God is with us and guiding our lives, in which we can openheartedly give ourselves completely to "Lord, how may I serve", without thought of any reward other than the joy of living for and serving God.

Swamiji himself said that he had chosen, in this lifetime, service over personal freedom in God. Many in the Ananda spiritual family, walking in Swamiji's footsteps, have made that same pledge. Swamiji has also said that he realized that these two ideals of Self-Realization and service to mankind are not separate, but one and the same.

The spiritual life is not about organizational affiliation, it is about personal transformation through *direct awareness of* and *participation in a conscious active relationship* with Life/God/the Universe. In all relationships, human or Divine, it is the quality and then the quantity of attention that we give to that relationship that will determine how much progress we make.

The Yoga Teachings that Paramhansa Yogananda clarified for the world offer practical tools and understandings about how to live a Spirit-centered life in the context of the scientific era and the advancing spiritual age of Dwapara Yuga. Swami Kriyananda has dedicated his life to helping others discover their spiritual potential and to support, in as many ways as possible, the efforts of each individual disciple. We must choose the level of interest and intensity that we want to give to the help that God offers us.

It has been my good fortune to be included in the spiritual family of the Masters of the Path of Self-Realization, for that I am grateful beyond what I can express. To you, the reader who has traveled with me to these final words, I encourage you, if you have not already done so, to inwardly request Life/God/the Universe, or whatever form of Universal presence that inspires you, to guide you to your guru and your spiritual family.

May your life be filled with the joy of God's presence and the blessings of spiritual family.

A Way to
Awakening

Swami Kriyananda

Reach
for the

Epilogue

"I give you my unconditional love… Will you give me the same unconditional love?" –*Autobiography of a Yogi*

Attunement is the essence of discipleship. The extent to which a person can share a sense of his guru's living presence determines the depth of his discipleship. –Swami Kriyananda

From the very beginning of the guru/disciple relationship the guru offers unconditional love to the disciple. That love is God's love flowing to the disciple through the channel of the guru. In this way the impersonal is also made personal. The disciple's challenge is to fully enter into that love through ever-deepening *attunement to* and *expression of* that love. As I look back at the portion of my life that has been shared in this volume I am reminded of the countless little and large ways that God through Paramhansa Yogananda and Swami Kriyananda have guided and blessed my life.

Through my participation with the Ananda spiritual family I have seen that same Divine love and blessings flow to and through hundreds of lives of Ananda residents and many thousands of lives in the worldwide Ananda Sangha. When people question whether or not there is a Universal God Presence (No matter what you call it.) and claim there is no proof, I can only say that that has not been my experience.

Every soul's incarnation is custom designed to be in harmony with the opportunities that best fit their spiritual needs. Our responsibility is to act and react in ways that lead to greater awareness of God's presence and to minimize the creation of new karmas that will require more future incarnations. The practice of the meditation techniques that Paramhansa Yogananda taught are life transforming tools for deepening our inner awareness, service to others is key to freeing ourselves from little self over-involvement and devotional satsang is one of the easiest ways to support and be supported in our spiritual quest.

On the outside the life of a disciple may look more the same than different from those who do not consciously choose to harmonize with the way that life is made from the inside out. But on the inside, there is a complete transformation of perspective. According to the unique features of each soul's relationship to Life/God/the Universe the reality of Universal consciousness and our nature as expressions of that consciousness becomes more accessible and with it the soul satisfying well-being that is the core component of every soul.

My life in India with Swamiji and beyond will be the subject of the third book in *The Journey of Discipleship Series,* titled *Serving with Swamiji*. When I arrived back in India to serve Ananda India I had no idea that I would live there for thirteen years or that my karma for finding trouble would lead me to live as a yogi in the Himalayan foothills for five of those years. It also came about that my natural talent for causing unexpected reactions in others was instrumental in the formation of the

Nayaswami Order that Swamiji initiated in November of 2009, of which I would become a founding member.

Modern India is an incredible blend of old and new, the ancient Vedic traditions are now trying to live side by side with worldwide corporate consciousness. India wants to integrate its spiritual traditions with today's world but has struggled with how to bring the two together. It became our mission, as representatives of Western success and efficiency to remind India that the solution to all challenges in life are best found by awakening and deepening our inner connection to Life itself. Paramhansa Yogananda's clear explanations of how the principles of outward and inward success are the same have become practical "Here is how you do it!" teachings.

About a year or so after arriving in Gurgaon I was talking with Swamiji in the upstairs office of his new home, our conversation was not of any particular import. At one point Swamiji paused and looked at me very directly and said, "Vijay, you have had lots of ups and downs in your life." It became one of those stretched out moments for me. I tried to think of what particular incidents he might be referring to but none came to mind. I didn't say anything in response, I just looked into his eyes and rested in the God/Yogananda/Kriyananda blessing Presence that came through him to me. This was one of the best signs that my life was headed in the right direction. I was no longer focused on the ups and downs of life, but on an ever-deepening experience that God is always present. That Presence is sweet, oh so sweet.

Toward the end of Master's life Swamiji asked him the following question, quoted from Chapter 38 of *The New Path*:

> 'Sir,' I said to Master one day, 'after you are gone, will you be as near to us as you are now?'

'To those who think me near,' he replied, 'I will be near.'

This is Paramhansa Yogananda's promise. A sacred vow that is held in perpetuity for those who choose to receive it.

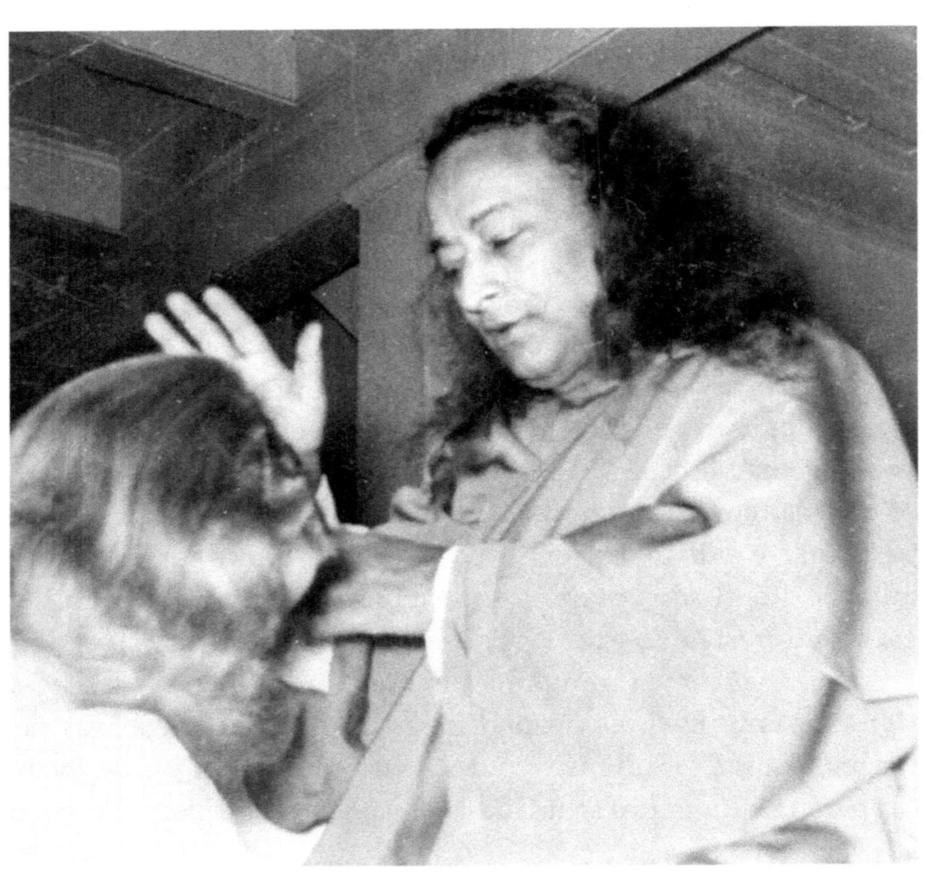

FruitgardenPublishing.Com

www.ingramcontent.com/pod-product-compliance
Lightning Source LLC
LaVergne TN
LVHW020647110826
845149LV00012B/1943

* 9 7 8 0 9 8 4 8 9 6 2 2 6 *